EDUCATION SYSTEM IN INDIA

Edited & Compiled by

DR. PREM SUNDER

Principal,
Darsh College of Education
Gohana (Sonepat),
Haryana

KSK PUBLISHERS & DISTRIBUTORS

7/26, Basement, Ansari Road, Darya Ganj, New Delhi-2
Phones: (O) 65190343, 43551324, 42564726
(Mobile) 9811088729 (Resi.) 47091605 (Fax): 011-42564726
E-mail: khelsahitya1@rediffmail.com
Website: *www.khelsahitya.com*

Published by:

KSK PUBLISHERS AND DISTRIBUTORS

7/26, Basement, Ansari Road, Darya Ganj, New Delhi-110002
Ph.: (Off.) 65190343, 43551324, 42564726
(M) 9811088729, (R) 47091605 Fax: 011-42564726
E-mail: *khelsahitya1@rediffmail.com*
Website: *www.khelsahitya.com*

I.S.B.N. – 978-81-89983-24-6

PRINTED IN INDIA 2009

Laser Typeset by:

Jain Media Graphics
Delhi-110035 (Mob.) 9911151534

Printed by:

New Gyan Offset Printers
Delhi-110035

PART-I
PRINCIPLES OF EDUCATIONAL SYSTEM
CONTENTS

PART-II
EDUCATION IN EMERGING INDIAN SOCIETY
CONTENTS

1

EDUCATION IN ANCIENT INDIA

Introduction

Education is not exotic to India. There is no other country where the love of learning had so early an origin or has exercised so lasting and powerful an influence. At no period of its history India has been altogether unenlightened country. Inscriptions on stone and copper, the palm-leaf records of the temples and in later days, all alike indicate not only the general knowledge, but also the common use of the art of writing.

The system of education generally advocated emanated from the vedas and was called vedic system of Education which insisted on a code of conduct both for the student and the teacher and placed the child under the care and direction of the teacher. The child was to live with his teacher as a member of his family and serve him in every way. At the close of student life, the teacher would advise his student as follows :

Speak the truth. Practise Virtue. Do not neglect the study. Make a handsome present to the teacher. Do not cut off the line of progeny. Become a householder and do not allow the family to go extinct.

Do not swerve from truth. Do not neglect the study. Make a handsome present to the teacher. Do not cut off the line of progeny. Become a householder and do not allow the family to go extinct.

Do not neglected the duty of God and parents and

the teacher in addition to these pieces of advice, would say a few more things of how accommodate oneself.

Vedangas

There are six Vedangas which are as good as treatises on science, and consist of grammar, astrology, poetry, etymology, sixty-four sciences and arts including astronomy, medicine, geometry, laws, etc. Vedangas are in the form of Sutras.

Vedangas are as under :

a. Jyotish : Astrology and Astronomy.

b. Chhandas : Prosody.

c. Nirukta : Philology.

d. Kalpa : Science of rituals.

e. Shiksha.

Characteristics of the vedas

1- Each veda is divided into four parts

a. Upanishads : Consisting of supreme science, and are more ancient treatises on philosophical teachings on the nature of God, man and nature.

b. Aranyakas : Books of and on forest dwellers.

c. Brahmanas : Consisting of prayers.

2. Vedas are in the form of shrutis, and are four in number. Rig Veda consisting of hymns, Sam Veda consisting of sacred chants : Yajur Veda consisting of invocation and sacrifice: Athava Veda is collection of sacred formulae and verses.

3. Profess and practice ideal moral life without seduction and sin. People were religiously and spiritually simple, king and honest.

4. Vedic outlook on life is revealed.

5. Vedic outlook on life is revealed.

6. Vedic outlook is optimistic and positive.

7. Worshiped on God whom the wise described as many. It was religion of Nature which held man central.

8. Vedic people had simple and pure living.

9. Vedas are representative of the Indian society and culture, and point to a unique socio-economic civilisation, where all are equal irrespective of status and gender.

Chief Characteristics of Hinduism

1. Modern Hinduism includes such socio-religious movements like Brahmo Samaj, Arya Samaj and Sarvodaya etc., making it alive to needs and aspirations of the contemporary society, all deeply rooted in traditional Hinduism.

2. Puranic and Tantrik trends add mysticism, yoga and siddis Led to Sophism and Bhakti-vad.

3. Morality is integral to Hindu way of life.

4. Progressive and tolerant; open to new ideas and trends.

5. Against caste system, basically liberal, assimilative and catholic.

6. Ahimsa, non-violence.

7. The concept of ideal man and relationships as depicted in Ramayana and Mahabharata : the Hindu Epics.

8. Varna Ashram : Brahmana, Kshatriya, Kayashtha, Shudra, Profession-Based.

9. Ethical actions are both personal and social. Dharma, Artha, Kama, Moksha as ultimate values.

10. Enlightened attitude, not dogmatic and uncritical, puts things to reason.

11. Variety of doctrines from Charvaka to Vedanta. It has six systems of thought called Shad Darshan.

Characteristics of Vedic Education

Terms such as knowledge, awakening, humility, modesty, etc. are often used to characterise Vedic education. Ancient texts refer to the uneducated person as an ignorant beast. Education is regarded as the source of light. The main features of Vedic education can be briefly enumerated as follows:

1. Accepting Aims : Education was self supporting in that student had to cater for his substance by seeking alms which induced humility and sense of social service among students.

2. Observance of Celibacy : Helped students exercise self control and live a simple and pious life.

3. Academic Freedom : Helped to develope original thinking and philosophical attitude giving depth and variety to student's approach to life-situations.

4. Gurukul- Centred : Propagation of cultural values and practices, and transmission of knowledge and skills were ensured through gurukul-centred system of education.

5. Vocational Efficiency : Earning livelihood according to one's ability and potential was another characteristic of Vedic education Practicality was the key word. Military science, agriculture, animal husbandry, Veterinary science, medicine, art and handicraft, Ayurveda, and education in commerce were popular subjects for vocational efficiency.

6. Spirituality : Education focused on the spiritual aspects of life. Nature was divine. Knowledge was means of salvation and righteous conduct was the essence of life.

7. Sublimation of Instincts : Man is the virtual slave of the instinctive drives embedded in his psyche. Obsessed by his senses, he often adopts the wrong path. The objective of education was to sublimate these instinctive tendencies and to turn the mind away from material distractions and enchantments.

8. Emphasis on Knowledge and Experience : The Gurukuls laid emphasis on knowledge and experience. During the Vedic period, the practice of distributing degrees did not exist. Students exhibited the knowledge obtained through discourses and discussions conducted in a concourse of scholars. Dr. R.K. Mukherjee opines that the objective of education was not merely reading, but assimilation of knowledge and experience.

9. Aims of Education : In the Vedic period, education had an idealistic form, in which the teachers laid stress upon worshiped of God, religiousness, spirituality, formation of character, development of personality, creation of an aptitude for the development of culture, nation and society. It is in this context that Dr. Altekar said that the objectives of education in ancient India were worship of God, a feeling for religion, formation of character, fulfillment of public and civic duties, an increase in social efficiency or skill, and the protection and propagation of national culture.

10. Knowledge, the third eye : Education is knowledge. It is man's third eye. This aphorism means that knowledge opens man's inner eye, flooding him with spiritual and divine light, which forms the provision for man's journey through life. Through education, the development of every aspect of human life becomes possible. Knowledge protects an individual like a mother, inspires him to follow the path of good conduct as a father does, and gives the pleasure that one's wife

provides.

Education leads to the development of personality. The word Veda originates form the word vid on which bears the meaning of knowledge. Sayana declares that the veda is a means to the obtaining of the adored, that which is worthy of worship, as well as a means to the banishment of the undesired, the evil. Knowledge of the four Vedas, Rig veda Yurveda, Samaveda and Arthaveda, along with new knowledge with broadened his intellectual horizon.

Aims of Vedic Education

1. Hinduism today stands for democratic and secular values and traditions emphasizing on tolerance, non-violence, freedom, equality, justice, brotherhood and harmony.

2. Child-Centred : Students were given special attention and treatment by teachers depending on their interest, aptitude, proficiency and performance, thus acting as the fore-runner of the modern theory and practice of education.

3. Natural - Oriented : The centres of education were located far from the populated and crowded areas, more in natural surroundings. Education should make man more with nature.

4. Individual-Centred : Education was for individual which was its chief concern. Education should, therefore, aim at overall development of an individual.

5. Religion- centred - Religion dominated every aspect of life in all national, personal, social and educative procedures and practices. Hence, education should be wedded to religion, giving unanimity and one-ness to the educative process without any contradiction.

6. Tamso ma Jyotirgamaya : Knowledge should

dispel doubts dogmas and darkness.

7. Make Living Worthy : Education should make life worth while, purposeful and relevant.

8. Education of Mind : Knowledge for creativity and pursuit of culture and civilisation.

9. Citta- Vritti-Nirodh - Education must aim at self-fulfillment and provide freedom from materials desires and attachment.

Salient Features of the Curriculum

1. However, alongwith the theoretical aspect of the curriculum, the practical was also given due weightage. Teacher affected the students through behavioural interaction and efficient education management.

2. The foundation of the education imparted in this ancient period was according to inherent tendency or aptitude. It is written in the Atharvaveda O Lord Indra ! fill us with that ability which a father imparts to his son. It is also stated in the Sabra Byshra, How a child learns is apparent from the fact that the chile of a Brahmin learns the vedic aphorisms while still at home. The imprint of these aphorisms upon his mind is indelible. Along with education, the performance of certain rituals was along regarded as essential. It was after these rituals that the child embarked upon a study of the subjects of his choice, though he was also required to study some other subjects. In this connection Sanat Kumar inquired of Naarada what he had studied. Naarada replied I have read the Rig veda, Yajurveda, Samaveda, Athraveda, the fifth Ved, history, the Puranas, I also know the Vedic grammar, the Veda of the Vedas, I am also read in rules pertaining to service of one's father, arithmetic, the science of time, knowledge of gods, the absolute, ghost, metrics, etymology, astronomy, knowledge of devas,

dance, music recreation and creation of fragrance. This sums up all that was possible to lean and could constitute curriculum.

3. Although the education of this period was dominated by the study of Vedic literature, historical study, stories of heroic lives and discourses on the Puranas also formed a part of the syllabus. Students had necessarily to obtain knowledge of metrics. Arithmetic was supplemented by a knowledge of geometry. Students were given knowledge of the four Vedas- Rig veda. Yajurveda, /samaveda and Arthrvaveda. The syllabus took within its compass such subject as spiritual as well as materialistic knowledge, Vedas, Vedic grammar, arithmetic, knowledge of gods, knowledge of the absolute, knowledge of ghosts, astronomy, logic, philosophy, ethics, conduct, etc.

Women in Vedic Education

Social refinement and cultural sophistication of a society is indicated by the status that it accords to its women population. History of social education is the story of women's emancipation and empowerment. In spite of their physiological constitution and obligations, women do not lag behind men in any intellectual and philosophical pursuit and activity. Women today occupy a variety of managerial and administrative positions at the highest level and are considered even more successful and dependable because of their inter-personal relationship ability, devotion to duty, and professional focusing.

Vedic education was no exception. It was an index of a very progressive and dynamic social order which afforded equal opportunities to women without any gender bias. However, general education include such subjects of domestic utility that may help hem take up their appointed role of motherhood and related household activities. But this in no way debarred them form taking up the highest of intellectual involvements should they ever chose to do so. Names such as those of Vishwavara, Jooha, Apala, Ghosha. Lopamudra, Sarswati and others are mentioned in this regard for taking up composing Names of Maitreyi, Gargeya, Kauanitiki and others are mentioned for participating in philosophical and intellectual discourses along with men of equal eminence and brilliance.

During the Vedic period, considerable attention was given to the protection and propagation of national culture. Knowledge and skills were transmitted to the succeeding generations through the medium of the schools, known as gurukuls. In essence, the achievement of the above mentioned objectives implies making the individual a complete individual. Knowledge leads to man's physical as well as spiritual development. It is knowledge that leads a man to his salvation. This times, strenuous efforts were made for the achievement of these objectives of education. Stress was laid on proper conduct. The student was prepared both for knowledge of the self as well as knowledge of the Absolute. Accepting as the foundation, primary was given to fire-sacrifices, rituals, prayers, and religious festivals.

The word Upnayana means to take close to, or bring in touch with. A ceremony called the Upnayana ceremony was performed before the child was taken to his teacher. This ceremony was performed at the ages of 8 , 11 to 12 for the Brahmise, Khshatriyas and Vaishays, respectively. The ceremony signalled the chil's transition from infancy of childhood, and his initiation into educational life. In this context, the term Upnayana means putting the student in touch with his teacher. With the passage of time, the ceremony came to be confined to the Brahmin class only.

In the house of teacher, the students was required to obtain education upto the age of 24, after which he was expected to enter domestic life. Students were divided into three categories :

a. Those obtaining education up the age of 24 - Vasu.

b. Those obtaining education up the age of 36- Rudra.

c. Those obtaining education up the age of 48- Aaditya.

In the Vedic Period, every teacher devoted himself to the integral development of each student. He aimed at the physical and intellectual development of his wards. The maximum attention was devoted to the individuals development of every students, but there was not provision for the education of the incapable and the handicapped, especially those who were lacking in mental and moral qualities or were known for more turpitude.

Teaching, making arrangements for the boarding and lodging of the students, medical treatment, taking care of the students, etc. were the major duties of a teacher toward his wards. Infusion of a spirit of piety and righteousness, formation of character, development of personality, inculcation of social and civic values, promotion of social efficiency, and spread of national culture may be described as the chief aims and ideals of ancient Indian education.

Teaching Methodology

1. Teaching followed some strategies such as

simple to complex, activity and skill-oriented procedures, Question-Answer technique and illustration. Self- study was considered more important.

2. Method of teaching was based on apprenticeship and was psychologically sound. Teaching was oral and habit of independent study was encouraged. Memorising naturally led to cramming where in Vedic verses were initially committed to memory without insight, and later mulled over and deliberated upon.

3. As mentioned above, the process of teaching was as follows :

a. Discussion for clarity of thought and diversity.

b. Emphasis on correct pronunciation, intonation and articulation.

c. Meditation after memorising to help assimilation.

d. Next step will begin only when the previous lesson is memorised.

e. Memorsing of lesson by student.

4. During the Vedic period, the Gurukul method prevailed, in which the student lived in the house of the guru, instead of living with his parents. Along with his colleagues, he led a celibate life and obtained education in the house of guru. Initially, in the vedic period, it was the teacher who occupied the primary place, but in the later period, it was the student who occupied the central place in education. The process of education passed through the three stages of comprehension, meditation, memory and nidhi-dhyasana. The Gurukuls were the centres of education, in which education was imparted only by individuals of character and ability. The student remained his Guru for 12 years. There were parishads or committees to satisfy the student's thirst for knowledge. Congresses of scholars were also

organised from time to time. In these awards were given to prominent scholars.

Education in Later Vedic/Brahmanic Period

Later Vedic Period -:

Also called as Brahmanic age, the later Vedic period was almost a refined extension of the Vedic education except that various types of educational institutions, such as shakha, charna, parishad, kul, and created. Sutra literature alongwith shad Darshan was also created during this period. Syllabus was determined according to the Varna Ashram system. Education became more restrictive as it was denied to shudras and women, an equation which continues, in whatever form, for centuries and became a curse of Indian Society.

Special Features

1. Free and universal education.

2. Free of state control.

3. Teaching methodology centred around listening, contemplation.

4. The educational calendar commenced on the full moon of Shravana, and culminated on the full moon of Paush corresponding to July-January session of the calendar. Full moon therefore, acquired methodology centred around listening, contemplation, comprehension, self-study, and recall.

5. Education was marked by such rituals as Vidya-arambha, upnayana, and samavartana.

6. Homely environment.

7. Fair and just: no discrimination of caste, sex and social status.

8. Gurukul- centred.

9. Character development.

10. Physical and mental development.

Objectives of Education

1. Preservation of knowledge and culture.
2. Propagation of purity.
3. Integrated personality.
4. Generation of sociability, or social awareness.
5. Development of character.
6. Self-control.

General Characteristics of Brahmanic Education

1. Primary was still given to the study of Vedas. The curriculum included subjects like grammar, arithmetic, geometry, astrology, economics, history, political science, agriculture, , military science and warfare, logic and philosophy, etc. The curriculum, as such, became place in the educational programme. Intonation was specially stressed upon as a special feature of language-learning.

2. Unlike the Vedic education where it remained oral, the art of writing was developed during the later Vedic/Brahmanical period. Purity of pronunciation and correct articulation was emphasized. Education was imparted through discussion, question-answer, clarification of doubts and concepts, etc.

3. Celibacy still remained an essential feature of the system.

4. Due to absence of collective education, Brahmanic education centred around individual, his growth and development.

5. Equitable attention to the two types of education: worldly and non-worldly. Education became preparation for life here and after.

6. Dominance of religion.

Causes of the Downfall

1. Lack of synthetic approach making education lopsided.

2. Rigidity of Varna ashrams acquired a narrow outlook resulting in loss of dignity of labour, hence disappearance of art and handicrafts from the educational curriculum.

3. Neglect of women's education imbalanced the social structure and control, and relegated women into obscurity.

4. Dogmatic faith in the Vedas and its rituals, making education exclusively Brahmanic, deprived of logic and consistency.

5. Deprivation of Shudra's right to education causing discrimination and interest and inequality in society.

6. Philosophy as a source of pure knowledge for salvation, deprived many to understand the real meaning of education as preparation for life here and now. Education became pedantic.

7. Religious dominance, occultism and stress on rituals resulted in less importance to material and worldly prosperity and development.

2

ELEMENTARY EDUCATIONAL PROBLEMS

Forms of Primary Education

1. Constitution refers to it neither as Primary, nor Elementary, but Compulsory education.

2. Some consider primary as a substitute for elementary.

3. Kothari Commission used the term primary, so did the NCERT.

4. Gandhi ji used the term primary for this stage.

5. NPE- 86 refers to it as elementary education.

6. Basic Education is envisaged as comprehensive and integral development of a child, and is based on handicrafts so as of education is referred to differently by different agencies.

7. Primary Education is also called general form providing for an education which achieves only the objectives of intellectual skill. John Ruskin describes the meaning of education as teaching people to conduct themselves in ways in which they do not behave. Education therefore, is modification of behaviour which is at its peak during the stage called primary wherein a child learns to interact in a social environment away from home.

Objectives : Kothari Commission

Junior Primary classes I to IV

Acquire a rudimentary knowledge of reading, writing and numbers and the appropriate skills. Learn and practice the basic principles of healthy living. Gain an elementary knowledge and appreciation of environment- social, physical and cultural. Appreciate, in a rudimentary way, their gifts of science in our every day life. Express freely and creatively through both verbal and no-verbal media. Lay proper foundations of intelligent patriotism though an appreciation of national symbols and national festivals. Learn to use his hands and also to develop a respect for dignity of labour .

To grow socially by acquiring habits of courtesy, cooperation and adjustment of working with others for a common purpose. Have respect for all places of worship, irrespective of the religion one follows. Learn in an elementary way important skills like listening, attentively, observing carefully and thinking logically. Acquire a spirit of inquiry in respect of the immediate environment. Gain some idea of the values to be cherished and also of the culture of the country. Appreciate the inter-dependence of people in all spheres of life inside the country and outside.

Senior Primary Classes V to VII

Acquire knowledge of basic facts and principles in different subjects and skills, and competence to apply them in appropriate situations. Express himself adequately through oral and written language to meet his everyday needs. Appreciate the use of number and the symbolic language of mathematics and to understand spatial relationships.

Learn the basic principles of personal and social health and to act upon them. Develop an appreciation of the unity that runs through our diverse culture practices. Develop a sense of healthy patriotism and legitimate pride in the nation- its past, present and future. Comprehend the ways in which science helps in our lives and to start using the scientific method in whatever he does. Acquire work-experience through the pursuit of crafts. Develop respect for religion other than his own to live and work co-operatively with others, regardless of all considerations of language, caste or religion.

Objectives of Primary Education : NCERT

1. The first objective is technocracy. The child should learn the method of enquiry in science and should begin to appreciate science and technology in the life and world around.

2. The Second objective is attainment of numeracy. The child should develop facility in the four fundamental numerical operations and be able to apply these in the life of the community to solve practical problems.

3. The first objective is literacy. The child should learn the first language, which would generally be his mother-tongue to a level where he can communicate easily with others through articulated speech and witting.

Aims of Primary Education

At the primary stage of education, the range of students in 6-14 years. The chief aims of education at this age are as under :

1. Creative Activities : Apart from the education of 3 Rs. children are also to be given training in manual work. At primary stage, basic education provides craft-centred education. It is activity centred and helps to

relate education directly with production. Thus, education at Elementary stage should help to create and construct something. It is similar to the concept of work-experience. But primary schools generally lack in this aspect of education. Education should be productive and help to develop skills.

2. Development of Virtues : It is common knowledge that in the education of a child, primary education acts as the foundation. A weak foundation would be dangerous. Therefore, while imparting education at this stage, inculcation of good habits and right attitudes among children is of vital importance. This will help to shape them into healthy and enlightened citizens. Only good teachers can help top generate these qualities among children.

3. Development of 3R : The chief aim of primary education is to provide education of 3R i.e., reading, writing and arithmetic. Mother-tongue is the medium of instruction at the stage. Children learn the language to read with proper accent, pronunciation and intonation. They are made to practice writing words badly and distinctly. These days children show much carelessness in learning the language. Teachers have to be very cautions with regard to the reading and writing of a language. The knowledge of Maths provide mental activity. All children are not well versed in it. They need incessant practice. Nowadays teaching of Maths require more understanding than cramming. While teaching this subject teachers are expected to adopt the technique of teaching Maths so the subject may become lively and interesting.

4. Study Environment : Apart from physical development, it is also necessary to acquaint the child abut the environment prevailing in and around the

family. They are expected to have a first and knowledge of the members of the family, neighbours, immediate community and the city etc. A study of school environment enhances their general knowledge and help to improve efficiency. The atmosphere of the school should be akin to healthy and attractive home environment. This will generate a sense of belongingness among children toward the institution and ultimately develop their personality on healthy lines.

5. Physical Development : At primary stage, there is need to give top priority to proper physical development of each child. For this, the institutions should be aware about their health. This entails proper arrangement of games and sports in the institution. Rousseau had stressed the need of a healthy mind in a healthy body. Games not only help in maintaining good health but are also a good means of recreation. Apart from this, they help to instill and imbibe other qualities, such as, team spirit and social and emotional adjustment among children.

Curriculum Related to Objectives

At the Lower primary level, the child should acquire control over the basic tools of learning such as reading, writing, counting, and in order to adapt himself to the environment, should study, in elementary terms, the social and material environment.

At the Higher primary level, education should be imparted in one language other than the mother-tongue, arithmetic, natural and physical science, history, geography, civics creative and constructive skills, and physical education. The Kothari Commission's outline for such curriculum is as follows :

1. Lower primary level - One language - mother

tongue or regional language. Arithmetic, Study of the environment, creative activities, work experience and social service, health education.

2. Higher Primary level - Mother tongue or regional language, Arithmetic, Science, social studies, art, work experience, physical education, education in moral and spiritual values.

According to the Kothari Commission, the first two classes of the primary school should be dovetailed into a unit, and wherever possible, the same arrangement should apply to the third and fourth classes also. For these classes, the proposed curriculum is very simple, and it reduces the burden of prescribed courses.

In order to develop learning, it is necessary to include in the curriculum such activities as study of the environment, conservation, social studies, science, self expression, music, art, drama, handicraft etc. It is also necessary to discover the student's eagerness for studying, as well as his ability. As far as the higher primary level is concerned, the study of the language, arithmetic, science, social studies, art, work experience, physical education, and teaching of moral and spiritual values in order to form their character and also the generate respect in their minds for other religions. For this, one or two hours in the week should be fixed, and the activities for social services should include participation in the local social life.

Objectives of Primary Education: Ishwer Bhai Patel Commitee

1. Development of the desire participation on productive work and to serve the community.

2. Development of social responsibility.

3. Development of aesthetic perception and creativity

through participation in artistic activities and observation of nature.

4. Acquisition of habits of cooperative behaviour within the family, school and community.

5. Acquisition of skills for planning and executing socially useful productive work with a view of making education work based.

6. Development of physical strength and team spirit through sports and games.

7. Acquisition of knowledge through observation, study and experimentation in the areas of social and natural sciences.

8. Acquisition of tools of formal learning, namely literacy, numeracy and manual skills.

Different contexts

1. Universality of Retention: University of retention pertains to the retaining every child admitted to the school till the last class of primary stage.

2. Universality of Enrolment: This aspect deals with the homogeneity of enrolment in a particular age-group. This requires enrolling every child of 6+ age group to class 1 restricting admission of a child of higher age-group to class 1. It would require pre-planning. The provision will save the child from the demoralising effect of stagnation.

3. Universality of Provision: The univesality of provision has something to do with providing the facility of school within an easy reach of every child. The school should be at a walking distance from home and should be suitably located. This would require expansion of primary education in balanced way. The population may also be a good basis for establishing primary schools in

the country. Thus, universality of provision deals with the availability of school facilities in terms of infrastructure.

Universalisation of Primary/ Elementary Education

Universalisation of education refers to any system of education that extends opportunities to population concerned regardless of any extraneous considerations like race, colour, caste, religion, sex, and ability. It implies that state is responsible for free, compulsory and universal elementary education to all children until they complete the age of 14 years. It may be noticed that whereas primary education is structurally known as Primary and Basic education, the Constitution refers to it as compulsory education. Article 45 of the constitution directed this to be provided by 1960. However, we are nowhere near the objective, in spite of Sarva Shiksha Abhiyan that vowed to send every child to school by 2003. Education for All has remained a mirage, distant on illusive. Article 29 and 30 provide certain exclusive educational and cultural rights to all, especially the minorities. Directive Principles of state policy emphasis the intellectual development of all citizens.

Hindrances of Universalisation of Primary Education

In spite of the best of intensions and efforts, the constitutional obligation under Article 45 is far from fulfillment even in the year 2004. Sarva Shiksha Abhiyan launched with great fanfare and enthusiasm had the target of Education for All by 2003, saying that no eligible child will be left out of school. Now, India 2020, a vision Document, has further extended probable date by which universalisation of primary education might be possible-a long distance away form 1960 as originally contemplated. What really is the malaise of primary education? Why has it not been a success? What are the hindrances to its application?

1. Inapplicability of a Uniform System : The geography of the country divides it into mutually unrelated and inhospitable segments making application for a uniform system of primary education impossible. As a matter of fact, primary education should be responsive to local needs and requirements in on overall plan of action. Nevertheless, the weather and terrain factors should not be allowed to blunt the movement.

2. Unrelated Educational Practices : While discussing aims, objectives and the learning experiences for primary education in a preceding section, we noticed that there is general disagreement with the ground reality. The curriculum is not realistic and, therefore lacks relevance and application. Inadequacy of suitable teachers and infrastructure further compound the problem. Even the programs like single-teacher schools and operation blackboard did not make any appreciable progress. Policy of schools exclusively for girls also inhibit the progress for primary education.

3. Social Apathy : External aggressions, compounding the problem of refugees and displaced families, and internal disorders hinder the progress of primary education as small children become a sitting dutch, and are therefore, made to stay at home for safety reasons. Lack of political will and contribution leaves a dismal impact as not much active consideration is given to this stage of a child's growth and development. Bringing education to the concurrent list might give

primary education is requisite thrust in the right direction. What really required is political and administrative involvement and obsession toward primary education. This spirit is woefully lacking presently.

4. Resource Crunch : Lack of financial resources and management, the target of one primary school in every village is still a far cry as most of these schools are located at a distance and are poorly strafed and housed. The problem becomes more severe in hilly and other inhospitable areas, Besides, children especially the girls, are kept at home for domestic management, and/or other errands at the time of harvesting etc. Primary education, thus, lacks that priority tag.

Comments

Primary Education should be taken up as a National Movement. That is what Sarva Shiksha Abhiyan connotes and aims at. With a little more will and ingenuity, the programme might click failing which universalisation of education would remain a distant dream. Efforts should be made to reduce the level of wastage and stagnation.

The Human resource development ministry refuses to by the rosy picture painted by the states, most of them congress-ruled, in achieving the Sarva Siksha Abhiyan and has asked them to come up with reliable and accurate data on the enrolment of children in schools. While estimates indicate that the number of children out school has reduced from 38 million at the beginning of the programme to around 10 million now, states were apprised of the need to carefully re-examine these so as to arrive reliable and accurate figures. HRD ministry sources said.

They said that states like Punjab, Jammu and Kashmir and Delhi have not yet fully put in place the necessary infrastructure for data collection and their estimates are, therefore, unlikely to be reliable.

Similarly, although UP has reported a sharp fall in the number of out-of-school children from 43 lakh at the beginning of the programme to 2.1 lakh today, these figures need to be carefully checked the sources said.

Stagnation

According to Hartog Committee 1929, stagnation means retention of a student for more than one year in class. Connected with student failure in class I, it results in decrease of number of students in higher classes successively till a very small number makes it to class V. Thus, primary schools become more of centres of failure wherein a child may be kept in a single class for two or three years due to failure. Efforts are now afoot not to have any failure till class V so as to meet the basic target of literacy and general education. The yearly level of stagnation in primary classes is between 30% to 50% and is a major hindrance to the success of universalisation of education.

Causes of Stagnation

1. Defective Examination System : Defective teaching methodology focussing on cramming, and once-a-year examination system also leads to projecting unreal picture of a child's performance causing failure and frustration, hence, stagnation. Secondary Education Commission pointed out defects of evaluation system at primary stage wherein a student demonstrates skills only at learning by rote, use of help-books and writing essay type answers which one can reproduce by rote. More stress on knowledge than on learning and

personality development, Passing the examination becomes the be-all of the entire education system wherein it becomes even an index of teacher competency. Kothari Commission recommended class I to IV as a single unit, hence no failures and no stagnation.

2. Irregular Attendance/Admissions : Admissions to most of the primary schools is almost continuous throughout the year thus affecting the teacher and class performance. Attendance is not given much priority and children remain away from school causing break in their studies, leading to stagnation as they to repeat the class due to failure.

3. Faulty Methods of Teaching : It is generally seen that even the elite public schools accept untrained teachers, only on their verbal communication skill, for the lower classes thinking that correct expression, pronunciation and intonation etc. are sufficient at the level, little realising that organising and presenting a lesson even at that stage is as important, if not more, than at any other stage of learning. Teaching should be systematic and interesting to convey the content/ activity in a manner that it leaves a lasting impression on a child's mind. The stress should be learning rather than on cramming.

4. Unsuitable Curriculum : Heady, dull, drab and uninteresting curriculum is responsible for stagnation to a very large extent. In spite of so much of research and revision, the learning experiences in most of research and revision, the learning experiences in most of the schools in the rural and urban areas generally remain traditional and unimaginative without any resource to child's ability, interest and attitude, with the result the child remains, by and large, uninvolved

and un-participative. That learning is fun, is absolutely foreign to the concept, forcing a child to hang on in the same class for more than the prescribed time.

5. Defective State Policy : Financial crunch and official apathy lack of insight and appreciation of educational expenditure as investment; general indifferent toward the problem of stagnation.

How to Eradicate Stagnation

1. Better means of communication so that children have no excuse to miss the school.

2. Change or mind-set and approach to primary education wherein parents should be educated by means of non-formal education.

3. Integrated approach to primary education.

4. Decentralisation of primary education.

5. Supervision and inspection should be revitalised and made more useful, direct and effective.

6. The methods of teaching and examination need drastic changes.

7. Poor children should get milk, maid-day meal, books etc. free of cost.

8. Facilities of games should exist in schools.

9. Suitable arrangement for the education of girls should be made.

10. The curriculum should be easy, practical and useful.

11. The principle of uniformity with regard to the age group of children should be preserved.

12. Education at the primary level should be free and compulsory and the principle of the universalisation should be implemented in letter and spirit.

Wastage

Hargog Committee 1929 was the first to consider the problem of wastage and stagnation in detail. The Committee was of the view that the problem is very grave in the field of primary education. On the basis of the available data it was found that if in 1922, 100 children got admission to class 1, only 18 were able to pass class V in 1927. It shows that rest of them either failed or left the school in one class or the other. The findings revealed that class 1 was a permanent stagnant pool where wastage was found to be the maximum.

It is amply clear that primary education will remain ineffective as long as each child did not remain in school for a minimum period of four years and achieve literacy. Though literacy is not education yet it is its root. Wastage, in this context, refers to dropping out of the child from the educational process , and involves a great deal of waste of human and material resources. According to Hartog Committee wastage means pre-mature withdrawal of the students from the class or school at any stage before completion of the primary course.

General Trends observed by Kothari Commission

1. Wastes is mor in the hills than the plains.

2. Rate of wastage varies throughout the country due to social and geographical factors. In U.P. it is approximately 60%.

3. Wastage is more in boys than in girls.

4. Wastage is maximum in class I and II.

According to a survey by UNESCO, wastage rage is very high in India wherein barely 50% children reap the full benefit of primary education.

Causes of Wastage

1. Lack of Space in Schools - Wastage also occurs in schools which have only make shift arrangements for housing the children. Another factor contributing to wastage is the fact that children are admitted to schools throughout the year. Besides, lack of attention toward attendance is another factor. It has been observed that wastage reaches the figure of 36% by the time we reach class 8.

2. Schools without Resources - Many schools are almost completely lacking in resources necessary for teaching and in the absence of these means the teacher cannot teach. Consequently, the children engage themselves in playing here and there, and in the absence of satisfactory results, soon leave the school.

3. Child Labour - Children living in villages are the property of their parents who can compel their children to labour and earn on the fields. For such parents, the money earned by the child is more important than his education.

4. Social and Economic Structure - India's economic and social structure is of a kind which inhibits parents to send their children for general education. Even today, our rural population holds on to the belief that a child should only be educated to the extent of being able to read and write.

5. Single Teacher Schools - Schools with single teacher make a special contribution to wastage. According to the report of the Indian Education Survey, these schools have played a significant role in this matter. It is difficult for a single teacher to handle five classes simultaneously. If he goes on leave, the school closes down. This makes the students reluctant in going

to school and soon they drop out altogether.

Wastage means dropping out of the child from the educational process. Stagnation refers to a child's stay in a class for more than one year due to failure. Discrimination of age of children in a class. Admission allowed throughout the year. Irregular attendance.

Evolved by Kothari Commission, integrated approach refers to a process by which various elements are brought near to each other, in a close relationship of education with the needs and aspirations of individual and society.

Decentralisation means handing over the foci of authority and responsibility to basic units or individuals instead of allowing them to rest with a few individuals. The New Education Policy will give the highest priority to solving the problem of children dropping out of school and will adopt an array of meticulously formulated strategies based on micro-planning and applied at the grass-root level all over the country. To ensure children's retention at school. This effort will be fully coordinated with the network of non-formal education. It shall be ensured that all children who attain the age of about 11 years by 1990 would have had five years of schooling, or its equivalent through the non-formal stream. Likewise by 1995, all children would be proved free and compulsory education up to 14 years of age.

The 10th five year plan was implemented in 2003 wherein free and compulsory education becomes the right of a child. Right to Education, therefore, acquires a constitutional guarantee.

3

MEANING OF EDUCATION

Introduction

Education is the process of development which consists of the passage of the human being from infancy to maturity and, the process whereby he adapts himself gradually in various ways to his physical social and spiritual environment. But even in this social process, the child needs support and freedom from an economic pressure, and that is why education requires long period of social as well as biological infancy when the young would live off the labour of others and be released from self support. However, assistance will be at least partially discounted unless education at the same time encourages wise and discriminating consumption. The child should bot become a parasite. He must pay back by realising the goals and objectives that education sets for him upto his optimal capacity, sincerity and honestly. Education must focus on total and optimal development of human resource.

Etymological Meaning

The word education is derived from the Latin roots as under -

Education, Educere, Educare. Education means to train- E means from inside and Doco means to draw out, to lead out or to bring up. Combining the two we get to draw form inside. Developing process of drawing out from within, to make explicit what is implicit, education is to draw out and develop powers and capacities to the optimal. Educare and educere also mean it is essentially a process of developing a child's inner dispositions, capacities and abilities to full use. It is a process of developing a continuous process of continuous development.

Wider Meaning of Education

In the wider sense, education is a process of development from cradle to the grave, a never-ending, continuous process of never ending, continuous development. In wider sense, education is experiential. What broadens our horizons, deepens our insight, refines our reactions and, stimulates thought and feeling, educates us. In wider sense, it is a process that goes on through life, and that is promoted by almost every experience in life. According to Dumvile, education in its widest sense includes all the influences which act upon an individual his passage from cradle to the grave. Education in this sense is intrinsic and unstructured.

Narrower Meaning of Education

In its narrow sense, education refers to school instruction. In this process the elders of the society prescribe to pre-determined aims to be realised during a specified time by providing pre-structured information to children through set methods of teaching. It is not drawing out, it is filling in, and thus hampers natural and full development of a child. Education in this sense is extrinsic and is in no way related to the child's endowments and capacities. In narrow sense, education may be taken to man any consciously directed effort to develop and cultivate powers.

Education as a Process

1. Education is a progressive process. Information and knowledge are transmitted and acquired progressively, gradually.

2. Education is a continuous process.

3. Education is an interactive process in which all the poles are mutually inclusive.

4. Education is a process. It is tripolar process.

To sum up

1. Education is a process of adjustment to environments.

2. Eduction is a process of producing change in the group.

3. Education is a process of development of individuality.

4. Education is a process of drawing out innate powers.

True Definition of Education

According to Raymond Education is that process of development which consists in the passage of human being from infancy to maturity, the process whereby the adapts himself gradually in various ways to his physical, social and spiritual environment.

Definition of Education

1. According to Socrates, "Education means the bringing out the ideas of universal validity which are in the mind of every man."

2. According to Mahatma Gandhi ji, "By education I means an all round drawing out of the best in child and man: body, mind and soul.

3. According to Freobel, "Education is process by which child makes his internal external."

4. Other, "Education is the manifestation of perfection already reached in man."

Components of Education

Education is a tripolar process. It has the following components-

1. Teacher, 2. Students, 3. Content. Hence, education is a tripolar and interactive process in which the instructional interventions bring in the desired behavioural change in the student. It is teacher John Latin.

Education and Training

Education :-

1. Education has various forms.

2. Education is lifelong.

3. Education affects the total life a pupil.

4. Education is comprehensive process.

Training :-

1. Training informal.

2. Training is restricted to specific area.

3. Based on a fixed, definite, pre-determined syllabus and includes only those experiences that help in the training of a specific task.

4. Training is a restricted activity.

Eduction and Instruction

Instructions :-

1. In instruction, cramming is encouraged. It is soon forgotten and thus, cannot be applied to meet the

challenges of life successfully.

2. Instruction prepares the child to pass in examination.

3. Instruction neglects interests, inclinations and capacities of the child. Ready-made dozes of knowledge are forced into his mind.

4. In instruction, the place of teacher is central. The role of child is secondary. Thus, the role is reversed.

5. Instruction means forcing into the mind of a child. Pre-determined dozens of knowledge in pre-planned way to achieve mental development. It is one-sided development and that too of memory only. Thus, its field is narrow in comparison.

Education

1. In education all learning is self-learning. It remains stable and permanent and can be applied to solve the problems of future life.

2. Education prepares the child for real life.

3. Education pays full attention to the interests, inclinations and abilities of the child. Nothing is forced into his mind without his will.

4. In education, the place of child is central, pivotal and of prime importance, pivotal and of prime importance. Teacher's role in subsidiary.

5. Education is the full development of all the innate powers of a child. Nothing is thrust into his mind by force form outside. It develops the child physically, mentally, emotionally and socially. Thus, its field is wider than that of instruction.

Education and Literacy

Literacy is concerned with the traditional 3 R'S., that

is reading, writing and arithmetic. It is related to acquiring knowledge of some subjects. Education, on the other hand, is related to 7 R's, that is reading, writing, arithmetic, rights, responsibilities and their relationships and recreation.

Literacy is mainly concerned with theoretical knowledge which can be evaluated through different types of questions- essay type, short answer type and objective type. But education cannot be evaluated through these to techniques. Education provides a way of life. It develops certain values. A person may posses high literacy and even high sounding degree but he may be labeled uneducated if he lacks human qualities. Education is concerned with the development of character and personality.

Balance Between Formal and Informal Agencies of Education

The truth is that none of the above discussed agencies is complete in itself. Each gives a certain type of education which is only a part of the whole. In really both the agencies the agencies of education are mutually complementary and supplementary for the complete and whole-some development of personality. Thus, both the agencies should co-operate in education the child. There must be a balance of working by both the agencies for the total development of the child. No one is to be neglected as both complete the desired development.

Importance of Education

Education is important from various points of view. Its field of activity is so wide that all activities and experience are embraced in tis sphere of work. Essentially, it is process of development, a development of the latent, inherent capacities of a child to the fullest extent. It sublimates the animal basic instincts in a child to socially useful activities, habits of thinking and behaving. It inculcate values, so that he is able to form a strong character useful to his own self and to the society of which he is an internal part. Further, education meets the immediate needs of a child and also social and refined patterns of behaviour. Not only this, is develops all his intellectual and emotional powers, so that he is able to meet the problems of life squarely and solve them successfully. It also develops the social qualities of service, tolerance, co-operation, fellow-feeling, inspiring the child to lay down all, even his life, for the glory and prosperity of his country. Last but not the least, education infuses in the child a spirit of dynamic citizenship which eggs him on in the service of his nation keeping in consideration the international understanding and well-being of humanity as a whole.

Forms of Education

1. Positive Negative - Positive education relates to scientific information about our environmental situations and experiences. For examples, imparting knowledge about the solar system; and such cardinal concepts like spacing the truth; hate if sin, not the sinner; without any direct experience there of, is called positive education.

Negative education is based on the child's own, direct experiences, and formation of his ideals based on these experiences. It is called negative because of its accompanying risk factor.,

2. General and Specific - Preparation for life is the keynote of the general education and it has no fixed and specific aim it covers the entire spectrum of world experiences. Specific education is related to some

specific and definite variation. It is preparation for livelihood.

3. Individual and Collective - Individual education is that form of education which is imparted by a teacher to a child in a direct manner keeping in mind the child's individual needs, abilities and potentialities. Collective education is imparted in a group where the norm is an average child, irrespective of the individual differences of the pupils.

4. Direct and Indirect - Direct education is the result of the mutual interaction between a teacher and a pupil. It is personal, structured and deliberated. Indirect education is acquired through free and unstructured experiences and environmental situations. It is also called impersonal education and is indirect.

5. Formal and Informal - In formal education pupils require information and other environment experiences in pre-specified manner in accordance with a fixed curriculum and in the precincts of a schools. Formal education is deliberate and specific.

4

EDUCATION IN BRITISH PERIOD (1800-1853)

Introduction

The British came to India during the Moghul period in 1600 AD primarily for trade and commerce. On the downfall of the Moghul empire, the British consolidated their hold and established East India Company under a Charter. The company acquired political dimensions yet retained its original trade-character in the early days. Later, the company ruled India for over 150 years bringing in its wake the best of western literature, science, culture and technology. The British organised education in India during various periods as under:

1. First Period : 1800-1853.
2. Second Period : 1854-1900.
3. Third Period : 1901-1919.
4. Fourth Period : 1920-1947.

First Period

Education in India was governed by the Board of Directors of the East India Company under section 43 of the Charter of 1813. Lord Macualay came to India in 1834 and was made chief of the Public Instruction by the then Governor General Lord Bentinck, a great reformer and visionary. Prior to Macualay, who considered Eastern education inferior to its western counterpart, the educational scenario in India was as under :

1. Indigenous Systems of Education : Actually Britishers came to India for trade in the year 1600. At that time, there was a net-work of large number of schools all over the country which were mostly single-teacher schools with multiple class teaching. Senior students acted as monitors and helped the teacher in the teaching work. Medium of instruction was Sanskrit, Bengali, Hindi, Urdu, Persial and Arabic etc. Practically each village had its primary school or Pathshala. In Bengal alone, it is said, there were about the year 1835 a hundred thousand such pathshala.

Despite a large number of indigenous institutions spread all over the country, their financial condition was far from satisfactory in terms of building, teachers pay scales and other infra-structure. The main reason of backwardness had been poverty, lack of teacher training institutions, death-knell of cottage industries and an attitude of indifference on the part of the government. The net result was that these institutions gradually disappeared from the scene. According to Western educators, the indigenous systems in India was of no importance and the British officers were justified in ending the same.

2. The Charter of 1813 : the increasing efforts of missionaries with regard to English education led to dissatisfaction among the masses. When the government took steps to check their activities, they lodged a complaint against it in Britain. The matter was raised in British Parliament. This results in the future policy of education to be followed in India and accepted the responsibility of the government for the spread of

education. A sum of rupees one lakh was earmarked for the education of the whole country.

Thus, the education of the masses was badly neglected. Only the Christian missionaries and a few Indian leaders were enthusiastic in establishing educational institutions privately and, with the passage of time, were successful in getting grant from the government.

3. Efforts of Christian Missionaries : With the establishment of East India Company, the supremacy of the Britishers in India increased but education in general was neglected. With the efforts of some Christian missionaries, only a few institutions were established which provided education through English medium, but they did not get any aid from the government.

According to Nurullah and Naik, the missionaries used education as a means of evangelisation. They propagated for the spread of Christian religion through English medium. Only the Presidencies of Calcutta, Madras and Bombay were the main centres of education at that time.

4. Anglicist - Classicist Controversy : A large number of controversial issues pertaining to the objectives, means and medium of instruction emerged with the implementation of the Charter of 1813. On the one hand, some Indians were in favour of imparting education through Sanskrit, Arabic, Persian and other classical languages, while on the other hand, some Westerners and others were pressing for English as the medium of instruction. This led to a controversy between the two schools of thought. The proponents of these schools were both British and Indian Philanthropists, and were called Orientalists and Occidentalists

respectively.

The controversy ranged around the problem of medium, responsibility and the education of classes versus masses. H.H. Wilson, H.T. Prince, other veteran Europeans and some Indian leaders, were in favour of classical system of education while David Hare, Lord Macaulay, Raja Rammohan Roy and other missionaries favoured English as the medium of instruction.

There is no denying the fact that the both schools of thought were unanimous of the propagation and spread of western science and literature, but they differed as to the objectives, medium, means and responsibility of education. The recommendations of Woods Despatch, 1854 ultimately ended the forty years long controversy by establishing the supremacy of English for education in India.

Special Features of 1813-Charter

The Charter of 1813 was reviewable in 1833 and had the following main features :

1. Missionaries from any foreign country would be allowed to come to India and they were supposes not to hurt the feelings of Indians.

2. Jobs would be provided to Indians in company's departments without any consideration of caste and creed. Only merit would be considered.

3. In 1813 Charter, the provisions of Rs. One lac was made for education, it is increased to ten lacs of rupees per year.

4. There will be a legal advisor in the council of Governor General, who will give legal advise.

5. Governor of Bengal will be the Governor General

and governors of some other provinces will work under him in some matters.

Need of Clarification of Section 43

The Orientalists Party led by H.T. Prince was arguing for correct interpretation of Clause 43 of the Charter Act of 1813 which read as under :

It shall be lawful for the Governor General-in-Council to direct that out of any surplus which may remain of the rents, revenues, and profits rising from the said territorial acquisitions, after defraying the expenses of the military, civil and commercial establishment and paying the interest of the debt, in manner hereinafter provided, a sum of not less the learned natives of India and for the introduction and promotion of a knowledge of the sciences among the inhabitants of the British territories in India.

The Clause implied three main issues :

1. Knowledge of sciences to be promoted among the Indians.

2. Literature to be revved and improved.

3. The learned natives of India are to be encouraged.

1. Another group of occidentalists or anglicists believed that oriental system was very slow and hence they did not appreciate the idea of drafting the new western leaning upon the old stock of oriental learning. They were of the opinion that Indians wanted to acquire European learning and that they desired to utilise the entire education grant for the purpose of diffusing western education.

On one point on which both the groups agreed was that the indigenous languages were summarily discarded as being crude and poor. Incapable of expressing scientific and literacy ideas essential for liberal education, they believed that the higher classes having being so educated, it is quite evident that education would ultimately filter down to the lower classes by their contact with them.

Due to this controversy, East India company could not determine its educational policy. Thus twenty years had passed and no decision was taken. Now was the time of review the Charter of 1813, after 20 years as stipulated.

2. He further said , There are many considerations which should project the Madras at least from any present demolition. It is the only ling through which the Government has at present any connection whatsoever with the instruction of the Muslim youth of Bengal/ It is not one of the passing institutions of recent establishment for the support of which funds are assigned from the Parliamentary lack of rupees but is an old established college endowed separately and efficiently performing the purposes of the endowment.

3. The Occidentalits interpreted all the three issues involved in clause 43 in the favour of English language and education and proposed to abolish oriental institutions. Orientalists especially argued for not doing away with Calcutta Madras which was established by Warren Hasting. Prince argued this: An endowment made by Warren Hasting. Prince argued thus : An endowment made by Warren Hasting more than 50 years ago and for the support of which certain funds, the land revenue of the Madras- Mughal part of which is included in the Barrackpore was specifically assigned. At first, the institution was left to uncontrolled management of the Moola placed by Mr. Hasting at its

head. The Muhal however, was under the Khas management of the Board of Revenue and the varying amount realised from it was placed at the Moolavee's disposal. Subsequently, the Muhal was made over at a fixed jama to the Raja Nudeca when he was restored to his estates of which this formed a part. Except, therefore, that the direct management of the lands was not in of hands of the Principal and Professors and Fellows of the college, this was assuredly as complete an endowment as any of the colleges of Oxford and Cambridge Universities.

Revised Charter - 1833

1. Educational grant was increased from Rs. 1,00,000 to Rs. 10,00,000 for strengthening the educational front.

2. This charter empowered the Governor of Bengal presidency to exercise his control over the rest of British India and was full authorised to direct the educational policy of these provinces.

3. Uninterrupted growth of English among all classes of society.

4. Missionaries of other countries got full freedom to carry on their work in India. Famous principle was announced- No native of the Said territories nor any natural born subject of His Majesty resident therein, shall by reason only of his religion, holding place of birth, descent colour or any of them, be disable from holding place, office or employment under the said company.

Downward Filtration Theory

A legacy of the Occidentalists who were against using oriental languages as the medium of instruction, Downward Filtration Theory believed that if the people of the higher social order are educated through the English language, their influence would gradually percolate to the masses who would take it up rather enthusiastically because of the class- effect. Education must filter down and permeate from above, drop by drop. From the Himalayas of the Indian life useful information was to trickle downwards forming in time a broad and stately stream to irritate the thirsty plains.

Some Extracts

1. Blood and Colour of Indians : We want a class of persons Indian in blood and colour but English in tastes, in opinions, in morals and in intellect.

2. Revival of Literature : It seems to be the opinion of some of the gentlemen who compose the Committee of Public Instruction that the course which they have hitherto pursued was strictly prescribed by the British Parliament in 1813. It does not appear tome that the Act of Parliament can by art of interpretation be made to bear the meaning which has been assigned to it. It contains nothing about the particular languages, sciences which are to be studied. A sum is set apart for the revival and promotion of literature, and the encouragement of the learned natives of India, and for the introduction and promotion of a knowledge of sciences among the inhabitants of the British territories . It is argued, or rather than taken for granted, that by literature Parliament could have meant at only Arabic and Sanskrit literature, that they never would have given the honourable appellation of a learned native to a native who was familiar with the poetry of Milton and the physics of Newton.

3. False Knowledge : We are to teach false history, facts, astronomy, false medicine, because we find them

in company of a false religion. We abstain, and I trust shall always abstain, from giving any public encouragement to those who are engaged in the work of converting the natives to Christianity. And while we act thus, can we reasonably or decently bribe men, out of the revenues of the state, to waste their youth in learning how they are to purify themselves after touching an ass or what texts of the Vedas they are to repeat to expiate the crime of killing of goat.

4 Universal Confession : The question now before us is simply whether, when it is in our power to teach this language, we shall teach languages in which by universal confession, there are no books on any subject which deserve to be compared to our own, whether, when we can tach European science, we shall teach systems which, by universal confession, whereever they differ from those of Europe differ for the worse, and whether when we can patronise sound philosophy and true history, we shall countenance, at the public expense, medical doctrines which would disgrace at an English boarding school, history abounding with kings thirty feet high and reigns thirty thousand years long, and geography made of seas of honey and seas of butter.

5. Language Claim : The claims of our own language are hardly necessary to recapitulate. It stands pre-eminent even among the languages of the West. It abounds with works of imagination not inferior to the noblest which Greece has bequeathed to us-with models of every species of eloquence, with historical compositions which, considered as vehicle of ethical and political instruction, have never been equalled with lively representations of human life and human nature-with the more profound speculations on metaphysics, morals, government, jurisprudence, trade-with full and

correct information respecting even experimental science which tends to preserve the health, to increase to comfort, or to expand the intellect of man. Whoever knows that language has ready access to all the vast intellectual wealth which all the wise nations of the earth have created and hoarded in the course of nine generations. It may safely be said that the literature now extant in the language is of greater value than all the literature which three hundred years ago was extinct in all the languages of the world together In India, English is the language spoken by the ruling class. It is spoken by the higher class of natives at the seats of Government. It is likely to become the language of commerce throughout the seas of the East.

6. Common Dialect : All parties seem to be agreed on one point, that the dialect commonly spoken among the natives of this part of India contain neither literary nor scientific information, and are more quarter, it will not be easy to translate any valuable work into them. It seems to be admitted on all side that the intellectual improvement of those classes of the people who have the means of pursuing higher studies can at present be effected only by means of some language not vernacular amongst them.

7. Public Faith : The admirers of the Oriental system of education have used another argument which, if we admit it to be valid, is decisive against a change. They conceive that the public faith is pledged to the present system and that to alter the appropriation of any of the funds which has hitherto been spent in encouraging the study of Arabic and Sanskrit will be downright stopped. It is not easy to understand by what process of reasoning they can have arrived at the encouragement of literature differ in no respect from the public purse for which are

made from the same purse for other objects of real or to be healthy. Do we thereby pledge ourselves to keep sanatorium the erection of a pier. Is it a violation of the public faith to the works if we afterwards see reason to believe that the building was useless.

8. Indian Literature : A single shelf of a good European library was worth the whole native literature of India and Arabia.

Macaulay's Minute

The beginning of British systems of education in India can be traced with Macaulay Minute. Macaulay was the first Britisher to ridicule and criticise the eastern system of education and culture. He opined a single shelf of good European library was worth the whole native literature of Indian and Arabia. Macaulay, was a staunch supporter of English language and literature and was very proud of it. About Indian education he said It was the duty of England to teach Indians what was good for their health and not what was palatable to their taste.

Thus, he strongly advocated the cause of English literature and science and he said, "We must at present do out best to form a class who may be interpreters between us and the millions whom we govern- a class of persons Indian in blood and colour but English in tastes, in opinions, in morals and in intellect. Macaulay advanced the following arguments in favour of the education of English literature and science in India.

1. It is every difficult to educate the Indian masses. In the beginning only the selected few can be educated and through filtration, by and by, education will percolate to the masses.

2. The study of English language is in the best

interests of Indians.

3. Indians themselves are eager to study English literature and science.

4. English is the main language of the west. In India also it is the language of the rulers and, therefore, the possibility of its being the language of the Far East are bright.

5. English language will go a long way in revitalising and rejuvenation the field of knowledge in the same way as Latin and Greek did for English in the past.

6. English is the key to modern gateway of knowledge and therefore, it is much more useful than the classical language like Sanskrit, Arabic and Persian etc.

In view of the above, Macaulay wanted to create a class among Indians as interpreters to carry out the work of administration and thus help in strengthening the British rule. It is because of all this that Macaulay is popularly known as the torch bearer of the British system of education in India.

Critical Estimate of Macaulay's Views of Indian Languages

1. Macaulay believe that English would bring renaissance in India as Greek and Latin had done in England. Macualay did not consider how limited his policy was. It appeared that he was making an effort to grow a temperate plant on warm plains. It may be possible for such a plant to survive under artificial environment but not to thrive. The fate of India was closely tied with the prosperity of Arabic or Sanskrit. He was also mistaken in the belief that English Education would anglicise Indian thoroughly. India can assimilate others

cultures but can not accept others cultures in place of her own. Has not his firm belief, which he expressed in a letter to his father that if his plans of education were followed up, there would be not a single dilatator among the respectable class in Bengal thirty years thereafter, come wrong?

2. Macaulay is justly blamed for his recommendation about use of English as the only medium of instruction. He totally rejected Indian languages as crude and unsuitable instrument for expressing scientific and literary ideas. It was an act of his negligence because he saw before his won eyes that some of the vernacular or other languages were being used as media of instruction for college education in Bombay presidency and a book like Bible could be effectively translated in them. Macaulay did not care to know the fact that number of Indian languages were in a flourishing state under the Mughals and were well equipped. He was perhaps misguided by local persons that the adoption of Indian languages as media of instruction was impossible. At a later date in 1836, as President of the General committee of Public Instruction, he, however, wrote, we are deeply sensible to the importance of encouraging the cultivation of the vernacular languages. We conceive the formation of a vernacular literature to be the ultimate object to which all our efforts must be directed.

It appears that Macualay admitted at a later stage, the utility of vernaculars as the media of instruction. It also appears from the above statements that he did not want English to continue for a long periods as medium of instruction. He wanted that Indian languages should supplant it, after becoming enriched. But the government misused the concession and English continued to be the sole medium of instruction.

Many Indian languages were rejuvenated by 1850. A number of educationist had started protesting against the use of English medium as the sole medium of instruction. But the Government of India did not pay any heed to it. It, on the contrary, reprimanded the Mumbai Government when they tried to improve local language through Poona Sanskrit College. It was only in 1904 that Lord Curzon drew the attention of the government to this policy. Ever since the cold breath of Maculay's rhetoric passed over the field of Indian languages and Indian Textbooks the elementary education of the people in their won language has shrivelled and pined.

3. Macaulay has been rightly criticised for his utter ignorance of Indian and Asiatic culture, A single shelf of good European library was worth the whole native literature of India and Arabia was a harsh and snobbish statement. The question now before us is simply whether, when we can patronise sound philosophy and true history, we shall countenance at public expenses, medical doctrines which would disgrace an English farrier, astronomy which would move laughter in girls at an English boarding school, history abounding with kings thirty feet high and reigns thirty thousand years long and geography made of seas of honey and seas of butter.

The above ridicules remarks show the narrowness of his vision and limitations of the grasp of the problem. His pronouncements says James are too glib, too confident, too unqualified and sometimes err against good taste. Macaulay wanted to cut Indians from their past heritage by forcing upon them a new language and a new culture and by snatching away from them their own. It did not occur to his mind at all that the urgent need of India then was acquisition of knowledge of western sciences and methods. Had he tried to give emphasis to the acquisition of scientific knowledge that west had so far amassed, India might have gained a lot. He simply tried to impose western learning, literature and history through a western language.

Place of Macaulay

1. Further, it is not correct to say that Macaulay was responsible for spreading western political ideas in India as he apprehended that having become instructed in European language, Indian in some future age may demand European institutions. How could person with such racial attitude contemplate of the well being and progress of India. The fact is, that spread of education through English was almost a fate accompli even before his arrival, and the rest was all a matter of circumstances. Indians like Raja RamMohun Roy were already demanding political leverage. In fact, it was the union of Lord Bentinck, Lord Macualay and Ram Mohan Roy that harnessed the existing socio-political condition in the country toward educations development. It was the glorious period- the period of Reforms, of the East Indian Company in India, and education was simply one of its aspects.

2. It is said the Macaulay was responsible for initiating a new educational policy, i.e., introducing European knowledge through the medium of English. He was not the originator of this system or policy. A vast majority of people were in favour of the policy. Raja Ram Mohan Roy and his colleagues, the new officers of East India company, and the Christian Missionaries, all

wanted westernisation of education. The ground was ready. It was Macaulay's job to add rich mineral to the soil. A large body of people have been reared: Indian in blood and colour, but English in tastes, in opinions, in morals and in intellect. A dawn of cultural renaissance had already begun for the educational policy had already gained momentum. It was for him to let go. The Government was also eager to introduce English education in India as needed English-educated India servants cheap. It wanted some connecting link of communication between the rulers and the ruled, and no other language seemed to be more appropriate. Hence, was the single-handed effort of Macaulay although he may be credited to trigger the process. The desire to learn the English language had already blossomed in the Indian hear.

English as a Medium of Instruction in India

On the basis of Macualay's Minute the educational policy of the country had finally been given a definite and stable shape. Hence, the Minute hold a permanently important place in the history of Indian education.

Lord Macualay was appointed the President of the General Committee of Public Instruction and was asked his views with regard to the ensuing revision of the Charter Act and its implementation, as well as, to suggest the ways and means by which the financial grant could be utilised. His views were in the form of Minute and are called Macaulay's Minute. Minute is a manner in which a suggested case is put up for the consideration and personal of the superior officer, in this case the Governor General of India and the British Parliament.

Macaulay interpreted the word literature in the Charter as English literature and discounted the use of oriental languages disdainfully called as Vernaculars whom he considered little developed for higher education. His claim for English as lingua franca was supported as under :

1. It has a great future to become the language of commerce throughout the sea of the East.

2. It is spoken by the higher class of local people in the Government who were called natives.

3. English was the only language spoken by the ruling class in India.

4. English stands pre-eminent even among the languages of the west.

Macaulay visualised that English would bring renaissance and revival in India just in the same manner as Greek of Latin did in England or just as the languages of Western Europe did in Russia. He further mentioned that the natives were themselves desirous and keen to learn English, a trend which contained ever since, and which made English as a world language. He firmly believed that education through English medium will churn out a class of people Indian in blood and colour but English in taste, outlook and culture Macaulay considered this class as the backbone of British empire in India and a source of filteration down of English to the masses. It led to the emergence of brown sahibs, a nomenclature that stuck on to the bureaucracy till the days of the Indian Civil Services, and even later.

Recommendations of the Governor General

William Bentinck, the them Governor General of India, and known for this reformist attitude, approved of Macaulay's Minutes and said I give my entire concurrence to the sentiments expressed in this minute:

and he passed the following order : His Lordship in the Council is of the opinion that the great object of the British Government ought to be the promotion of the European literature and printed for the purpose of education would be best employed on English education alone.

The resolution promised to supply Government with English educated Indian servants, and the hopes came true in a big way.

Evaluation of Macaulay's Education Policy in India

Macaulay's Minutes have a number of defects, no doubt, but it may have to be accepted that it was a very important document.

1. To denounce Macaulay as an evil genius would be unjust because the movement for western education had already started in India long before Macaulay wrote this Minutes. Perhaps, the Government of the time used his Minutes as a handle to suit their convenience. Macaulay, however, may be held responsible for perpetuating a class of educated Indians who having been brought up in western culture, lost total contact with the general Indian masses, creating a schism between the class and the masses. Perhaps that was Macaulay's vision of divide and rule which the British were so apt at during centuries of their hold on this great nation.

With regard to his views on Indian languages, he seemed to have reviewed his earlier stand in one of his letters to his father in 1836 in which he lamented on the ill-effect of English education on the Indian youth who forsook their religious faith and even embraced Christianity. Macaulay considered it as an alarming trend. It is quite likely that his won religious fold. Hence, teaching through English did not remain restricted to political gains alone : it transgressed into religion as well. Further, he realised the value and richness of the Indian languages which had flourished and progressed during the Moghul period, and were considered suitable and worthwhile for translating Bible into them.

Nevertheless, great emphasis and importance was attached to Macaulay's Minutes by the then Government of India and the Crown, and it became a Magna Carta of educational development in India with far reaching assumptions, and consequences : it was, infact, a vision document, in spite of its short sightedeness and micro presentation.

Salient Features of Bantinck Resolution -1835

Lord William Bantinck was the Governor General of India since 1828. Because of his open-minded and reformist attitude he was popular among the Indian elite of the time and was successful in bringing about the sea change in the socio-economic structure and control of society. He had appointed Lord Macaulay to submit his considered legal opinion about the matters educational consequence to the revision of the Charter Act in 1833. He accepted Macaulay's Minute whole heartedly and considered them to be a landmark in the development of educational system in India. The Minute became the policy document on education during his time.

On 7 March 1835, Lord William Bentinck accorded his approval to the Minute, and published it in the form of a resolution having the following salient features :

1. The money saved in this manner should be utilised in work of disseminating English literature and

science among the natives of India through the medium of English language.

2. In future, books on Oriental languages should not be published, for money had inordinately been spent on them.

3. The oriental institutions should not be abolished. Their teachers should be given salaries and students stipends as formerly.

4. The great object of British Government is to promote European literature and sciences in India. Hence all educational funds should be spent on English Education.

With the policy of Bentinks, Orientalists got a great setback. He declared his policy for the promotion of European languages, literature and science in India. This was the first declaration of British Government which determined aims, content, medium of instruction and promotion of western science and literature. Lord William Bentinck was satisfied with the arguments of Macaulay in favour of English education. So he accepted Macaulay Minute in the Resolution dated 7 March 1835 and observed thus: I give my entire concurrence to the sentiments expressed in the Minute.

The Governor-General of India in Council has attentively considered the two latter from the Secretary to the Committee of Public Instruction, dated the 21st and 22nd January last, and the papers referred to in them.

First : His Lordship in Council is of opinion that the great object of the British Government ought to be the promotion of European literature and science among the natives of India: and that all the funds appropriated for the purpose of education would be best employed on English educational alone.

Second : But it is not the intention of His Lordship-in-Council to abolish any college or school of native learning, while the native population shall appear to be inclined to avail themselves of the advantages which it affords, and his Lordship-in-Council directs that all the existing professors and students at all institutions under the superintendence of the committee shall continue to receive their stipends not stipend shall be given to any student that may hereafter enter at any of these institutions: and that when any professor or oriental learning shall vacate his situation, the Committee shall report to the Government the number and state of the class in order the Government may be able to decide upon the expediency of appointing a successor.

Third : It has come to the knowledge of the Governor General-in-Council that a large sum has been expended by the committee on the printing of oriental works; His Lordship-in-Council directs that no portion of the funds shall hereafter be so employed.

Fourth : His Lordship-in-Council directs that all the funds which these reforms will leave at the disposal of the Committee be hence forth employed in imparting to the native population a knowledge of English literature and science through the medium of the English language: and His Lordship-in-Council request the Committee to submit to Government, with all expedition, a plan for the accomplishment of this purpose.

This was the first declaration of the British Government in the sphere of education in India. It eventually determined the aim, content and the medium of instruction in India. Promotion of western sciences and arts was acknowledges as the avowed object.

Adam's Report

William Adam lived in India for 27 years. Through journalism and educational investigations he tried to serve Indian people. He studied the educational situation of Bengal between 1835 and 1838 and submitted important reports.

William Adam was born in Scotland in 1789 and became a priest in 1815 in a Baptist Mission Society. In 1818 he reached Sereampore and studied Bengali and Sanskrit. He came in contact with Raja Ram Mohan Roy in Calcutta. They were influenced by each other. Adam was so influenced that he broke his relations with the Church in 1821 missionary to survey the educational conditions of Bengal. Adam submitted three reports between 1835 and 1838. He took help from Raja Ram Mohan Roy, Ishwar Chandra Vidya Sagar and other in this regard.

First Report (1835)

It contained educational data. In it, he had described indigenous elementary schools in the following manner:

By this description are meant those schools in which instruction in the elements of knowledge in communicated, and which have been originated and are supported by the natives themselves, in contradiction from those that are supported by religious or philanthropic societies. The number of such schools in Bengal is supposed to be very great. A distinguished member of the General Committee of Public Instruction in a minute on the subject expressed the opinion, that if one rupee per mensem were expended on each existing village school in the Lower Provinces, the amount would probably fall little short of 12 lakhs of rupees per annum. This supposes that there are 100,000 such schools in Bengal and Bihar and assuming the population of those two provinces be 40,000,000 there would be a village school for every 400 persons.

Second Report (1838)

In the second report with Rajshahi district, Nattore Thana was selected for investigation. The report says that the population of the Thana was 195.296 of which 123,640 were Muslims and 65,.656 were Hindus. There were 48 villages. Only 27 elementary schools were there with 262 students. Out of these schools 10 were Bengali schools with 167 students, 4 were Persian schools with 23 students, 13 were Arabic School with 42 students. There were 1,588 families belonging to 238 villages giving instruction to 2,342 students. Average age of admission was 8 years and that of leaving school was 14 years. The average pay of teachers was Rs. 5 to 8 per month.

Third Report (1838)

In this report Adam admitted that his statistics were underestimated. He has written thus: Although I believed that the returns I receive are in general worthy of confidence as far as they to, Yet I have no security that they are not defective. In traversing in district, my agents could not visit all the villages in contained, amounting to several thousands. This was physically impossible without protracting the enquiry beyond all reasonable limits. The were, therefore, compelled to depend either upon their personal knowledge, or upon the information that could be gathered from others as to the places possessing schools, every one of which was invariably visited and examined; but that in no instance a village- institution has been over-looked is more than I dare affirm, and in point of fact I have sometimes discovered instances in which such institutions had at first escaped attention.

Adam's Suggestions

William Adam had appointed to enquire into the state of indigenous education in the Presidency of Bengal. He submitted three reports at different times. He was a nobleman with honest motives and wanted to bring about regeneration of the country through the expansion of education. His educational policy was quite free from politics. He put forth certain wise suggestions with respect to the education of the country.

1. It was further suggested that books in indigenous languages should be published for the students and teachers and an Inspector of Schools be appointed in each of the districts to examine the progress of education. Normal schools, according to the plan, were to be established for the training of the teachers and proper text-books were to be provided to them to educate children on the basis of the books. Examination of the teachers should be conducted afterwards and their remunerations fixed so that they might settle in villages to educate the rural children. It was further suggested that the Government should award small grants of land for the maintenance of those schools.

2. Adam prepared a plan in which it was suggested that as an experimental measure, some districts must be selected in the first instance where a thorough enquiry might be instituted in the field of education.

3. He recognised the utility of the existing Oriental institutions and desired that Government should patronise them. These were very schools which had been

satisfying the educational needs of the country for a considerably long period of time. Hence it was essential to promote the cause of indigenous schools to make the national educational plan success. These institutions can be regarded as to the foundation upon which have to erect the huge fabric of high education. All schemes for the improvement of education, therefore, to be efficient and permanent, should be based upon the existing institutions of the country. Transmitted from time immemorial, familiar to the conceptions of the people and inspiring them which respect and veneration. Adam recommended in this connection that existing native institutions from the highest to the lowest, of all kings and classes, were the fittest means to be employed for raising and improving the character of the people; that to employ those institutions for such a purpose would be the simplest, the safest and most popular, the most economical and the most effectual plan for giving that stimulus to the native mind which it needs on the subject of education and for eliciting the exertions of the native themselves for their improvement, without which all other means must be unveiling.

4. He believed in mass-education; consequently, he vehemently opposed the Filtration Theory of education, which aimed at the education only of the people of higher class. He observer, Children should not go to colleges only to learn the alphabet; to make the superstructure lofty and firm, the foundations should be broad and deep.

Adams's Views on Organisation of Education

Adam was full of appreciation. Adam had remarked about these indigenous institutions as follows:

1. Again, if the maxim that the tendency of

knowledge is to descend, not to ascend, requires us to have first zilla, next pergunnah and then village schools, it follows that we ought not to have even zilla schools till we have provincial colleges, nor the later till we have national universities; nor these till we have a cosmopolitan one. But this is an application of the maxim foreign to its spirit. Improvement begins with the individual and extends to the mass, and the individuals who give the stimulus to the mass are doubtless generally found in the upper, that is, the thinking class of society which especially in this country, is not composed exclusively, of those who are highest in rank or who possess the greatest wealth. The truth of the maxim does not require that the measures adopted should have reference first to large and then to small localities in progressive descent. On the contrary the efficiency of every successive higher grade of institution cannot be secured except by drawing instructed pupils from the next lower grade which, consequently by the necessity of the case, demands prior attention, Children should not go to colleges to learn the alphabet, to make the superstructure lofty and firm, the foundation should be broad and deep; and thus building from the foundations, all classes of institutions and every grade of instruction may be combined with harmonious and salutary effect.

2. Instead of beginning with schools for the lower grades of native society, a system of government institutions may be advocated that shall provide, in the first place, for the higher classes on the principle that the tendency of knowledge is to descent, not to ascend, and that, with this view, we should at present seek to establish a school at the head-station on every zilla, afterwards pergunnah schools and last of all village

schools, gradually acquiring in the process more numerous and better qualified instruments for the diffusion of education.

The primary objection to this plan is that is overlooks entire systems of native educational institutions, Hindu and Mohammedan, which exited long before our rule, and which continue to exist under our rule, independent of us and of our projects, forming and moulding the native character in successive generations. At the face of this palpable fact, the plan assumes that the country is to be indebted to us for schools, teachers, books- everything necessary to its moral and intellectual improvement, and that in the prosecution of our views we are to reject all the aids which the ancient institutions of the country and the actual attainments of the people afford towards their advancement. We have to deal in this country principally with Hindus and Mohammedans, the former one of the earliest civilized nations of the earth, the latter in some of the brightest period of their history, distinguished promoters of science, preserving a profound love and veneration for learning nourished by those very institutions of which I have spoken, and which it would be equally improvident on our part and offence to them to neglect.

Fate of Adam Reports

Macualay who had some other plan in his mind opposed Adam's plan vehemently. He wrote a very scathing criticism of that plan. Consequently when this plan was submitted to the Government, it was rejected by Auckland. The Committee regarded Adam's plan as quite impracticable. Adam, in sheer disgust with the attitude of the Government, tendered his resignation immediately. In this way another valuable opportunity for the expansion of mass education was lost.

This report has been dubbed as myth or a legend by some students of educational history while others maintain with equal force that it is substantially correct. The argument chiefly centres round two points, first, the two sides differ in the interpretation of the word school. One side uses the expression in its modern sense, viz., and institution of a more or less permanent nature conducted by a person who teachers a certain number of the children of the locality in return for fees and perquisites from the pupils and/or remuneration from the community. If the word is used in this sense, it is correct to conclude that the idea of 100,000 schools in Bengal is a fantastic exaggeration of facts.

But the other side contests this interpretation. It argues that in those days, the word school was used to mean a place where instruction was given and included the centres where the system of domestic instruction prevailed. According to this view, a family where the teacher was employed to give education to its children or where the father thought his won children, with or without other children form the locality, was also a school as understood in those days. In support of this theory, it is pointed out that Adam collected all statistics of families giving domestic instruction as part of his enquiry about school and scholars.

There are no indigenous colleges conducted by Muslims, But Adam found 38 Sanskrit colleges with 397 students. The average age of the admission was 11 years and the average age of completing the course was 27 years. Of course 397 students, 136 belonged to the villages where the colleges were situated and received free education, while 261 students belonged to other villages and received food, lodging and education free of charge from their teachers.

Thomson Plan

Though Adam's work could not convince the Government and was turned down in Bengal, it had a far reaching effect in North-western Provinces. Thomsome adopted his scheme only 5 years later. In 1842 the North Western Provinces were constituted and were separated from Bengal. The new province followed an educational policy quite different. It rejected the downward filtration theory. It advocated the use of mother-tongue and not of any foreign language as medium of instruction. If recognised the local demand for indigenous education. It regarded the education of the masses as its primary objectives.

In 1843, James Thompson was appointed as Lieutenant Governor of the Provinces He carried out to complete his plan to multiply and improve the village schools by supervision, advice, encouragement and by the distribution of elementary books suited to their wants. Therefore, he is regarded as the father of elementary education in India. In 1845 he issued a circular and asked all district collectors to supply a detailed information about the existing condition of education in their respective district. The enquiry revealed the depressed state of education and so he submitted a plan to the Government for organising vernacular education.

The main points of the original plan were :

1. If the zamindar agrees to outline the money for the maintenance of the teacher, this bit of land may be surrendered to him.

2. The teacher should be remunerated by grant of small jagirs of 5 to 10 acres of land of annual rent value form 20 to 40 rupees.

3. A school should be set up in every village of 200 houses.

A second plan was submitted in 1849 when the Directors did not approve of jagirs to teachers. The new plan made the following recommendations:

1. The plan, to be followed first on experimental basis, was to be spread later throughout the province.

2. The work of the visitors was be supervised by visitor-general.

3. Indigenous schools should be supervised by Inspectors who were required to advise, assist and encourage indigenous school education.

4. A comprehensive curriculum, considering the importance of reading, writing, accountancy, mensuration, history and geography should be formed.

5. The government should establish a tehsil school to function as a model for schools in the neighbouring areas.

Thompson not only wanted to improve indigenous education through advice and guidance, but he wanted that primary education should come within reach of common people. With the help of one of his collectors of Mathura, he opened a new school in each halka of villages at a central place to that boys may come to that village school. The zamindars also cooperated. They contributed 1% of the revenue for the benefit of the school. Such an idea was caught up by neighbouring district of Agra, Bareily, Etah, Etawah, Manipuri, Shahjajanpur. Thus we can say that Thompson laid a firmer foundation for elementary education in his province.

The Charter of 1813

The increasing efforts of missionaries with regard of English education led to dissatisfaction among the masses. When the government took steps to check their activities, they lodged a complaint against it in Britain. The matter was raised in British Parliament. This resulted in the enactment of the Charter of 1813. The Charter threw light on the future policy of education to be followed in India and accepted the responsibility of the government for the spread of education. A sum of rupees one lack was earmarked for the education one of whole country.

Thus, the education of the masses was badly neglected. Only the Christian missionaries and a few Indian leaders were enthusiastic in establishing educational institutions privately and, with the passage of time, were successful in getting grant form the government.

Efforts of Christian Missionaries

With the establishment of East India Company, the supremacy of the Britishers in India increased but education in general was neglected. With the efforts of some Christian missionaries, only a few institutions were established which provided education through English medium, but they did not get any aid from the government.

According to Nurllah and Naik, The missionaries used education as means of evangelisation. They propagated for the spread of Christian religion through English medium. Only the Presidencies of Calcutta,

Madras and Bombay were the main centres of education at that time.

Anglicist-Classicist Controversy

A large number of controversial issues pertaining to the objectives, means and medium of instruction emerged within the implementation of the Charter of 1813. On the one hand, some Indians were in favour of imparting education through Sanskrit, Arabic, Persian and other classical languages, while on the other hand, some Westeners and others were pressing for English as the medium of Instruction. This led to controversy between the two schools of thought.

5

EDUCATIONAL ADMINISTRATION: CONCEPTUAL BACKGROUND

Introduction

The concept of educational administration has a long history of origin and development. Many of the concepts used in educational administration have been borrowed from business and public administration. Therefore, historical perspective may help in understating the conceptual base of modern education administration.

Periods of Development

1. The Period Between 1900-1935 - Kimbrough has described this period as traditional era, while others have termed it classical period. It was during this period that several professional persons and academicians wrote profusely on administration and its practices. One of the central doctrines of this period emphasized that policy-making and policy-execution should be kept separate. In their view, administration should be confined be kept separate. In their view, administration should be confined to those activities, powers and techniques which are necessary to carry out policies set by policy makers.

Talyorism or Scientific Management Approach : Frederick W. Taylor, developed a theoretical approach to management which became popular as the Scientific Management in the 1880s and early 1900s. The approach was based on six important principles which, would maximise the use of available human and material resources in achieving the goals of the organisation. The principles soon became popular in all organisations as they aimed at lowering the unit cost of factory production by increasing the efficiency of the management. These principles were:

a. Principle of Functional Management : It requires the management to be so designed that it serves best the purpose of improving coordination of activities among various specialist. Discipline should be established and objective must be achieved.

b. Principle of Scientific Methods of Work : It means that the management should scientifically determine the best methods and should train the workers accordingly.

c. Time-Study Principle : It provides that a standard time limit should be established for all work to be done: and that all productive efforts be measured by accurate time-study. It aimed at finding out how a piece of work could be done efficiently and effectively.

d. The Principle of Managerial Control : It means that the managerial staff should be trained and taught to apply the scientific principles of management and its control.

e. Principle of Separation of Planning from Performance: Under it the management should take over the responsibility for planning the work from the workers. Workers should be made to execute the task.

f. Piece-Rage Principle - It allows wages to be proportional to output.

2. Posdcorb - Luther Gullick in his book the Papers

on the science of Administration adapted Fayol's analysis and defined the job of manager as the letters POSDCORB; that is, planning, organisation, staffing, directing, coordination, reporting and budgeting.

Thus, Fayol, Gullick and all others who came after them attempted a precise definition of the functions of administration and described administration as a process. This theory had a lasting impact on the process of administration. Max Weber, a German sociologist, in his book The Theory of Social and Economic Organisations, focussed on the structure of organisations and considered bureaucracy as the best form of administrative organisation capable of attaining the highest degree of efficiency. He conceived of a pyramidal type of organisation in which authority is vested in the highest position at the top and chain of authority run directly from the top to bottom. Weber described a number of elements of an ideal bureaucracy as under:

a. Span of Control,.

b. Selection and promotion based only on technical competence.

c. Unity of command.

d. A system of departmentalisation either on the basis of purpose, or on the basis of process or clientele or place.

e. A system of procedures for dealing with work situations.

f. Division of labour.

Thus, classical approaches of administration provided a sound based of administration in early decades of the last century wherein Taylor, Fayol and

Weber led the way in the early efforts to solve the problems of administering organisations.

3. Fayol's 14 Principles of Management - A French industrialist, Henri Fayol, basically a geologist and mining engineer was the founder of the classical management school of thought and had powerful ideas of his own when Taylor's ideas were popular in America. He focussed his attention on the manager and separated the process of administration from other operations in the organisation such as production, etc. He emphasised the common elements of the process of administration is different organisations. He is called the father of the administrative process. His major contribution was his element of management. He identified fourteen principles. Collectively, all these principles constitute classical organisation theory. These principles are:

1. Esprit de Corps.

2. Stability of Staff.

3. Subordination of Individual Interest to the Common Good.

4. Unity of Direction.

5. Unity of Command.

6. Discipline.

7. Authority.

8. Remunerations.

4. The Period Between 1935-1950 - Kimbrough calls as the Transitional Era Oweas has put this under the title, Human Relations Movement. This shifts of emphasis separates it from the Traditional Era. Instead of focussing on the structure and the process, the administrative thought during this period focussed on

people and their relationships in organisations. The dimension of human relations was added to the earlier concepts of Tylorism. Fayol's Process Theory and Waber's Bureaucracy which continued to be used in theory and practice of administration. Elton Mayo and his associates in his book The Human Problems of an Industrial civilisation in 1924-1933 at the Hawthorne Plant of Western Electric Company near Chicago found that increase and decrease in production depended very much on how the people working in the plant were manipulated and treated and provided the empirical base on which this movement was founded.

But, the leading protagonist of the movement was Mary Parkar Follett who dominated the field for about thirty-two years and she claimed in her blood Creative Experience that all problems of administration and management were, ultimately, the problems of human relations. So pioneered a theory that was later known as the contingency theory of management. Her writings and ideas presented an antithesis of classical traditional view of management. Following major themes emerged during this period and moulded the administrative thought:

a. This was the dominant concern during this period. This focus was central to Follett's thought. This meant that management is an ever-changing and dynamic process in response to emerging situation. It was determined by four fundamental principles as the key to the effectiveness of an organisation:

(i) Coordination as a continuing process.

(ii) Coordination by direct contact of the responsible people.

(iii) Coordination as the reciprocal.

(iv) Coordination in the early stages.

b. It was emphasised that building and maintenance of harmonious human relations in the organisations depended very much on meeting their psychological needs.

c. Authority Based on Knowledge, Participation and Reasons : Follett, Barnard, Mc Greor and several other writers and scholars advocated the concept of functional authority which is based on technical skills, professional knowledge, social approval, group-acceptance and competence of the leader. Amitai Etizioni, in his book Modern Organizations, held a view that in professional organisations like hospitals, schools, colleges, universities, etc., the traditional line-staff authority should be reversed. He said that to the except there is a line-staff relationship at all, professionals should hold the major authority and administrators the secondary staff-authority. Rensis Likert, in his book The Human Organisations, advocated horizontal control and group centred leadership. Many new terms to indicate the new authority-concept came into vague such as group decision-making, democratic leadership, participative democracy, situational leadership, authority based on acceptance, collegiality. They all aimed at presenting an alternative to the traditional notion of authority from top to the bottom.

d. F.J. Roethlisberger and William J. Dickson, members of the Mayo team said, limits of human collaboration are determined far more by the informal than the formal organisation. Several other writers also stressed that working in collaboration is contingent upon many such factors as social codes, conventions, traditions, social pressures, etc., which form the basis of informal organisation within a formal organisation. It is a widely accepted fact that keeping an eye on these informal organisations and manipulating them in the interest of the organisations Barnard also described the importance of informal organisation. He held the view that functioning of formal organisations lis very much influenced by informal organisations that happen to develop within them.

5. The Period 1950 Onwards - It was the synthesis of the classical and the human relations movement and is considered by R.G. Owens, in his book Organizational Behaviour in Education, as the organisational behaviour. It borrowed adapted concepts and knowledge from various social sciences and behavioural disciplines such as psychology, anthropology, political science, management and social psychology and applied them to management and administration. A number of behaviourists published important works which substantially influenced the development of the field of administration. The study and management of organisational behaviour was the major theme of this period.

The writers of his period emphasised on organisation and on people working in them. The study and understanding of organisational behaviour is mor important. Organisational behaviour is the human behaviour which is an outcome of an interaction between the organisation and the people. Hence the organisation and the people are important if organisational goals are to be achieved.

Aims and Objectives of Educational Administration

Story of mankind is the story of its development.

Man develops new ideas, tries them out and rejects or modifies them in the light of his experiences. Therefore, aims and objectives keep changing and they are influenced by age, time and prevailing conditions. In the world of P.C. Wren, School administration which does not facilitate education is a parasite and a debauchery of public funds. School administration, therefore, exists only for the people and its efficiency must be measured by the extent to which it contributes to teaching and learning. The aims and objectives also vary from place to place, from time to time and from society to society. But they always serve the purpose of upliftment, growth and development of the existing system of education. The following are some of the aims and objectives of educational administration :

1. Expansion of Education : The target of universalisation of education has not yet been realised. It is one of the important objectives of administration to see that expansion takes place according to targets. The selection of places for opening of new schools should be done keeping in view the academic considerations only.

2. Persons in the Key posts as Educational Administrators - The educational administrators, such as Education officials, whose single major objective is to improve upon what is being done in the classroom, should look to the following factors to perform the task of education efficiently :

(i) Proper supervision to stimulate, coordinate and guide the continued growth of the teachers in school, both individually and collectively.

(ii) Recruitment on the basis of merit.

(iii) Secure active cooperation of the department of education.

(iv) Provide proper guidelines to teachers.

(v) Encourage better understanding and inter-personal relations amongst students and teachers.

(vi) Develop the morale of teacher.

(vii) Encourage teachers to use improved teaching methods and make teaching effective.

(viii) Along with conservation, facilities must be provided to generate new ideas among the teachers.

3. Implementing the Educational Plans in the Efficient and Effective Manner - Planning is a significant management technique. Educational administration can achieve all the goals of education fully and comprehensively by preparing ideal plants.

4. Justice - A teacher, being an intellectual worker, can work better if he feels satisfied with the way he is being administered. Unless he gets the peace of mine, he cannot teach in the class. Educational administrator should aim at giving justice to the teachers is respect of recruitment, promotion and transfer. For this, he must frame fair just rules to guide him and put a stop to any favouritism and bias. Effective teaching can be stimulated by right method of recruitment based on worth and merit, uniform rules or transfer and promotion for every teacher, as it creates an atmosphere of peace and satisfaction.

5. Encouragement of Direct Democracy in Schools - Direct democracy should be encouraged in school administration. Important matters should be decided in the presence of the staff and students, and not by the headmaster alone. The headmaster of a school should deal with each aggrieved student or aggrieved party directly, and not through any other agency.

6. Encouragement of Direct Democracy in Schools - Direct democracy should be encouraged in school administration. Important matters should be decided in the presence of the staff and students, and not by the headmaster alone. The headmaster of a school should deal with each aggrieved student or aggrieved party directly, and not through any other agency.

7. Understanding Mass Psychology - A Director of Education or an Inspector of School or a Headmaster must frequently meet the young students to get a feel about of their changing moods, needs, emotions and fancies. No officer can rule the young on the strength of power alone. He has to set right things by correcting emotional imbalances by understanding their psychology. The authorities of school administration must understand mass psychology of students and teachers, and provide necessary leadership.

8. Integration of School Administration - Integration is the demand of school administration. The administrative officers, staff, students and other employees in the field of education, should learn to work for the common good. There should bot be any division among them. Democratic administration believes, above all things, in the capacity of each individual to share and participate effectively in all policies and activities that concern him.

9. Providing Proper Facilities, Freedom and Encouragement to the Meritorious Teachers - It should not the teachers like clerks or another limbs of administration. It should accord special consideration and status to them. The teacher as a builder and creator has to be allowed a lot of freedom of action. An educational administrator should learn to accept the

brilliance of a junior teacher. The educational authority should enlist the cooperation of the teacher community.

The administrative authorities should realise that every teacher wants to express his opinion on the policy and problems of the school he serves and is frustrated, when he is unable to do so. As a result of this, teacher may be provided with proper facilities, freedom and encouragement to work for the progress of better education, and must behave as the first among equals. His duty should be to promote initiative, positive activities, great virtues and research which bring great credit to him.

10. Providing High Chairs to the Best Fitted Persons - Educational administration in the emerging Indian society should aim at providing high positions on the basis of merit and fitness. In some quarters people think it fit to appoint IAS officers as directors of schools and college education. But it is a fact of experience that civil servants moving from one department to another, cannot have the emotional commitment to education or that deep understanding of the problems and needs and classroom situations, which would come naturally to a teacher or a educationist. In school administration, be is a Director, Inspectors of Schools, of Headmaster, must essentially be a teacher.

It is seen that biological seniority brings to high positions the old times and not those best fitted brilliant younger staff, capable of doing great things for the reconstruction of education. Some old timers are exhausted men and women, whose main business would be met and satisfied with the pension case finalisation and post-retirement benefits.

11. Good of Education : Educational administration,

should aim at the good of education. Graham Balfour has stated very aptly, the purpose of educational administration is to enable the right education from the right teachers, at a cost within the means of the state, which will enable students to profit by their learning. Kandel opines, fundamentally the purpose of educational administration brings pupils and teachers under such conditions as will more successfully promote the end of education.

Relationship Between Educational and Educational Administration

Educational administration is the dynamic side of education and deals with the educational practices. Educational administration must be directed towards the fulfillment of the objectives of education as set forth by the society. Traditional educational administrative systems were designed primarily to serve as caretaker, regulatory and supervisory role in an era when education and the world outside were moving slowly by today's pace and when the size and diversity of educational tasks were much smaller.

Meaning of Educational Administration

Society establishes various institutions or organisations so as to carry on its multifarious activities, such as government, industry, trade, defence, education, etc. By administration we mean the machinery and procedure through which an organisation in different situations is managed. Thus, we can say that administration is a comprehensive effort to direct, guide and integrate associating him and strivings which are focussed towards some specific end of aim. Educational administration deals with the educational practices.

It is the dynamic side of education. It deals with educational institutions from the schools and colleges to the secretariat in a comprehensive effort to achieve some specific educational objectives. It is concerned with both human and material resources. The human elements in educational administration include :

(i) Equipment and instructional supplies.

(ii) Money.

(iii) Other employees in general.

(iv) Parents and Teachers.

Beyond these two elements are ideas, laws and regulations, community needs, and so on. All of these have a bearing on the educational process. The integration of these elements into a whole is educational administration.

Definitions of Educational Administration

The following are the important definitions of educational administration :

1. According to Authur. B. Moehlman, "Administration is the comprehensive effort to direct, guide and integrate associated human striving which are focussed toward some specific ends or aims administration is conceived as the necessary activities of those individuals in an organisation who are charged with ordering, forwarding and facilitating the associated efforts of a group of individuals brought together to realize certain defined purposes."

2. According to Stephen J. Knezevich, "Educational administration is a specialized set of organisational functions whose primary purpose is to insure the efficient and effective delivery of relevant educational

services as well as implementation of legislative policies through planning, decision-making and leadership behaviour, that keeps an organisation focussed on predetermined objectives, provides for optimum allocation and most prudent care of resources to ensure their most productive uses, stimulates and coordinates professional and other personnel to produce a coherent social system and desirable organisational climate and, facilitates determination of essential changes to satisfy future and emerging needs of students and society."

3. According to S.N. Mukherji, "Educational Administration is concerned with the management of things as well as with human relationships, i.e., the better working together of people. In fact, it is more concerned with human beings and less with inanimate things."

4. According to Jesse B. Sears, "In education, administration contains much that we mean by the word government and is closely related in content to such words as superintendence, supervision, planning, oversight, direction, organisation, control, guidance, and regulation."

5. According to Henry Fayol, "Like other administrations, Educational Administration is a process of five elements as - planning, organising, direction, coordination and control."

From these definitions we conclude that educational administration is:

a. Rendering service of society towards its progress and that of the individuals comprising it including the teacher, student, parents and public, and coordination of their efforts.

b. Assisting in the realisation of the predetermined

aims and objectives of education.

c. Making efforts in unison.

Characteristic of Educational Administration

The chief characteristics of educational administration are as follows :

1. Educational administration seeks cooperation of all the concerned personnel in determination of policy and programme.

2. The objective of educational administration is to bring about professional development in the educational workers.

3. Much importance is give to practicability in educational administration.

4 The role of educational administration is dependent on utility.

5. The objective of the nature of educational administration is to bring about improvement in the working of the school.

6. The form of educational administration is always dynamic.

7. The from of educational administration is in both centralisation and decentralisation.

8. The nature of educational administration if functional and controlled.

9. Educational administration is a human process.

10. Educational administration is an integrated process.

Classification of Educational Administration

1. Democratic Educational Administration -

Kilpatrick explains the purpose of democratic educational organisation in these words : Everything connected with the whole school system centres on this one-thing, the educative development of the pupils. For that the budget exists; for that everything is done that is properly done; for that the superintendent receives his salary, a large salary than others get, because- it is believed- this differential best proves to promote the purpose for which he is appointed namely, to advance the better education of the young.

John Dewey states, Democracy is more than a form of a government. It is primarily a mode of associated living, of conjoint communicated experiences. The democratic theory of educational administration strikes at the harmonious balance between the extremities of centralised and decentralised types of educational administration. Basic principles of Democratic Educational Administration are :

a. Principle of freedom.

b. Principle of sharing responsibility.

c. Principle of egalitarianism.

d. Principle of respect for dignity of man.

2. Autocratic Educational Administration- Educational administration based on this theory considers that state as the all inclusive social category. Ross makes the following observation: It seeks education as the most powerful means of achieving its end and therefore enforces a rigid systems of education with no loose ends. It is supreme of dictate what shall be taught and how it shall be taught. In curriculum and methods, the watchwords are always discipline, organisation, a willing acceptance of authority, a damping down of

individuality. The totalirian educational administration emphasises the concepts and principles which are as follows :

a. Crushing down of individuality.

b. Rigid conformity to rules and regulations.

c. Willing acceptance of authority.

d. Centralised authority.

Scope of Educational Administration

The scope of general administration can be defined under five headings viz., Production, Assuring Public Use, Finance and Accounting, Personnel and Coordination. Thus, the following is the scope of educational administration :

1. Coordination - Ensure the close inter-relations and integration of different functional activities of the organisations such as personnel, finance and, production of desired results for integration of realization of the desired goals.

2. Personnel - Personnel are especially important for the educational enterprise where the whole work is centred round the impact of one type of human beings,, the teachers, upon another type of human beings, the students. The scope of educational administration, therefore, spreads over the personnel.

3. Finance and Accounting - Educational administration is also concerned with receiving and spending money necessary for the operation and activities of the educational machinery with proper maintenance of records.

4. Assuring Public Use - It means that the product of the organisation, its goals and services are so

produced, that they become acceptable to the public for its use and benefit.

5. Production - It means realisation of the goals of education set up by the society. Educational administration has, therefore, to interpret the aims of education to the education workers such that they may shape the final product of education in the desired from and shape.

Types of Educational Administration

Educational administration can be classified into two types :

1. External Administration - In India the framework of rules and regulations besides prescribing the curriculum and textbooks, scales of salaries of various categories of the staff, terms and conditions of their service, code of conduct, tuition fees for various classes, fixation of the duration of the school session and determination of financial aid and regulation other matters for the welfare of the staff and students, flow from the Education Department of the government. The schools have to teach the material as prescribed or recommended for different classes by the Educational Department.

Under such a system, the teachers, administrators and educationist function in a team spirit. This hinders the teacher's initiative. The best from of administration system therefore that in which the teacher effectively participate in the affairs of the schools. Only as a result of the corporate functioning of all these, can the objectives be attained for which the particular institution is started.

2. Internal Administration - It is necessary that the

heads of schools are given an opportunity to have their say in educational matters. If they are not granted the freedom in dealing with these matters, they would not be able to make use of their initiative and would only be following the line detracted by higher authorities. The internal educational administration means the system under which the headmaster of a school manages and directs the day-to-day programs and activities with the help of his colleagues and students in accordance with the general rules and regulations laid down by the Education Department.

A democratic outlook should be brought to bear on the internal management of the school so that not only educationists, administrators and teachers but also the students be held equally accountable for the administration of the school if balanced coordination is to be established between their activities] and functions. Therefore, when India has chosen the path of democracy, it becomes desirable that the schools should be allowed some autonomy in regard to the selection of textbooks and teaching methods.

Functions of Educational Administration

Educational administration is the process through which the functions of the school are discharged and service rendered to the school and society in the task of achieving the educational goals by coordinating the efforts of the people engaged in the task. Educational administration has, therefore, to perform some definite function.

1. Control - Control is the application of the power and authority to hold the workers responsible for their actions. Control is required in all sphere of the educative process, aims and objectives, teachers and students,

instruction and equipment, finance and public relations, etc. This is the process of directing or funding and activity and also judging it. It is closely related to the elements of the administrative process, such as planning, organisation, etc., and contributes to these elements.

2. Coordination - The educational administrator has to reckon with many physical, social and economic forces. He has to carry on a wide variety of activities. Coordination is putting things together in a harmonious relationship so that they may function more effectively.

Coordination is necessary to attune all these factors and forces to forge a unity in diversity of relationships to produce a unified and integrated total effect. For this, deliberate efforts have to be made. Coordination depends upon the nature of particular problem, circumstances and availability of resources and the final goal. The administrator should possess a good skill for harmonising all these diverse relationships. Coordination is required in all fields of administration, such as planning, organisation, etc. It is also needed in respect of purpose, time and place of the various activities like laying down policies, preparing the budget, selection of staff and development of the curriculum, etc.

3. Direction or Supervision - Direction is the release of energy to guide action towards desired goals. It originates with planning issues in activities and closes with evaluation of results. In the narrow sense, direction is only a part of the activity. It begins with the start of the act, indicates what is to be done and ends when the activity is over. In the broad or general sense, direction means the responsibility for running a number of

activities.

It is very important because it sets the plans and organisation into action. It is the enterprise in operation. It needs coordination as lack of coordination may result in poor administration. Good direction means getting the best possible work done with the least possible expenditure of time, energy and money. Direction depends on several factors, such as the prevalent circumstances, staff, equipment, finances, etc., as well as the knowledge and skill of the administrator.

4. Execution - In executing or working out plans in practical terms, the educational administration has to perform three important tasks or responsibilities in principle : Direction or Supervision, Coordination and, Control.

5. Integration - Integration should be used to arrive at the possible findings or recommendations which are easy for application and future improvement.

6. Development - Development of methods should answer what instruments or tools of appraisal are to be used, such as, tests, rating scales, questionnaires, schedules, surveys, observation and interviews, etc.

7. Formulation - Formulation of objectives and purpose of evaluation in clear and definite terms, regarding why and what, of the evaluative process in integral to administrative activity.

8. Evaluating - Evaluation is a necessary process by which the superior adjusts the junior staff. By constant appraisal of procedures, evaluation suggests their modification in the light of experiences gained, and to adjust the forces and methods accordingly. The administrator should recognise the impact of evaluation

on the people. He must use it only for its legitimate purpose- to improve the individual and the group, offer them psychological security, to help the organisation fulfil its purposes, measure its progress, and secure public understanding and support.

The administrator should encourage self-appraisal by the workers so that they are able to judge the quality and quantity of their individual contribution to the group effort. It should be remembered that workers do not appreciate appraisal when they feel their security and status are threatened.

9. Influencing - Sometimes situations may arise where due influencing has to be exercised over the junior or senior staff in the hierarchy so as to bring abut the desired results.

10. Planning - Planning is useful because it clarifies what is to be accomplished. It saves time, effort and money, and increases efficiency and effectiveness. Planning is necessary for translating purpose in action. Planning is the selection of a good course of action out several alternatives. It is, therefore, fundamental to the administrative process and a vital step of the enterprise.

The success depends upon other individuals understanding and willingness to cooperate, i.e., upon their identification with the activity, its purpose and success. Planning for others does not bring good results, for the a method of approaching problems, and as the latter changes and differs from time to time and situation to situation, planning should also respond by being continuous, dynamic and flexible. Plans and ideas are to guide and direct the workers efforts and activities.

11. Decision Making - Having made suitable organisational programs, it is necessary to make

decisions in order to realise the predetermined goals.

12. Communicating - Communication is a sine qua non in any administrative situation. All routes to communication with the personnel situated up or down the hierarchy line should be maintained for proper and effective administrative control over various aspects.

13. The Forty-fifth Year Book, Pt. II by the National Society for the Study of Education, has mentioned the following functions which educational administration should perform :

a. Utilise maximally the special capacities of the personnel and the material resources.

b. Delegate authority and responsibility.

c. Determine policies and implement them.

d. Secure the goodwill of personnel, public, education department and other social agencies and institutions.

e. Implement a democratically determined programme.

f. The procedures and techniques for the performance of work, including the policies deal with the theory and practice of administration.

The Difference Between Administration and Supervision

The two concepts of administration and supervision are somewhat new to the field of educational administration. The role of education in an educational institution is to administer the classes, building, playground, library, laboratory, etc., but the purpose of supervision is different from it. According to Twillian T. Melechior, Administration of school begins with getting the citizens to providing building and grounds, continues through maintenance, securing teachers and supplies and providing general oversight of the situation in which teacher and pupil are together in a classroom. Supervision in institution begins with the teacher at work in the classroom; it ends with reports to parents and with interview.

Administrative functions are concerned primarily with the material facilities and the operation of the schools. Supervisory functions are concerned with improving the learning situation. Supervision is a service particularly concerned with institution and its improvement. It is directly concerned with the teacher and learning and with the factors included in and related to these process- the teacher, the pupil, the curriculum, the material of instruction, the socio-physical environment of the situation.

The difference between administration and supervision can be enumerated in the following words :

1. Division of time into periods, sending teachers to the classes as may be needed, determination of time for co-curricular and extra-curricular activities are decided by the administration; while supervision strives to bring progress to all elements in the process of teaching, such as pupils, teachers, teaching aids, etc.

2. The responsibility of construction of institution - building, library, laboratory, etc. lies with the administration; while supervision is directly concerned with the teaching work to be carried out in the institution.

3. The chief function of education is integrated in the operation of institution, while supervision takes care of the progress of the teachers running the institution.

4. The function is to make provision of material facilities in an institution, while the attention of supervision is concentrated on facilitating means of progress of educational process.

Features of Educational Administration

Chief objectives of educational administration is to make educational process effective and efficient. S.N. Mukherjee has stated, Educational administration organises human relations and resources of equipment. The efforts are made jointly by human relations and resources for best performance. Educational administration is more concerned with man than matter. The following are the chief features of the nature of educational administration.

1. It is centralised as well as a decentralised process.

2. It is related to all aspects of child development.

3. It is a dynamic process. It changes according to country, time and situations.

4. It requires cooperation, sympathy and positive attitude.

5. It is a human process under social, philosophical, psychological, political and economic situations.

6. It influences the social change and social mobility.

7. It is an objective- oriented process.

8. It controls the organisation of physical resources for desirable change in human behaviour.

9. It includes the process or research and development.

Theories of Educational Administration

Meaning of Theory- A good theory is one which reveals uniformities in the subject matter of the theory; which enables one to predict precisely; that is, in accordance with establish criteria and guides to action or answers which work is to be done in terms of standards determined by the profession and occupied by the public. A theory which performs these tasks for the practising administrator has a great value. A theory must have a theme and must be logical and consistent.

1. It assists an individual to collect facts concerned with a theme.

2. It is helpful to explain a phenomenon under examination.

3. It should have the qualities of validity and reliability. Advantages of having a theory.

4. It should be built up deductively and inductively.

5. Theory should be as explicit as possible.

Features of Educational Administration in a Democratic State

It is truism to say that men and communities thrive best in an atmosphere of freedom. If a system imposes a rigid uniformity of ideas and practices, it commits a crime against the law of God and the spirit of man. The social philosophy which underscores most of the philosophies of education is neither fascism nor communism but democracy. Democracy is considered to be system of government and a way of life which offers greater scope than any other system for the development of human personality and the varied talents which nature has given to individuals and groups.

Without proper knowledge and training it would be almost impossible to achieve that aspiration to self-rule.

Therefore, education should be so oriented in its ideology, methods and organisation, that it will develop the basic qualities of character, which are very much essential for the successful functioning of the democratic life. The central point the democratic philosophy of education can be best understood from its etymological derivation Demos, which means the people and Kartis which means power. Thus the comminution of these two Greek words means rule by the people. If people are to rule themselves they must educate themselves for the task.

In a totalitarian system of government the state becomes the end and individuals the means. Liberty under such a system is not to provide the means for individual self-realisation and self-expression, but rather for self-sacrifice for the interest of the state. The aim of education in totalitarian pattern is not to equalise educational opportunities. It rather increase the social distance to the privileged few from the masses. Democratic philosophy of education, on the other hand, is not only adapt education to democracy, but to make democracy itself safe for education.

Factors Influencing Educational Administration - Educational administration of a country is influenced by educational philosophy, social system and form of the government. In our country education is a state subject. The administration behaviours or factors are of two types :

1. Environmental Factors Affecting Educational - The educational institutions are organised according to social environment and social conditions. The institutional environmental factors include social, economic, political and other forces. These are as under

a. Nature of Community - If include- Nature of community, Impact of other communities, Complexity of the community, Power conflicts in the communities, Standard of families, Characteristics of community.

b. Social Philosophy - Educational administration has to provide for inculcating ideals and values of the society. Educational administration is also influenced by social philosophy of the society. Educational system should be representative of the culture of a society.

c. Social Customs - It includes - Complexity of life, Physical resources, Status of management, Quality of family life, Power conflicts, Institutional organisation.

d. Nature of State - It has the direct control and influence on educational administration. In a democratic state, the nature of educational administration is a decentralised system. It includes the following factors - Financial provision or grants-in-aid system, Statutory provision of education, Government functioning, Form of government.

2. Personal Factors Affecting Educational Administration - The personal factors determine the administrator, teachers, staff, students, institution and organisation. The administrator is the nerve centre of educational administration, others are dependent factors. The following are the personal factors operation in educational administration.

a. Physical and intellectual abilities should be considered in assigning responsibilities and accountabilities of various personnel associated with it.

b. Interference of authority by the state and centre influences the educational administration.

c. Objectives of administration influence the organising, directing and controlling of activities.

d. Educational objective has the important role of designing the programs for an institution.

e. Diagnosing abilities is also essential to diagnose the cause of problems of educational administration so that remedial action can be taken.

f. Assigning the duties according to the abilities of the workers and teachers.

g. Cooperation is essential for functioning. It requires group decision about the problems and activities.

h. Attitude, values, habits include perception and beliefs of administration and other workers.

i. Administrative ability includes the activities of perception or observation, vitality, motivation or encouraging workers, emotional stability, following the rules and social qualities of responsibility.

Principles of Democratic Educational Administration

The system of administration, which is authoritarian administration, but administration which emphasises on democratic principles. Administration is nothing but the management of the affairs of an organisation. The principles of management of the affairs of an organisation. The principles of management are dominated by the prevailing philosophy of the people. The philosophy of democratic management emphasises on cooperation, coordination, mutual goodwill, combined efforts, etc. Some of the important principles of administration are :

(i) Principle of Research - Proper techniques and procedures can be adopted for research in the field of educational administration. Therefore, the Indian Education Commission recommended that the Ministry of Education should establish a National Staff College of Educational Administrators. It should have a research wing for conducting studies in problems of educational administration and function as a clearing house of administrative procedures and practices in the states and Union territories.

(ii) Principle of Recognition of the Individual Growth - Competent personnel should be entrusted with the task of administration. Everyone cannot be an efficient administrator. Hence, competent persons should be identified and chosen on the basis of their identified competence, and not on the basis of biological seniority.

(iii) Principle of Participation - An administrator, who recognises the dignity and worth of every individual, should recognise that certain teachers are better in classrooms while there are some who achieve outstanding success in co-curricular activities. Such merits should also be recognised and their competencies should be utilised in the specific field by seeking their participation.

(iv) Principle of Competency - Democracy believes, among other things, in the capacity of each individual to share and participate effectively in all policies and activities that concern him. The school administrator should realise that every teacher wants to express his opinion on the policy and problems of the school he serves. He becomes frustrated when he is unable to do so. As such, it is necessary to provide opportunities to every teachers to bring his individual intelligence to bear most fully and appreciably on the solution of common problems.

(v) Principle of Equality - Democratic administration should provided equal opportunity in the fields of education. But it would be quite unfair to give equal opportunities to the students of unequal abilities. The principle should be just rather than equal. The headmaster should not keep himself aloof from others. He is the first among equals. So he should look upon his colleagues as equal to him. They are his co-workers, not his subordinates. He should take his colleagues into confidence in running the school, in decision making and in other important matters. Educational psychology has clearly established that individuals differ among themselves in every respect. The capacities and attitude of each are unequal. It, therefore, follows that equalisation of educational opportunities should be provided on the basis of individual differences. R. R. Kimaria writes, A democratic administrator should look upon the personnel as socially equal to himself; he should not take decisions by himself; but with his colleagues; he should make them feel responsible and share in administration; he should have a code of set rulers of administration which he and his colleagues should follow rigidly, making no discrimination in their application; and lastly he should want no special privileges.

(vi) Principle of Cooperation - The principle of cooperation is the basis of democratic administration. Dewey once said, A society which makes provision for participation in the good of all its members on equal terms and which secures flexible judgement of its institutions through interaction of the different form of associated life is so far as democratic.

A cooperative spirit must be reflected in every activity of the school. Full understanding goodwill should prevail between parents and school, and between school and controlling authorities. Ryburn writes, The pupils of the school, if they are to develop the characteristics of co-operativeness must live when in school, in a society which in a practical way provides living example of the cooperation. The running of a school is not one man's job. It needs the working of many hands and heads. Therefore, persons concerned with the process of school administration must follow the principle of cooperation.

(vii) Principle of Evaluation - The principle of evaluation should be adopted to assess the success and failure of a programme of administration. It helps to understand the defects in the programme and to modify them by changing the nature of educational administration.

(viii) Principle of Flexibility - A democratic administrator believes in changes, not in rigidly. He modifies his plan of action in the light of his experiences and also on the constructive advice of his colleagues. Democratic administration should not follow any stereotype ideas to bring about better results in Policy and approaches.

(ix) Principle of Sharing - Mutually shared purposes have two important aspects sharing the largest number and variety and purposes among the persons involved in the process of administration, and sharing with other groups. Development of policies and the planning of educational programs become a joint responsibility of all those who participate in the process. The participants must have to share in planning, executing and evaluation the process of administration. The teachers, the students, the administrators and the public share responsibility to achieve success in the field of education. The success and failure are also equality shared and each is held responsible for his part in the joint enterprise.

Theory of General Administration as Presented by Benard

1. The understanding of the three factors- physical, biological and social are necessary for the study of normal organisations.

2. Cooperation depends upon leadership, which is another name for high personal capacity for technological attainment and moral complexity.

3. Wrong decisions are made due to wrong perception of the above factors of the environment and they limit the scope and success of cooperation.

4. Society is made up of complex organisations.

5. Social integration depends upon development of leadership. In the preparation of leaders mistakes have been committed. In the past, morality was more emphasised than technological capacity. At present, greater emphasis is laid on development of technological proficiency than on morality. In both cases the result is the same- imbalance and disequilibrium. Both are equally important and necessary for good administration.

6. Disturbance in cooperation results in false ideologies, prejudices, interests, etc., of the leaders of formal organisations.

7. An increasing degree of cooperation implies an increasing degree of complexity of morality. High degree

of moral complexity cannot be attained without high technological efficiency.

8. Cooperation is a synthesis of three basic factors -- physical, biological and social.

9. Informal organisations are found within all formal organisations. The formal units are essential for maintaining order and consistency and the informal for vitality. They are mutually dependent and both are necessary for enlisting cooperation.

10. Dynamic expression of leadership is more to do with creativeness which depends upon technological proficiency and development of techniques in relation to it.

11. These false ideologies cause four types of errors - over simplification of organisation life; disregard for the necessity for informal organisation; wrong emphasis on subjective rather than objective aspects of authority; and confusion of morality with responsibility.

12. Good administrators and executives take into account the specific situation, which include not only the physical, personal and social factors but also the utilities related to each of them and the utilities attached to them by the organisation.

Scope of Aspects

1. Public Relations - Educational administration should maintain effective public relations. It involves and bulletins about past achievement and future proposals. Administration should encourage community visitation and secure its participation and cooperation by a process of give and take.

2. Physical Facilities - Important pupil services, such as health and recreation and psychological

services to testing and records, guidance and counseling and co-curricular activities, etc. have to be organised and administered for the benefit of the young. It comprises of the area dealing with the problem of provision and maintenance of the school plant, equipment and supplies, their production, purchase unkeep and accounting, etc.

3. Curriculum - Administration has to pay close attention to the teaching-learning programme and process and to matters of preparation, selection and supply of textbooks and other instructional material. Educational administration has to deal with curriculum construction and its day-to-day development. It has also to took after the continuous evaluation and progressive improvement of the educational programs which are urgently called for in view of the constantly and rapidly occurring scientific, technological and social changes.

4. Finance - It includes income and expenditure and their accounting and auditing. Rules and regulations have to be framed for budgeting, spending and controlling of funds and resources. Decisions have to be taken abut sharing of the cost of education among the centre, the States and the Local Bodies. The policy of taxation and prescribing fees, etc. has to be formulated.

5. Personnel - Manpower plays the key role of education and proper attention has to be paid to them. Good services conditions, attractive salaries, security of tenure, welfare, services and retirement benefits have to be offered of bring in the best available talent. Schemes for their direction, guidance and supervision have to be drawn up. They have to be selected, recruited and trained and their qualifications and standards have to be prescribed.

6. Pupils - They are focal point of the educational enterprise. It is for them that the entire process of education and its constituents exist. Rules of their admission, promotion, discipline, etc. have to be framed and implemented. It is therefore, necessary to determine the individual and social purpose and procedures with their needs, interests and capacities and the demands of society.

7. Legal Structure - It refers to the law, rules and regulations to be framed in order to determine the agencies of education, their types, powers and standards of educational institutions to be run by them, and to decide the question of decentralisation of management and to set up organisational and administrative machinery.

6

BASIC FUNCTIONS OF ADMINISTRATION (PLANNING, ORGANISING, DIRECTING AND CONTROLLING

Introduction

By Planning is meant to predetermine who will do which task at what place and how. The administrators have to take due steps for successful execution functions of the school from time to time. The meaning of planning is choosing the best out of various alternative objectives, processes, policies and programs. The significance of planning lies in arranging the specialist training programs and deferent personnel and attached to the educational institution and also the functions which are undertaken in realising such objectives and aims. In fact, the educational planning is a progressive process. It does not only deep in view the present requirements, but also looks into the future for different needs that are likely to arise in the coming times due to change in perception, scientific development, technological improvements and new inventions besides social thinking and political changes.

The judicious process of planning is a process which keeps in view the past experiences and guidance and hopes for future progress by keeping in tune with the present. While taking the level of planning into consideration, it is necessary to know the objectives which have to be accomplished. It should also be made clear what processes, techniques and methods would be adopted in realising those objectives. It is also necessary to classify the aids and systems to be used in it. The administrator must keep in view a special thing, that is to make the planning process quite flexible, so that he is able to change with the dynamic changes in the environment and overcome hindrances in realising the objectives due to one or the other reason. However, it may be known that excessive flexibility on the part of the administrator tells about his weakness.

Various activities and functions of administration are done under planning. Different kinds of problems arise before the administration in its day-to-day functioning of the school where the administrator has to take such decisions. It is necessary for a proficient administrator to take such decisions with justice and without prejudice. He should take into consideration various aspects of a situation including the objective which would be served by taking a particular king of decision. He should also collect and collage all related information and statistics for analysis and, evaluate the available alternatives before taking the final decision.

1. According to Hayens and Messy, Planning is that function of administrator in which he decides in advance what he will do. It is decision-making process of a special kind it is an intellectual process in which creative thinking and imagination are essential.

2. According to M.E. Hurley, Planning is deciding in advance what is to be done. It involves selection of objectives, policies, procedures and programs from among alternatives.'

3. According to William H. Newman, Planning is

predetermination of what is to be done in the future generally. In this view, it is to include extensive and expansive form of human conduct in it.

4. According to Koontz and O' Donnel, Planning is a mental activity, is a conscious determination of doing a work in a particular way. It is base of decision on the basis of objectives, facts and pre-conceived thoughts,

Nature of Planning

The following can be included in the nature of planning:

1. Based on forecasting.
2. Selective process.
3. Futuristic.
4. Basis of proficiency in administration.
5. Universal process.
6. Intellectual and continuous process.
7. Foremost function of administration.
8. Inseparable part of an organisation.

Objectives of Planning

The chief objectives of planning are as follows :-

1. Achievement of Objectives - The final and most important objective of planning is to continuously proceed and try for achievement of the objectives of the organisation so that the final ends cab be attained while working in the right direction.

2. Proper Knowledge of Main and Sub-Objectives - One of the chief objectives of planning is to inform the workers and other concerned personnel abut the goals and sub-objectives of the organisation. Planning not only

informs them about the goals and aims of the organisation, but also how to achieve them.

3. Providing Appropriate Direction - Having made the future planning, appropriate direction is given to the future course of events of the organisation. Thus, great difficulty is averred with planning.

4. Establishment of Coordination and Equality - Planning helps in establishing coordination and quality in various activities of the organisation.

5. Certainty in Work - Attempts are made in administration to bring about certainty in the future works so that the objectives of the organisation are met.

6. Accurate Forecasting - The objectives of planning is to forecast the future needs correctly. So, forecasting is considered as the essence of planning.

7. Economy in Management - When the planning of future events has been finalised, the attention of the administration is diverted toward its execution, so it beings about economy in execution.

Functions Related to Planning

Functions related to planning are as follows :

1. Control on Irrational Decisions - The greatest advantage of planning is that the decisions done under it are done prudently and after due consideration. Thus, it helps control imprudent and hasty decisions.

2. Knowledge of Duties and Responsibilities of Officers - Planning produces organisational power and energy. Planning helps the workers and executives to realise their duties and responsibilities easily.

3. Benefit of Future Possibilities - Future originates in the present and is the source of possibilities of

development. Planning can help find out the future possibilities and take benefits from them. According to the opinion of Koont and O' Donell, planning is such selected and chosen path which coordinates of collective works of administration into one effort.

4. Focussing Toward Achievement of Objectives - Planning helps centralise the administrators toward achievement of goals proficient. With the help of planning, every department focuses on achievement of goals of the organisation while coordinating with one another. It makes the effort of different departments complementary, and not competitive. Thus, planning helps the administrators focus on achievement of objectives.

5. Elimination of Ambiguity - Lack of planning means absence of objectives, policies, programs, processes, etc. In the absence of all these, the functions of the administration would become aimless, disorderly and uncertain. It would result in losses and end of the profession. Planning helps inspire achievement of the goals of the organisation in an orderly and scientific manner. It helps replace disorderliness with orderliness and management.

6. Minimising Uncertainty and Risk - The fundamental basis of planning is forecasting, and not merely guesses and conjectures. It is based on the available facts and statistics and on the analysis of the situations and facts. As such, it makes the risks and uncertainties reducible to almost nil if proper planning has been made. Thus, planning is preparation for the future events which results in benefits.

7. Establishment to Effective Control - Having decided the measurements of forms and execution of

various functions, planning makes evaluation of the actual achievements possible. The process of reformation can be initiated on finding a difference between the planning and actual achievement. It helps exercise control over the situation.

8. Increase in Managerial Efficiency - the complete planning of the processes of an organisation directs the functions of the organisation toward clear objectives which makes organisation and administration easy. Coordination and control of different functions is completed by the planning process which helps in cooperation of administrative functions.

Organisation

Definitions of Organisation

The word organisation is quite an extensive word and does not admit a definite and universal definition. Various scholars have, therefore, defined it differently. The chief ones are as follows:

1. According to E.F.L. Brich, "Organisation is that part of management which is concerned with the definition of the structure of the responsibilities by means of which the activities of the enterprise are distributed among the personnel employed in its service, and the forms of interrelations established among the personnel by virtue of such responsibilities."

2. According to Prof. L.H. Haney, "Organisation is a harmonious adjustment of specialised part for the accomplishment of some common purpose or purposes."

3. According to Dr. S.P. Singh, "Organisation is an art of establishing coordination and cooperation between various elements of production for the attainment of definite goals."

4. According to Mejarland, "An identifiable group of people contributing their efforts toward the attainment of goals is called organisation.,"

Functions of Organisation in Administration

The functions of organisation in administration are as follows :

1. Optimum Use of Technical Improvements - An able organisation makes it possible to make use of the latest technical and scientific achievements as a result of research and technological advancement. The objective of every organisation is to achieve maximum production with minimum effort which is possible if latest devices are used.

2. Optimum Use of Resources - A healthy organisation arranges for training of its employees. The trained manpower is suitably employed on the posts and talks which they have been trained to perform thus increasing their efficiency. Besides, their ability can be measured by delegating them authority and to ascertain whether such staff can be promoted to shoulder heavier responsibilities.

3. Easy Delegation - Some administrators keep busy doing such things which is fact should be done by their juniors. It reduces time available with them for performing the other important functions which they and no other should do. It burdens them unnecessarily. An able organisation frees such a person by defining the work field of the administrators clearly and marks their boundaries under which they have to work while allotting the work to all functionaries according to their efficiency and ability. It also provides for allotment and delegation of duties which can be done by the junior staff, thus keeping the seniors free to plan and do more

important fuctions.

4. Easiness in Coordination - Coordination among various departments of an organisation is established with the help of the organisation. The general objectives of different departments are kept in view and coordinated with the objectives of the other departments and of the whole organisation.

5. Helpful for Development of Administration - A healthy organisation arranges for the training of its employees. The trained manpower is utilised in various posts in the administration. Besides, their proficiency and ability is used for development of their skill and ability.

6. Increase in the Speed of Development - A healthy organisation makes such a structure by which self-development of the organisation takes place naturally. It is necessary in the modern times to develop its activities and expand them so that progress can be made rapidly.

7. Motivation for Creative Work - The functions are distributed and arranged on the basis of priority in an organisation Alternatively, the fuctions may be arranged on the basis of their importance. It makes the workers do the work creatively and they encourage the creative work in organisation.

8. Motivation for Specialisation and Classification - The role of organisation in the present times is all the more vital as it inspires specialisation and classification. Under the modern organisation, every person is allotted the duty which he can efficiently and ably do while keeping his interest alive.

9. Moral Restriction on Corruption - A good

organisation makes the workers hard-working, honest and devoted and awaken them to the needs of the organisation and their own duties. It helps curtail corruption with moral implications. When the organisation is inactive, the workers do not want to work resulting in less production and inefficiency. An organisation should always remain young and energetic else its young workers too would become old and energetic. An efficient organisation makes its workers progress high values and moral character.

10. Increase in Managerial and Administrative Efficiency - Proficient, effective and able organisation makes the function of administration easy and comfortable. It increase management and capacity of administration. An able organisation takes advantage of the proficiencies of the workers according to their abilities. Besides, it delegates and distributes duties according to the capacities of the workers to make administration efficient. On the other hand, an inefficient organisation keeps itself busy in aimless works and wastes its time due to which hardly any time is left for fruitful activities.

11. Other Advantages - Besides the above, the following can be the causes of the importance of organisation :

a. Helpful in national security.

b. Enhancement of moral character.

c. Easiness of communication.

d. Easiness in control.

Thus, we see that the important of an organisation is great. The opinion of Lanvary Fish is very important. According to him, organisation is far more than a simple chart. It is such a process by the medium of which administration directs, coordinates and control the business. In fact, it is the foundation of the administration.

Control

Control is an important function of administration. The administration exercise it to know whether the tasks of the organisation are being executed according to plan or not, and if not, what are the causes behind it. Besides, control helps increase in production, decrease in costs, control over quality, and development of the employees. Various scholars have defined control variously. Some of them are as follows :

1. According to Koontz and O' Denell, "The managerial function of control is the measurement and correction of the performance of subordinates in order to make sure that the objectives and plan devised to attain them are accomplished."

2. Marrycushing Niles, "Control is to make balance toward directed activities of the organisation toward a definite aim or a group of them."

Functions of Control in Administration

The functions of control in an organization can be enumerated as follows :

1. Safety from Risk - Every function of the organisation is fully checked under the process of control and the risky and fallacious points are found out to reform and correct them for future control of risk.

2. Helpful in Delegation - An organisation is made when suitable delegation of authority is effected. The duties and responsibilites of the personnel are decided according to them. It is possible by the control process

whether those duties and responsibilities are being executed properly or not.

3. Helpful in Coordination - The process of control helps establish coordination in various activities of the departments of the organisation and ends the friction occurring between them. It helps achieve the objectives of the organisation successfully.

4. Source of Motivation - A successful control mechanism can help the organisation know who are the proficient employees and those who are not. The proficient employees can be motivated to increase their production further while the unproficient ones can be suitably admonished or punished or motivated to enhance their proficiency to attain the standards set by the organisation.

5. Basis of Future Plans - The process of control is the basis of future planning. It helps the organisation beget such information and facts on the basis of which suitable and proper planning for the future strategy of the organisation can be made.

6. Discipline in Organisation - The process of control is important in bringing about discipline in business and institution. Control can be exercised to reduce the instances of dishonesty, idleness, improper conduct, etc. and their possibilities to a great extent. It cultivates an atmosphere of discipline.

Direction

The word direction means to take work from others. In other words, direction is to guide or direct a function toward the desired direction. Direction is also called by the terms of operation, guidance, etc. The chief definitions of direction are as follows :

1. According to Theo Haimann, "Directing consists of the processes and the techniques utilised in issuing instruction and making certain that operations are carried on as originally planned."

2. According to Koontz and O' Denell, "Direction is a complex function that includes all those actions which are designed to encourage subordinates to work effectively and efficiently in both the short and long run."

3. According to Marshall E. Denmock, "The heart of administration is the directing function which involves determining the course of giving orders and instructions, providing the dynamic leadership."

Functions of Direction

The following functions are performed under the process of direction:

1. Provide able leadership to the subordinates and motivate them.

2. Make communication effective.

3. Raise the moral of the subordinates.

4. Make control effective.

5. Guide and train the subordinates from time to time.

6. Establish coordination among various functions.

7. Order the subordinates.

8. Inspect the works of the subordinates.

Work of Direction in Administration

Direction has important place in administration because in absence of it, the administrative works of different nature fail to achieve targets and objectives, besides they lack control and coordination. As a boat cannot be steered without on oar, an army cannot fight without a leader, a vehicle cannot be driven without a driver, so an administration cannot function without direction. According to John Seymour, "Direction in administration is akin to strategy in war. This function concerns itself with the disposition of resources, the points at which special efforts are to be concentrated and survival among the stresses and strains of practical life of the administration."

Characteristics of Good Direction

The characteristics of good and effective direction are as follows:

1. Direction is a continuous process.

2. There are two chief objectives of direction- to make the employees work and to prepare the administrators take responsibility.

3. Direction helps make inspection, supervision and evaluation of the subordinates effective.

4. Direction is a necessary and important function of administration.

5. The need of direction is felt at every level of administration.

6. Direction inspires and stimulates the employees toward fulfillment and achievement of the objectives of the institution.

7

EDUCATIONAL MANAGEMENT: HUMAN BEINGS AND INPUT, PROCESS AND OUTPUT

Introduction

Educational management consists of designs of institution. The desired objectives cannot be achieved on the basis of learning theories alone. Therefore, teaching-learning structure, teaching theories and structure of the content have been developed. Instructional designs are the sum of these things. The development of educational designs. Glaser states that professional skills and efficiency can be developed with the help of instructional designs. The experts and specialists are attempting to investigate the level of professional skills to be developed. L Carter found in his investigation that instructional designs are an effective tool for developing group professional efficiency than of an individual. Educational management has the main assumption that teaching is not only an art but also a science; and teachers are not only effective by birth but can be made effective through training programs as well.

Institutional designs emphasize on structure of the task. The content is analyses for its structure and for ascertaining its characteristics. The learner's responses are analysed in view of objectives and levels of learning.

The entering behaviour is considered for providing a new stimuli to have desired responses of the learner. The appropriate teaching strategies, techniques and tactics are selected for presentation content so that desired learning structure may be generated. The techniques of motivation are employed for leading the teaching. The measuring instrument is constructed for evaluating the performance level of the students so that decisions may be taken about the objectives of learning.

Uuwing has defined instructional design thus : Instructional design is concerned with an application of modern skills and techniques for the requirements of education and training. This includes facilitation of learning by manipulation of media, methods, and the control of environment of so far this reflects on learning.

Such type of thinking took place in 1950 and different approaches were evolved for the problem of education and training but the following three approaches are most popular :

1. System analysis.
2. Cybemetic psychology
3. Training psychology.

The three approaches of Instructional Designs are supplementary to one another toward solving the problems of education and training. They are closely related to deal with the input, output and process aspects of educational technology.

Training Psychology emphasises on task analysis and design of inter-related training components. Training psychology is concerned with input aspect and its main function is task analysis. It evolves the structure of teaching and learning. Cybernetic Psychology focuses on dynamic feedback and self-regulation. The second approach of cybernetic deals with the process aspect of education and its major function is to provide reinforcement for leading the teaching. System Analysis focuses on system or output. The third approach of system analysis concerns with the development of organisation and administration on the basis of output aspect of these approaches are being described in detail in the following paragraphs.

1. Instructional designs should be conducted by means of a systems approach. Briefly, systems approached in instruction means planned and organised use of all available learning aids including instructional media, in order to achieve the desirable learning objectives by the mots efficient possible way. If focuses on the learner and his performances first and then decisions are made regarding content, learning experiences, instructional media and instructional strategies for realising the objectives.

2. Instructional designs have phases that are both immediate and long range. Design in the immediate sense relates to the preparation of the design a few hours before the instruction is given. The long range approach takes time to plan and prepare not only the design of a particular topic but the whole course itself or the entire instructional system. This approach involves more complex and varied designs. Such designs are undertaken by individual teachers, a team of teachers, curriculum planners and textbook writers.

3. Instructional designs must be based on knowledge of how human beings learn. Consideration should be given not only to what the students should learn but how they should learn. Instructional design must take into account learning conditions.

4. Instructional designs must aim at aiding the

learning of the individual. The instruction may be oriented to the individual in spite of the fact that learners may be in large or small groups.

5. Systematically designed instruction greatly affects individual human development. A nurturing environment is not adequate to develop an individual. Planning and directing are essential aspects of learning. As instructional design should ensure that no one is educationally disadvantaged.

Kinds of Instructional Designs

Instructional designs can be classified into five categories :

1. Objective based.
2. Skill based.
3. Model based.
4. Learning Style based.
5. Competency based.

Teachers should make an attempt to reduce the factors that do not encourage good learning styles such as anxiety, frustration and emotional instability, dependence on teachers and parents, not memory and convergent thinking. The college teachers surmise first, the existence of different styles of learning adopted by students and secondly, the effect of these styles on the learning styles, where the planning, preparation and conduct of a lesson emphasises learning style of the students. The teacher's design of instruction should provide opportunities to the students who use different learning patterns.

Functions of Instructional Designs

The sequence of teaching acts or events that a

teacher plans, organises and carries out in order to create a learning environment for the college students if called the instructional design. Instructional designs provide the scientific basis for the instructional system. It develops the professional skill and efficiency for the teachers. Glaser has enumerated the following functions of instructional designs:

1. Learner's responses are analysed for the structure of the content of learning. The entering behaviours of the students are studied for appropriate stimuli for better performance.

a. Provide performance.

b. Provide feedback.

c. Gain and direct attention.

d. Activate recall.

e. Inform the learner of the objectives of learning.

f. Review the process on the basis of assessment.

g. Enhance retention and transfer.

2. The performance of student's is assessed in order to find out if the objectives of learning have been realised.

3. The instructional task is analysed for the structure of the content.

4. Teaching strategies, techniques and approaches are selected by the teachers for presenting the content so that the desired learning structures result.

Instructional designs, are therefore, concerned with the structuring of the content to create a suitable learning environment, the selection of appropriate teaching strategies and methods, and the assessment of the performance level of students. When a college teacher designs his instructional hours, he should be conscious of the need to motivate the students not only at the beginning of the class but right through, whenever the opportunity arises. The learning experiences thus provided may be assessed for replanning the instructional design.

Through motivation, attention is sought and the teacher adopts several ways to maintain it. Some of these steps may include listing the objectives of learning for the particular class or topic, enhancing retention of material learnt during the class by active questioning and providing feedback on the responses given by the students. The questions should not only aim at recall responses but also include reflective thinking, reviewing, generalising and reasoning. Selected instructional aids and media may also be used for better learning outcomes.

Cybernetic Psychology

The second approach of instructional designs, namely, cybernetic has denoted the discipline associated with the research of communication and control. It suggests concern with component elements of a system which may function together to produce the most effective integrated system. The term cybernetic was used by Norbest Wiener associated with the physical system and physics.

The instructional system also has three major elements and can also be considered as a cybenetic system. A cybenetic instructional system would also include knowledge of results to the leaner and some record of students's response. Its input consists of library material, subject matter content, learner characteristics and objectives. The students responses function as feedback for input. The procedure controls the presentation and modifies the presentation or display of knowledge or results on the basis of students responses corresponding to the objectives. In the cybernetic system of instruction, following is the order of input, output and procedure.

The first essential input is the content or material to be presented, i.e. library material or library input which is inclusive of any written material or audio-visual material, programmed instructional system are the objectives by which the system is designed to accomplish. A third input of a cybernetic instructional system is the formation concerning with the individual characteristics of the students. Because this is a cybenetic system, the fourth type of input consists of the feedback aspect, without this an instructional system is not able to adjust the presentation and to produce the change in behaviour specified by the objective input. It may be noted here that in most of the instructions in the schools the inputs of students responses are ignored.

The first essential output for an instructional system is the display of the learner which may be oral such as lecture explanation, visual, written, and so on. A display is any stimulus situation structured and presented to the learner for the purpose of establishing some responses. In a cybernetic system, third type of output which may or may not be used in a particular instructional situation will be the record of each student's response. The procedure is the selection mechanism which presents and displays in a linear fashion, on following the other. Movie or filmstrip presentation is a good example of such a system.

Feedback theory evaluates the techniques of self-instruction according to how well they conform to the principles of cybernetic design. In order to optimise feedback control of symbolic knowledge and skill, original presentation should be more varied and flexible than permitted by most of the teaching machines and programs. Especially organised systems of reference are also important. However, self-instruction is useful for drill and review in specific details. The mechanism of feedback devices are most effective for the modification of teacher behaviour. These mechanisms are based on the principles of cybernetic.

Models of Teacher Education

The development of teaching concept is based on teacher education model. The teachers are prepared by determining the nature of training task which they have to perform in classroom teaching. A number of teacher education models have been developed and these models are based on the principles of training psychology. The teacher education models can be classified into three groups. On the basis of teaching tasks, the following classification of teacher education models has been made :

1. Product Factors Models - The third type of teacher education models are based on output system. These models are used for improving the outcomes of learning where educational internship may be employed for this purpose in a teacher education programme.

2. Process Factors Models - The Process factors models training tasks are organised in such a way that their focus is on the development of the internal abilities and efficiency of teachers and main emphasis is given on the mastery of content and development of right type of attitude toward teaching.

a. The Toledo Model of Teacher Training.

b. Regional Laboratory Model of Teacher Training.

c. The Georgia Model of Teacher Training.

d. Teacher College Model of Teacher Training.

This type of teacher education models orient the training task for developing teaching skills or teacher behaviour in the classroom interaction. The Georgia and Toledo models are the examples of this type of model. Pre-service and in-service programs are organised in Indian conditions for developing this factor.

3. Presage Factors Models :

a. The Wisconsin Model of Teacher Education.

b. Syracuse Model of Teacher Education.

c. Florida Model of Teacher Education.

d. Michigan State Model of Teacher Education.

Training Psychology

The main objective of training psychology is to improve to activities in which a learner performs function. The learning outcome cannot be improved by learning theories, therefore, training psychology prepares on outline for task by analysing its components. Training psychology is mainly concerned with the problems of teaching, learning and training. Out training institutions cannot produce effective teachers with help of learning theories. Moreover, they have failed to provide substantial solution for teaching and training problems. Training psychology is a approach for these problems and has come through investigation on complex problems of training. The task components are organised in such a way that the desired objectives may be achieved. The crucial aspect of training psychology is the Task Analysis. It is an approach to teaching process rather than learning theories. The main assumption of this approach is that learning is a dependent variable whereas teaching is the independent and variable wherein learning can only be improved by developing teaching task.

Principles of Training Psychology

The principles of training psychology are useful for developing teacher-education models can also for developing instruction. The training psychology has been developed for the practical problems of teaching and training. It has a greater scope of application in the area of education and training. Norman A. Crowder has propounded branching programme in which main stress in given on task analysis and identification of difficult elements. The diagnosis is done for the difficulty of elements. The diagnosis is done for the difficulty of elements and designing of remedial instruction. The principles of training psychology can provide scientific basis for designing individualised or remedial instructions and development of curriculum. The curriculum and instructional material can be made specific and relevant to the objectives and to the competence and skill to be developed in the leaner.

The branching programme is originated from human training and form principles of psychology. The task elements are performed by each learner according to his won needs. This strategy has its own requirements for each and every learner.

The principles of training psychology are being used for improving present training programme by developing models to teacher education in our country. The principles of training psychology may be helpful for pupil-teachers in:

1. It is assured that every task element can be performed effectively.

2. The elements are organised in such a sequence which may generate appropriate learning conditions. 3. The elements are identified and analysed for the performance of last task.

The principles of stimulus- response of military psychology having failed to give the solution for the complex problems of training the Task Analysis approach has been followed for the development of training. Robert Gange has explained that the human task can be analysed in its elements. He further assumed that these elements are quite different from one another. The task elements can be performed by employing different tactics. The task elements function as a mediator for the last task. The functions of an elements function helpful in the transfer of learning and training. The shortage of task elements reduces the transfer to zero.

These statements convey the meaning of the principles of training psychology which are broadly associated with task analysis.

Relevance of Cybernetic in Education

The concept of cybernetic is most useful for developing design of training programs for complex behaviour. Most useful concept in the cybernetic is that of feedback which has far-reaching implications for teaching, learning and training.. The classroom instruction, a school or the programme of teaching can be considered as a dynamic system. This stresses on the principle that teaching is resultant activity of the combination of forces, factors and conditions. The teacher has to take into consideration all these factors to generate appropriated teaching situation. The following are the major implications of cybenetic:

1. Teacher education programme can be improved by employing the mechanism of feedback devices for the modification of teacher behaviour.

2. The input, output and process units of teaching enable the teacher understand and analyse teaching in more scientific manner.

3. The principles of cybernetic are applied for classroom instruction, group as well as individual learning.

4. It provides the basis of self- education. The feedback control is used to develop programmed instructional material.

5. The teaching activities can be made highly structured and well organised in view of leaning objectives.

6. The innovative practices in teacher education programme such as micro-teaching, simulated social skill teaching and inter-action analysis are based on the theory of feedback.

7. It enables the teacher to understand some of the fundamental mechanisms that control learning.

8. The cybernetic principles are used for developing remedial instruction or individualised instructional material.

Cybernetic Theory

Cybernetic theory views an individual as a feedback system which generate its activities in order to detect and control specific stimulus characteristics of the environment. Cybernetic can be considered as a branch of training psychology. It conceptualises human being in engineering terms considering him like an electric machine which uses the process of sensory feedback to control and modify its behaviour.

It analyses intrinsic mechanism by which control is established and maintained by sensory feedback and self-regulation. The system can be of two types- an open loop system and a closed loop system. The closed loop system is often referred to as cybernetic system. In the open loop system the output is returned to the system and consequently affects future output of the system. It is the one which places a boundary around the system.

All systems include at least three basic elements - input, process and output. The input unit provides some process by which material or information is entered into the system. The process unit acts on the material or information to modify it in any way. The output unit consists of some techniques for discharging the results of process from the system. The output from a system which returns as an input to control future output is called feedback.

Procedure of System Analysis

To accomplish a system analysis a number of steps are followed. The following steps must be utilised for conducting the study of system analysis :

1. Block Diagram - The problem area is a final step in the analytical stage of the systems analysis. A block diagram is prepared for all functions of the subsystem that make up the problem area. It denotes logical structure of the sub-system operations and is similar to the block diagram.

2. Specify Operations in the Problem - After identifying specific problem, it is necessary to review the operations within the problem area. It is much more comprehensive than the original review of the total operation. It helps to understand quickly the relationship

of all facets of the problem to the total operating system.

3. Isolation of the Problem - The administrator does not always know exactly the main problem; therefore, it is necessary to follow earlier steps in order to isolate specific problem of the system. The collection and analysis of data helps in identifying and defining the problem.

4. Analysis of Data - Analysis of data is done to make it meaningful. The analysis of data is employed to experiment paradigms to study the effect of independent variable upon dependent variable. In system analysis study, an objective analysis is made for determining the influence of variables. The investigator is concerned with interaction of many variables. The Primary concern is to obtain correlation not necessary to establish the cause and effect.

5. Collection of Data - The review of system for identifying the main problem yields the data within the problem area. The collection of data basically involves the statistical techniques and procedure. In many situations the aspects of system analysis are the application of classical statistical procedure.

6. Review of System Operation - The second step in system analysis includes a comprehensive review of the systems operation. System analysis is problem-oriented and it is necessary to understand completely the systems operation. The administrators fall in some problems but these do not always turn out to be main problems.

7. Formation of Objectives - The most important and difficult aspect of the entire system analysis study is to formulate the specific objectives to be achieved. To state objectives in general terms is totally inadequate. An objective may be written in behavioural term of fiscal

functions.

System Analysis

System analysis is known as the third approach of instructional designs which is closely related to both training psychology and cybernetic. It has greatly influenced management decision-making in business, industry, government departments and military organisation. This new technology is known by several terms, but one term that has gained considerable standardization in System Analysis.

The term System analysis actually emerged from the scientific management concept. In general, System Analysis involves utilisation of Scientific mathematical techniques applied to organisational operation as a part of management decision-making activities. System technology brings the educational management a scientific quantitative approach for solving complex educational administrative problems. It is essentially based on mathematics. The word system has been derived from the field of engineering.

A system is the sum total of agents working interdentally and dependently together to achieve the required goals. The term system conveys the meaning of analysis and development. It has the assumption that no comprehensive system development can take place without prior system quantitative methods for analysing management problems. The field of educational administration is becoming set with the quantitative-scientific techniques that help the educational administrators in the decision-making process.

Relevance of Systems Analysis

The system analysis provides scientific and quantitative basis for studying the problems of educational system and has greatly influenced the educational administration and organisation. The educational implication of systems analysis have been enumerated as follows:

1. It enables the educational administrator to identify the actual problem and abstains from a verified solution of the problem.

2. Any change in the educational system can be brought objectively, empirically and economically with great utility by the help of system analysis.

3. It brings to educational management a scientific-quantitative approach for solving complex education administrative problems.

4. The sub-system of education is analysed to understand the actual problem and tentative solutions can be verified to test on a segment of the system.

5. The training programs can also be improved with the help of system analysis. The new concept of management may be implemented in training programs.

A system is a inter-relation of parts each having a specific function. Educational technology can be viewed from the systems approach. A system may be defined as the assemblage of components each having its own purposes. The parts and their functions are inter-related in specific ways so that they perform adequately to achieve the purpose of the system as a whole. The whole is more than the sum of the parts. The system is designed on the objectives to be achieved and objectives being defined in terms of obtainable outputs. Inputs are transferred into desirable outputs. For this transformation, interaction takes place with the components. It is synergistic, e.g., a bicycle, car, school, college, etc.

The educational system includes students and teachers, and refers to curriculum content, instructional material, instructional strategy, physical environment, and the evaluation of instructional objectives. Each component has its own functions and interactions. These functions and interactions are more important than their description.

The systems approach is a rational problem-solving method of analysing process and making it more effective. The simple system representations show how the inputs into a system undergo some process of transformation into a product output and the effects of the outputs on the environment are monitored so as to modify future inputs. Colleges can be thought of as places where the process of education works on the minds and personalities of all the members and the product is the effect of this educational process which will thus be qualitative as well as quantitative. The system approach in instruction is an integrated, programmed complex of instructional media, hardware and personnel, whose components are structured as a single unit with a schedule of time and sequential planning. It is a strategy which utilises analysis design a management to attain the stated goal effectively and efficiently. The feedback loop represents the information on which the educational process is modified to better provide for the needs of learners who are entering the college or leaving it for work situations.

Combination of Teaching Strategies and Instructional Designs

Teaching strategies include teaching methods, approaches and techniques such as lecture method, tutorial approach, case study technique, demonstration method, term-teaching approach, programmed instruction, etc. The teaching strategies have the high probability of generating effective learning in students. Practising teachers may have to bring about some modifications, minor changes and adapt them to further increase the probability of their success in helping students learn more and better. In planning an instructional design such as objectives, skills, competencies, models or learning styles. Teaching strategies aim at establishing relationship between teaching inputs and learning outcomes, mainly in terms of realising the learning objectives. In doing so, he focuses attention on the type of design he is to prepare.

The teaching strategies used to elaborate the content or subject matter of that unit or topic have to be spelled out in that particular design. Teaching strategies have been introduced in this book for large groups, small groups and individual instruction. Teaching strategies when designed with clearly spelt-out objectives and effective means of achicving them with in-built evaluation techniques, are known as educational technology. Application of technology will ensure the achievement of objectives with the minimum effort and time required. When teaching result is effective learning of all the students taught. Then any strategy that is applied to achieve this can be called educational technology.

8

STATE

Meaning of State

Fed up with barbarous way of life, people rose above their selfish interests and organised themselves into sorts of associations investing them with power and functions. These early associations formed a super association which controlled and directed the other associations in a manner that befit all. The super association is not only numerous but powerful, and all other associations and their members implicitly recognise and honour its writ. This body is called State, and the following four elements-

1. Sovereignty - The body so formed must have sovereign rights over the territory and people that comprise it. The government and the population defend the territorial integrity of their state generally called country. No other similar body, state or country, should have any counter interests in this regard. To safeguard their territorial interests, these independent bodies may forge into a bigger association, such as, League of Nations or, the United Nations.

Definition

1. According to Garner, "State is community of persons, more or less numerous, Permanently occupying a definite portion of territory, independency of a foreign control, and possessing an organised government to

which the inhabitants render a habitual obedience."

2. According to I.L. Kandel, "State may be defined as an organised political community with government recognised by people".

Critical Estimate of State Control

Merits -

1. Impart better quality of education because of its power, vision and resources.

2. Achieve national objectives of education in a concerted manner.

3. Inculcate necessary attitudes keeping in line with its national and international requirements.

4. Secular education, to develop understanding and respect for all religions.

5. Uniforms standard of education. Underline the principle of equality.

6. State control on education will ensure free, universal and compulsory education to enable it discharge its constitutional obligations.

Limitations

1. Stifle growth, development and expression.

2. May lead to a totalitarian form of state neglecting and sidelining the individual.

3. Education will become extraneous, and may amount to mere filling in from outside with no relevance to the individual.

4. Deprive citizens of their right to equality and freedom.

5. Deprive Family of its legitimate right to supervise

education of tis children keeping in line with their traditions ethoes.

6. Myopic outlook on the importance, nature and extent of the aims of education.

7. Mechanisation in educational content and process with no scope for any variation, enterprise and ingenuity.

8. Teachers committed to the state's way of thinking and approach may benefit at the cost of those with benign and liberal outlook.

9. May become an instrument of state indoctrination. Education may cease to be a welfare measure.

10. Neglect of individual differences, abilities, needs and aspirations due to emphasis on uniformity and universality alone.

11. May lead to lopsided growth and development of the individual.

12. Unhealthy, dangerous and dubious political influence and control may vitiate the free educational atmosphere in the country.

Educational Functions of State

State, however, has the following functions to perform in a democratic, progressive and altruistic set up -

1. Educational Research and Application - The state must encourage fundamental and action research in all areas of education, such as, science, humanities, engineering and medicine. Efforts must be made to get this work published at state expenses. Such central bodies like U.G.C., I.C.S.R., N.C.E.R.T., respective I.I,Ts

various subject-wise councils such as Indian Council of social Science Research, university research cells, should be provided adequate funds, facilities and resources to conduct research and publish findings. The state must take on thereafter and ensure that the research finds application in various educational programs and projects.

2. Scholarships - The central and state governments must encourage exceptional children by providing awards and scholarships at the national, state and district level. National Talent Search programme is one such provision at the national level.

3. Provision of standard books at subsidised rates.

4. General Control and Direction - The state and local administration should exercise control on the content and process of teaching, evaluation procedure, and conduct of school activities according to the local conditions, and law and order situation. Defaulting institutions should be penalised, or at least ticked off. But it should not go to the extent of Delhi administration which can called +2 affiliation of a prestigious session extra by one day. Rightly, the state Governor intervened and cancelled this ridiculous order. But one must sit up and take note of the control that a state might exercise even in a democratic setup and, that too in the national capital.

5. Red Cross and First Aid Training - Training in the First Aid, and Red Cross procedures should be encouraged by the state among the students so that they may help during disaster management.

6. Scouts and Guides Training - Planned at the national level, Scouts and Guides training is a state subject, and is supervised by trained personnel at the

district level. One week's Scouts and Guides training is made compulsory for the prospective teachers and is an integral part of their teachers training programme.

7. N.C.C. Training - This comes under the purview of the central government, and is organised in various states at the college level by the state N.C.C. directorates, and is funded by the central exchequer.

8. Training of Efficient Teachers - State should open teachers training colleges for the training and preparation of teachers for all levels of teaching in government, private and public schools.

9. Encouragement of Guardians - State should give necessary incentives to parents to sent their children to school. It could be by way of free-ships, subsidised books and uniforms, mid-day meals, etc. The Government has proposed a sum of Rs. 12,000.00 per year, to be excluded form the Income tax liability of the parents for the financial year 2003-2004. Such concessions will encourage parents to sent their children to school. More concessions should be considered with regard to the girl child.

10. Provide Educational Institutions - State should provide schools, colleges and universities, and take upon itself, directly and on directly through its various autonomous and voluntary bodies. It will meet the basic need and requirements of the society. It may also encourage other association and organisations to open schools by providing technical knowhow funds and recognition.

11. Training in Citizenship - Quality of a democratic setup will depend on the quality of the citizens. Education should, therefore, be such that it produces qualified, progressive, dynamic citizens who would take

to the statecraft in the manner best suited to them and to the country, State should, therefore, oversee that its educational policy gives adequate and relevant knowledge, develops necessary skills, and inculcates socially and culturally desirable attitudes, that may help an individual go about in a successful and useful manner, both for himself as well as the country. Training in Citizenship is, perhaps, the basic function of the state.

12. Construction of a National Education Policy - Construction of a National Education Policy to be in consonance with its directive principles, ensuring equal opportunities to all citizens without any bias and discrimination.

Historical Retrospects in India

We shall presently touch upon, in brief, the history of relation between State and Education in India-

1. Vedic Period - There was no relation between the state and education during the Vedic period in India. Statecraft, art of governance, proficiency in the use of weapons, knowledge of scriptures, philosophy, logic, rituals, medication, etc., Were provided by the saints in their own ashrams located away from the din and noise of the city life, and where the environment was chaste, pure and conducive. One may remember that the three components of education, i.e., teacher, content and pupil, vary in the order of their superiority from time to time. Education in the Vedic period was teacher-centred without any fixed programs, curriculum, and expensive sprawling infrastructures. Maintained by the society, these gurukuls, the family of the guru, had independent existence where the writ of the guru was the only worthwhile constraint. Even the mightiest of the rulers visiting such ashramas paid respect and obeisance to

the teacher in a befitting manner thus acknowledging the supremacy and competence of the presiding guru.

2. Brahmanic Period - There was no direct state control and education was sponsored by private agencies through donations and grants, and other measures to encourage and sustain deserving students. It , however, lost that glorious touch of the Vedic period where it commanded absolute respect and obeisance. Education became a professional and commercial activity. This necessarily led to the shift from teacher to the institution. The university of Taxila came into being, which was renowned for its depth, range and influence. Education moved into the hands of the priests, and acquired a state ritual.

3. This period witnessed further privatisation and commercialisation of education institutions. Universities, such as, Nalanda, Nadia, Vallabi, and Vikramashila came into existence, and were run by associations. These institutions were great seats of learning, and enjoyed total freedom, without any state control.

It may be observed that hitherto there was no contradiction between social and individual approach to education, hence no one really thought of exercising any constraint. The whole environment was Indian, hence smooth and congenial. Education, in the succeeding ages of historical evolution, slowly moved toward state control, influence and indulgence, primarily because the cause was no longer Indian, Foreign influences had their own axe to grind, and did not permit education to have its own way,

4. Muslim Period - Most of the Muslim rulers looked beyond the borders of India for inspiration, and

education was no exception. The emphasis on preservation of their own culture necessitated state patronage. Education, generally, consisted of teaching of the Quran and Shariat through the means of Maktabls and Madarass. As Islam was the religion of the court, state intervened to exercise control and direction. Moulivis and Ullemas gained social and political advancements by accepting grants by the state which, in their wake, brought many a rider, unshering in direct and indirect state control on education in India.

5. British Period - In spite of the direct state control on education during the British Period, education also prospered in the hands of private associations, religious bodies and cultural organisations who had a reasonable degree of freedom of thought and action. Wood's despatch and Macaulay's minutes, made into the educational system by opening departments of public instruction to be presided over senior officers to be called Directors of Public Instruction, and supported and assisted by district level education officers.

This department had a direct role in planning and supervision of these schools, and exercised extensive control on these institutions. It was in 1882 that Hunter Commission dissuaded the state in t is regard to permit private and voluntary agencies to run such schools on grants-in-aid basis. There was a spate of government and Normal schools, at least one in each district, and institutions opened by Missionaries, Muslim, Kish, Aryassmajis, Christians and other religious and cultural bodies in the interest of their own respective communities. Islamia Colleges/schools, Khalsa College/ Schools, D.A.V. Colleges/ Schools, Christian College/ Schools, Mission Schools/ Colleges, took pride in offering specific education to their communities on the lines they considered best for them. Education became almost autonomous except that these institutions had not abide by the government directives/orders/ instructions and to accept their supervisory role.

6. Modern Period - Education was accorded a special status in free India. Our Constitution bears testimony to this. There have been amendments to make education more dynamic and relevant. Education, which was earlier a state subject, is now upgraded to the Concurrent List wherein both the central and the state governments do their bit to improve and streamline the quality, extent and content of education, in a spirit of mutual dependance and cooperation. Educational institutions are, more or less, autonomous, and devise ways and means to make their programs relevant and useful. The concept of central and deemed universities has caught on in a progressive manner.

At the district level, the Inspector of School/ Education officer carries out supervisory functions, in-service teacher development programs, and even exercises financial control on the government programs, and even exercised financial control on the government and aided schools. To guard against malpractices, teachers are paid their salaries through nationalised banks, wherein the principal forwards the monthly salary bill to the DIOS for approval and clearance. Within this control, the educational institutions have a fair amount of freedom of action.

The so called public schools, which are, in fact, privately managed schools, do not receive financial grant, yet have to subscribe to the remote control of the government orders/directives, directly or through state boards of education, or other central examination of

Secondary Education Certificate, in matters of curriculum, teaching schedules, student welfare, teacher working conditions, etc. This may be, by and large, and administrative control, leaving the educational institutions free in their academic work.

The Central Government may, however, appoint commissions to update and streamline the National Education Policy and curriculum framework, from time to ti7ramount and absolute. Within these parameters, education is free to enunciate and practise its concepts and precepts, for the all round growth, development and prosperity of its people. Even the state funding of educational institutions does not hamper their freedom of thought and action. Central Advisory Board on Education, National Council of Education, Curriculum Revision Forum, and a host of other national and state council and bodies, are there to help in the formulation and execution of educational policy, norms and parameters, so that education has a progressive, dynamic, secular and scientific outlook.

This healthy relationship between the state and education is for the betterment of both, and should be taken as a via media or a middle course between the two extreme views on distribution of power mentioned above, and round development of its people, and for the prosperity and development of the country in a spirit of mutual respect and trust. The function of the state is to protect and promote, not to absorb or take the place of family and the individual.

The great Indian ethoes and psyche, and a long chain of benign thinkers prepared the ground for individualistic and democratic way of life in all matters relating to the school. It is this respect for the self and its culmination and realisation that manifests itself in our outlook on education in India today, where the major agencies of education have a free interplay of approach and output. In spite of occasional aberration in the Indian society, there is near unanimity that education should be free of any direct state control, and should be left to the educationists to shape it in a manner they consider best for the total uplift of society, taking care of all its sections, opinions and aspirations.

Influence of State of Education

Even in a benevolent state, education would deplore entrance and meddling of state in educational matters and for the fear that educational policies will then be determined by considerations oblique or even irrelevant to the meritorious development of education itself. It is primarily, perhaps, for the reason the state is most powerful, and nothing may stop it if it ever decides to take control of matters educational. This is the basic fear that lurks in the mind of the schoolman. However, the influence of the state on education may be in direct proportion to its ideology on distribution of power.

There may be instances where the basic constitutional structure may give definite directions in this regard, when a system of education would have uphold and be in line with the directive principles. For example, any system of education in India would have to cherish and circumscribe itself to the basic directives enshrined in the Indian Constitution. No educational theory and practice could run counter to the principles of Freedom, Equality, Fraternity, are Justice as enshrined in our Constitution, but would these directions not act as a guiding principle circumscribing all educational thought and philosophy in the country?

Similarly, the French and American Declarations ascribe certain dignity and status to man, and would foreshadow educational policy in line with that. To this extent, education should be the advocated that education should flourish under the State guardianship. The nature and extent of this guardianship would however vary with the current political thought of an era. To major currents of thoughts in this direction are as under -

1. Individualism and Collectivism - Individualism and Collectivism also called the Doctrine and Laissez faire, advocates complete freedom to the individual and forbids the State from interfering with matters, such as education, and to ensure complete decontrol and decentralisation in this regard. Locke, Mill and Benthem are such thinkers who advocate total freedom to the individual in educational matters. Collectivism, on the other hand, considers education to be under the state control so that it has trained and skilled manpower available, in a manner that it considers prudent, for the growth and prosperity of the state, Mathew Arnold, Carlyle and Ruskin are the chief exponents of this point of view.

2. Democratic State - Holding the opposite view, a democratic state does not regulate education. As a matter of fact, a democratic state binds itself with the principle of sharing of power; sharing power with its citizens, for the progress and betterment of all. Democratic state is a welfare organisation wherein education is a welfare measure as most of the educational institutions are funded by the government. Education in a democratic state is decentralised and aims at the fulfillment of the aims and objectives considered integral to the overall development of the

people; irrespective of caste, creed, region, religion and gender. The state may issue some general directions in this regard, besides which education is autonomous with complete control over the content and process. The only rider is, that not educational policy should violate and run counter to the directive principles. As a matter of fact, these directive principles are also given by the people to themselves at some point of time in their social and political evolution, and the State simply ensures their compliance.

3. Totalitarian State - The totalitarian state considers the state as the ultimate and absolute power, at the same time encompassing and transcending the people, with total control on its citizenry. It realises the importance of education to perpetuate its ideology, and insist that education should play a subservient role, and inculcate such tendencies and attitudes that support their viewpoint, and help in achieving a society as conceived by them. Education, therefore, is centralised in this form of State, with total control on content and process. It is an extremist view that completely neglects the individual, his needs, aspirations, requirements, desires and, competence. The State is above all, and the rest play a subservient role, as mere tools to establish the supremacy and efficacy of the State. The view may also be called Socialistic, where the control is total, both qualitative and quantitative. Pinkervich considers public education aiming to mould the future citizens as mighty instrument which a government cannot pass onto others. Education in this sense, is mere tool, a tool of governance.

Limitations

1. Neglects other social institutions and agencies

that may have legitimate stakes in the education of a child.

2. Aims at the total indoctrination of the citizens.

3. Does not help conservation of culture and values, as the total emphasis is on the art of governance under a totalitarian ideology.

4. Upholds perpetuation of the State at total neglect of the individual.

5. Entails a long term investment with uncertain and dubious results.

9

SECONDARY EDUCATION: MAJOR PROBLEMS

The advent of the East India Company brought in its wake the fruits of western education as the Company wished to raise a body of the Indians, qualified by their habits and acquirements to take a large share and to occupy high positions in the civil administration. Macaulay Minutes are a landmark in this regard. Lord William Bentinck gets full credit for giving his approval showing far-sight and understanding of things to come, as the policy laid the firm foundation for the subsequent British empire, later getting a further fillip form Wood's Despatch. The British educational policy created employment opportunities for the Indians so as to make them actively participate in the empire building exercise with honour and dignity, and a great sense of involvement.

Wood's Despatch 1854 played a vital role in the growth and development of secondary education by proclaiming that the people of India should be made familiar with the works of European authors, with the result of the thought and labour of Europeans on the subjects of every description and, to extend the means of imparting this knowledge, must be the object of any general system of education.

On the basis of this approach, universities were set at Bombay and Calcutta in 1857. These universities began to control and administer secondary schools on the basis of the matriculation examination and thus created a foundation for a colleges.

In 1882, the Hunter Commission suggested various syllabi for secondary schools, It suggested that the higher classes for the secondary schools should be divided into two parts- one should prepare students for the matriculation examination, and the other prepare youth for commercial and non-literacy activities.

However, these schools were under direct control of the universities, and the education department had no say in their functioning and programs.

In 1904 rules for the matriculation examination were framed in accord with the Indian Universities Act., and as a consequence, the secondary schools passed even more firmly into the hands of universities. This trend changed during the period 1905-1917 when the schools were subjected to control by the universities for granting recognition as well as to the education department for granting aid to them. Later it was decided that the education departments alone will exercise control over the secondary schools. It was a big leap forward which determined the nature and scope of secondary education in India for next over hundred years. The subsequent commissions and Reports further consolidated it and made it more formidable, pragmatic, progressive and life-related.

Objectives of Secondary Education : Ishwar Bhai Patel Commitee 1977

1. Participation in and promoting social activities in the school and community in such a way as to combine democratic values, and work for equality and upliftment on the work and under privileged.

2. Exploring the world of work, understanding the realities of life in order to prepare for a confident entry into the world outside the school.

3. Developing aesthetic appreciation and creativity

through participation in artistic activities.

4. Developing health-consciousness through participation in games, sports, and athletics for the maintenance of physical fitness.

5. Acquisition of broad based general eduction consisting of science, mathematics, social sciences, languages and socially useful productive labour.

6. Acquisition of skills and habits of self-learning.

Structural Changes : Kothari Commission

The effect of the recommendations of Mudaliar Commission soon wore off as the shift from the Intermediate to higher secondary was neither profitable nor practicable in the absence of a uniform policy at the national level. The reality underlying this change over was that uniformity must be imparted to the whole educational organisation in the country so that national unity and social unity can be awakened. Education should include programs for social service and national service which would have immense potential for the comprehensive and positive development of the child. Its recommendation of 10+2+3 educational system is a step in the same direction.

Structure of Secondary Education: Mudaliar Commission

Secondary Education Commission 1952-53 discovered a variety of forms of secondary education in the country which made the Commission sit up and formulate a smooth and uniform structure for Secondary education on a national basis. The commission considered various levels of education as independent units, all inclusive by themselves. Secondary education thus also became a complete unit by itself and not merely a preparatory stage, so that at the end of this period the student should be in a position, if he so desired, to enter the responsibilities of life and take up some useful vocation.

The Commission suggested the following structure:

1. At places where the higher secondary syllabus cannot be taught, and in the colleges which have a four year syllabus i.e. a two year syllabus for the intermediate and a two year syllabus for the degree course, provisions should be made for introducing a one year pre-university course before granting admission to the university. The syllabus should be implemented in colleges.

2. The Commission clearly found that the intermediate system of examination was defective. It argued that the intermediate examination destroyed the continuity of college education and created difficulties in the planning of the syllabus for the degree course. Adding one year to the secondary level will bring about an increase in skill and efficiency, while an additional one year with the degree course will generate educational skill. In this way, uninterrupted progress continues to take place over a three year period.

3. In the same way, the degree course should be of three years durations. Thus, the entire secondary level is broken up into two parts- (i) junior secondary, (ii) from class 9 to 11.

4. There should be a 4 year syllabus at the higher secondary level. The Commission suggested changing the existing intermediate system into the higher secondary level, comprising four years of education inclusive of one year of the intermediate level.

5. There should be a 3 year syllabus at the middle school, junior high school or senior basic level.

Features of Curriculum Reconstruction Kothari Commission

1. Curriculum should be designed to train students for work and for leisure.

2. Curriculum should not be split up into a number of isolated and uncoordinated subjects. It must ensure coordination, unification and interplay of all subjects.

3. Curriculum should be vitally and organically related to community life.

4. Curriculum should have variety and flexibility to cater for individual differences needs and interests.

5. Curriculum should be life-related and touch upon the needs and aspirations of students so as to help development of balanced personality.

Upgradation of Curriculum

1. The formation of subject Teachers Associations in the different school subjects will help to stimulate experimentation and upgrading of curricula. The State Education Departments, State Institutes of Education and NCERT should help the associations in their educational activities and coordinate their work.

2. Advanced curricula should be prepared by state Boards of School Education in all subjects and introduced in a phased manner in schools which fulfil certain conditions of staff and facilities.

3. Schools should be given the freedom to devise and experiment with new curricula suited to their needs. A lead should be given in the matter by training colleges and universities through their experimental schools.

4. The Commission suggested that school curricula should be upgraded by:

a. The orientation of teachers to the revised curricula through in-service education.

b. Preparation of textbooks and teaching-learning materials.

c. Revision of curricula based on such research.

d. Research in curriculum development undertaken by University Departments of Education, Training Colleges, State Institution of Education and Boards of School Education.

Multipurpose School

Mooted by Mudaliar Commission and supported by Kothari Commission, multi-purpose school meets the twin requirement of variety and flexibility of curriculum wherein a diversified syllabus is available to students in accordance with their ability, attitude and interest.

Objectives of Multipurpose Schools

K.G. Saiyyadian expressed the profound view that if a student, in the absence of proper counselling, takes up humanities instead of science, or vice versa, it is not only his school-life which is ruined but also his entire future because of a faulty choice of profession. In order to overcome this shortcoming stress has been laid upon the setting up of multipurpose schools.

The main objectives of multipurpose schools are the following-

1. Providing education in social and constructive or creative activities.

2. Creating skill in handicraft.

3. Guiding them to train the abilities and talents of students for the creation of national character and national wealth.

4. Making continuous efforts for the multi-faceted development of schools.

Need for Multipurpose Schools

The Mudaliar Commission stressed the need for establishing multipurpose schools on the basis of the following arguments :

1. In such schools, it is possible to organise courses of study which are in harmony with social, economic and psychological needs of the student and society.

2. Multipurpose schools can fulfil country's need for technicians, and contribute to the development of technical education.

3. In such schools, there are arrangements for teaching of a variety of courses making the students undergo comprehensive development.

4. Students who fail to progress in one class can easily be transferred to a more suitable class or course. Without there being any need for transferring to anther school.

5. In such schools, the child is free to choose subjects in accordance with his interests.

6. These schools destroy the feeling of inequality in the child's mind and help to develop human qualities and values in him.

7. In the U.S.A. Multipurpose schools had proved more successful than schools which had only one purpose: unit-purpose schools.

Vocationalisation

Kothari Commission recommended vocationalisation of secondary education and related vocationalisation with productivity. Hence, education should be productivity-oriented to meet the future needs of society restructuring of education on the following lines : mission suggested restructuring of education on the following lines:

1. Laying special stress upon agriculture and related sciences, scientific and technological education at the university level, should be developed.

2. Education at the secondary level should be vocationalised in order to meet the needs of industry, agriculture and trade.

3. Work experience should be integral part of general education.

4. Science should be an integral part of general education.

Education should help create self employment so that it enables one to get along with the responsibilities of life immediately after completing secondary education, if one of so desires, for fulfillment and well-being of future needs and aspirations. Secondary, education is the backbone of country's educational system and constitutes culmination of a phase developing multiple abilities and habits in an individual for success in life laying a solid educational and attitudinal foundation.

In view of the importance it attached to the vocationalisation of secondary education, the Commission proposed that the Central Government should aid the state Governments in implementing such a programme. Citing the example of the U.S.A. the Commission had thrust the entire responsibility for the vocationalisation of secondary education upon the union government.

At present, the existing system of secondary education does not make provisions for vocationalisation which may satisfy the needs for skilled workers in the next twenty years.

At the secondary level, these school satisfy only 30% of the need. In 1965-66 there was an increase of 2.2%. The Commission projected that by 1985-86, there should be an increase of 20% at the lower secondary level. For the next twenty years, the Commission made provisions for the admission of 24,13,000 students to vocational schools. In the same manner, the projected figurers of admission to total number of students. The Commission set for itself the target of 50 percent. It was indeed a major thrust toward vocationalisation of secondary education.

Guiding Principles of Work-Experience

1. Job oriented - Work experience should be job-oriented. The term job in this context, should be taken to refer to one complete unit of work in any occupation, for instance, construction of furniture, joining together various parts of produce a complete chair, carpentry, weaving etc.

2. Full Awareness - From the educational viewpoint, it is desirable that the child should be made aware of every activity concerned with a particular mode of his own effort.

3. Family Occupation - Children who enjoy facilities for obtaining work experience at home should be encouraged to learn their family occupation. If the school, college or university can assist the student in improving this occupation, it should extend help.

4. Use of Other Sources - In rural areas, where schools do not have their own land, students can obtain work experience by working on the farms of private individual at a time when there is additional demand for labour, for instance, during the sowing and harvesting seasons.

5. Teaching of Technology - Whenever opportunity is available, the use of technological means should be taught in work experience.

6. Help from Retired Persons - In places where industrial training institutions or polythenic institutions are available, the retired teachers from such institutions could be made use of. With the help of these institutions, some general tool kits can be prepared for use in work experience.

7. Division of Time - The division of time in work experience will be in accordance with the nature of the activity. In agricultural activity it will be sowing or harvesting duration in the week may be adequate.

8. No part of curriculum - Work experience will not be

a part of the curriculum. Hence, arrangements will be made in the time-table to ensure that the regular teaching time-table is not disturbed.

9. No Compulsion - Any scheme of work experience should not be made compulsory for any school.

10. Profit - The profit from work experience should flow to those who have worked for it. In other words, the cost of the raw materials involved should be deducted from the income and the profit handed over to the students.

11. Vocational Basis - Every activity engaged in must have a vocational basis. The income or production obtained from work experience, must in every case, be more than the expenditure incurred on it.

12. Less Expensive - In preparing a programme of work-experience, it must be remembered that a scheme involving vast expenditure is not to be considered. Instead the programme must envisage the maximum utilisation of the facilities commonly available in schools.

Work Experience: An Integral Part of Vocationalisation

The Commission suggested that work experience was essential for arousing loyalty toward the vocation. In its view, work experience can be defined as any productive activity which contributes to productive work in the school, house, laboratory, fields and factory or at any other place. The Commission recommended that work experience should be introduced at every educational level. The concept of work experience is based on the principle that the process of generating knowledge and wealth should be co-existent.

The reality is that work-experience evolves an attitude of loyalty toward the profession. Because of this liberal attitude, it is proposed that, at the higher secondary level, a variety of specialised courses should be available. The student should be allowed to make his choice according to his interests and inclinations, can thus be prepared to choose a career of his linking. This will also facilitate his adjustment in life.

Utility of Vocationalisation

1. Science and technology will be accepted as the foundation stones, and so, in modernisation, religion and work will be harmoniously blended.

2. The vocationalisation of secondary education will make possible the best utilisation of the country's resources and circumstances in Hunter Commission had proposed a plan of education very similar to the present one in 1882.

3. Students will be convinced that education is purposeful, and that they, too are needed for nation building. The Commission values this change as the most significant.

4. The Commission hope that, in this way, every educated individual will be given a job along with his certificate.

5. The country's economic condition will improve and its man power will be upto constructive use.

6. The individual will depend, for his livelihood, upon his limbs rather than upon offices.

7. Direct relationship between employment and education.

Liberalisation of Scholarships for Vocationalisation

The Commission suggested that provisions for scholarships on a large scale are desirable, with a view to promoting vocationalisation of secondary education. It said that in vocational colleges, there are more provisions for scholarships and that the proportion there is greater than in general education. For future progress, the following principles should be adopted:

(i) an increase in the amount of the scholarships.

(ii) liberal policy in granting admissions.

In the country like India, the majority of parents cannot afford vocational education for their children because of poverty. It is because of this that the Commission had sought to make the programme of vocationalisation of education successful through liberalisation of the number and amount of scholarships.

Expansion

Specifications of Secondary Education in NPE-1986-

In National Policy of Education in 1986, the expansion programme for secondary education was adopted and worked in full swing. This programme was based on traditions as well as innovations and fulfillment of future needs.

Following are the specifications of secondary education in this policy :

1. Development for self employment.

2. Vocationalisation of secondary education in different courses.

3. Establishment of pace-setting schools free of cost.

4. Expression of different roles of the students of humanity, science, social science etc.

5. Cooperation of NCERT and NIEPA and Institute of Educational Technology will lead secondary education.

6. Deciding minimum level of learning.

7. Common curriculum.

8. Adoption of common school system.

9. Adoption of 10 +2 system at national level.

Problems in Expansion

1. Absence of royalty, devotion and sense of purpose on

the part of those associated with secondary education.

2. Imbalance in the allocation of funds to secondary education.

3. Inadequate improvement in teacher's salaries and perks.

4. Lack of growth in the number of institutions.

5. Lack of proper management by respective school management bodies.

6. Lack of clarity in defining objectives in the Five year plan programs.

Qualitative Development of Secondary Education: Fifth Plan

1. Opening of Teachers Centre in every tehsil for teacher's welfare and professional development, construction of houses on a cooperative basis, provision of medical and other facilities, and encouragement to research.

2. Development of selected schools.

3. Development of teaching in science and mathematics.

4. Strengthening of guidance and counselling services.

5. Vocationalisation of secondary education.

6. Introduction of work experience at the secondary level.

Kothari Commission on Expansion

1. Education of girls should spread. At the lower stage, this proportion should be 1:2 and at the secondary stage 1:3. There should be separate schools, hostel and scholarships for girls.

2. Provisions for part-time as well as full time vocational education should be made from class 7 to 8. The education

of girls should emphasise training in domestic activities.

3. By 1975-76, 20% of the secondary schools should become institutions providing vocational training. By 1985-86, there should be a 50% increase in such institutions.

4. Students should be chosen for admission to secondary schools on the basis of self-selection. In this, attention must also be paid to the school record.

5. Programs for the spread of secondary education should be implemented in a planned manner at the district level so that existing schools may achieve the desired standards.

6. For the next 20 years, secondary education should expand in the manner outlined below :

(i) Brilliant students should be identified and selected.

(ii) Admissions should be based on available facilities.

(iii) Schools should be located at suitable places.

Expansion of Secondary Education: Seventh Five Year Plan 1985-90

The Government of India presented in 1985 a document called Challenges of Education: A Policy Perspective, which acted as a springboard to national policy on Educational 1986 as a part of 7th five year plan wherein 1201 crore rupees were allocated for the secondary education. Besides, the objectives of secondary education were stated in the following terms:

1. Toward vocationalisation, 5000 secondary schools during the plan period.

2. Search for talent.

3. Science, Environment and value-based education.

4. Vocationalisation.

National Education Commission

The National Education Commission 1964-66 was set up in response to the following rationale, aspirations and expectations:

1. Educational policy in India should be indigenous and alive to its needs, requirements and aspirations, and emanate from Indian experience and conditions.

2. To arrive at a global perception of education rather than fragmented efforts yielding limited and partial results.

3. The Government of India considered education as the key to national development, prosperity and welfare to commensurate with investment of human resources in this regard. Education, therefore, needed a face-lift, relevance, outlook can context so that it was in tune with national growth and development.

4. There was a great need of social and economic change. A new-look educational policy was considered necessary to gear it up and usher in desired change expeditiously.

5. In spite of educational expansion there was marked dissatisfaction about several aspects of educational development, organisation and management.

Main Considerations of the Report

The main features of this report were:

1. Education for agriculture and research in agriculture and allied sciences to be given a high priority in the scheme of educational reconstruction. Energetic and imaginative steps were required to draw a reasonable proportion of talent to go in for advanced study and research in agricultural science.

2. Special emphasis on the training and quality of teachers for schools.

3. Strengthening the centres of advanced study and setting up of a small number of Universities which would

aim at achieving highest international standards.

4. Vocationalisation of Secondary Education.

5. Stress on moral education and inculcation of a sense of social responsibility. Schools should recognise their responsibility in facilitating the transition of youth from the world of school to the world of work and life.

6. Introduction of work experience which includes manual work, production experience, etc., and social service as integral part of general education, more or less at all level of education.

Special Features

This was the Sixth Commission in the history of Education Commissions in India. The unique feature of this Commissions was not to limit its inquiry to any specific sector or aspect of education as the earlier Commissions had done but to have a comprehensive review of the entire educational system. The Commission, consequently, tried to cover every field and aspect of education. Another feature of the Commission was its firm belief that education is the most powerful instrument of national development. The report has appropriately been entitled Education and National Development. The third feature of this Commission was its international composition.

The Commission set up 12 task forces and 7 working groups. It interviewed about 9000 men and women distinguished in public life; educators, scientists, industrialists and scholars in different fields, and others interested in education. It received and scrutinised over 2400 memoranda and notes. The Commission spent about hundred day in visiting universities, Colleges and schools and held discussions mission began its task on 2 October, 1964, Mahatma Gandhi's birthday, and submitted its report 29 June 1966 to the Union Education Minister. It provided a detailed plan of two decades, 1966-86, for development of education in the country.

Structure of the Report

The whole report is divided into four parts. In First Part problems are general, such as

1. Toward Equalisation of Educational Opportunities.
2. Enrolment and manpower.
3. Teacher's Education.
4. Teacher's Status.
5. The Educational system: Structure and Standards.
6. Educational and National Objectives.

In the Second Part of the report, the following discussed:

1. Adult Education.
2. Vocational, Technical and Engineering Education.
3. The Governance of Universities.
4. Higher Education- Objectives and improvement.
5. School Eduction: Administration & Supervision.

Third part of this report deals with the implementation of the suggested from recommendation under the following captions: Educational Planning and Administration, Educational Finance.

In the Fourth Part supplementary papers and other information which throw light on the working and methodology of the Commissions were included.

Bridging Isolation of Teacher Education

1. Intensive efforts should be made to remove the existing separation among the institutions preparing teachers for different stages of education or, for special fields, such as art and craft, physical education, by implementing a phased programme of upgrading all training institutions to the college standard with ultimate objective

of bringing all teacher education under the University, and by establishing a State Board of Teacher Education in each state.

2. To remove the existing isolation of Teacher-education from schools, Extension work should be regarded as an essential function of a teachers training institution. Extensions Services Department should be established in each institution. Effective alumni association should be established to bring old students and faculty together to discuss and plan programs and curricula. Practice teaching for teacher under training should be organised in active collaboration with selected school which should receive recognition special grants for equipment and supervision. Periodic exchange of the staff of the co-operation schools and of the teachers training institutional should be arranged.

3. To remove the exiting isolation of teacher education from University life, education as distinguished form pedagogy, should be recognised as an independent academic discipline and introduced as an elective subject in the B.A., B.Sc., M.A., M.Sc. degree coursed school of education should be established in selected universities to develop programs in teacher-education and studies and research in education in collaboration with the other University disciplines.

4. In order to make the professional preparation of effective teachers, teacher-education must be brought into the main stream of the academic life of the Universities on the one hand, and of school life and educational development on the other.

Structural Guidelines : Higher Education

1. Transfer of Pre-University courses from the university to the school to be completed by 1975-96 under the alleges of the U.G.C.

2. Scholarships to those who opt for longer courses.

3. Bridge courses between the existing and the new/ longer courses to be formulated.

4. Three years special courses for the first degree beginning at the end of the first year of the existing three-year degree course, should be started in selected subject and in selected institutions.

5. Universities may start graduate schools with a three years Master's course in certain subjects.

6. Duration of the first degree course to be of three years, and that of second degree from two to three years.

Structural Guidelines: School Education

1. Class XI to XII should provide specialised studies in different subjects.

2. Providing 11 to 12 years course.

3. Providing 10 years course.

4. Two types of secondary schools.

5. No streaming/specialisation till after class X.

6. First public examination at the end of 10 years formal schooling.

7. Age at the time of admission to class I should ordinarily be not less than 6 years.

Development of Social and National Integration

Social and National Integration was one of the major objectives of Report and the Commission suggested:

1 Promotion of National Consciousness : A re-evaluation of our culture heritage is needed. For this there should be well organised teaching of languages; literature, philosophy, religions, History of India, Indian architecture, sculpture, painting, music, dance and drama. Camps, summer school etc. should be organised without any barrier. Creation a faith in the future would involve an attempt as

a part of the courses in citizenship. The educational programme in schools and colleges should be designed to inculcate democratic values.

2. English will be a link language in higher education for academic work and intellectual inter-communication. It is Hindi which can and should take this place in due course.

3. The teaching and study of English should continue right from the school stage. Other languages, particularly Russian, should be encouraged for international communication.

4. The regional languages should also be made the language of administration for the regions concerned.

5. All-India institutes should continue to use English as the medium of education for the time being. The eventual adoption of Hindi should, however, be considered in due course, subject to certain safeguards.

6. Energetic action is needed to produce books and literature, particularly scientific and technical, in regional languages in the universities with the help of U.G.C. Also all the important scientific and technical books in English and other foreign languages should be translated into regional languages.

7. Mother tongue should be the medium of instruction in school and higher education.

8. Development of an appropriate language-policy can materially assist in social and national integration.

9. N.C.C. should be continued in its present basis till the end of the Fourth five-year plan.

10. The common school system of public education should be adopted as a national goal and effectively implemented in a phased programme spread over the period of 20 years.

National Objectives of Education

1. Education about Religion.

2. Development of Social, Moral and Spiritual Values.

3. Education and Modernisation.

4. Social and National Integration.

5. Education and Productivity.

Structural Changes

The Commission suggested the following elements with regard to structure and duration of education :

1. Utilisation of available resources to their optimum.

2. Quality of teachers, curricula, methods of teaching, evaluation, equipment and infrastructure.

3. Duration covered by different stages.

4. Division of the educational pyramid into different with regard to structure and duration of education.

Religious Education

Secularism and Religion - In a multi-religious society of ours, it is necessary to define the attitude of the state towards religion, religious education and the concept of secularism. The adoption of a secularist policy means that in political economic and social matters, all citizens, irrespective of their religious faith, will enjoy equality of rights, that no religious community will be favoured or discriminated against; and the instruction in religious dogmas will not be provided in state schools. But it is not an irreligious or anti religious policy as it does not belittle the importance of religion as such. It gives to every citizen the fullest freedom of religious belief and worship. It is anxious to ensure good relations amongst different religious groups and to promote not only religious tolerance but also an active reverence for all religions,

In such a society, however, one has to make a distinction between religious education and education about religions. The former is largely concerned with the teaching or the tenets and practices of a particular religion, generally in the form in which the religious groups envisage them, whereas the latter is a study of religions and religious thought from a broad point of view- the state with many religions to provide education in any one religion. It is however, necessary for multi-religious democratic state to promote a tolerant study of all religions so that its citizens can understand each other better and live amicable together.

Teacher Education

1. The Government of India should make provision of funds in the centrally sponsored sector to assist State Governments to develop teacher-education which was outside the universities.

2. U.G.C., in collaboration with NCERT, should set up a standing committee for teacher-education consisting of eminent educationists devoted to the cause of teacher-education.

3. Allocation of substantial funds to the U.G.C. by the Government for improvement of teacher-education in the universities.

4. The U.G.C. should take upon it the responsibility for maintenance of standards in teacher education at national level, as well as for raising of standards at the state level.

Curriculum

Essentials of Curricular Improvement:

1. At the secondary stage, courses should be provided at two levels, ordinary and advanced beginning with class VII.

2. At the higher stage, enrichment programs should be provided for the talented children. It may take the form of additional subject or greater depth in the same subject.

3. At the higher secondary stage, courses will be diversified in such a manner as to enable pupils to study any three subjects in depth with considerable freedom and elasticity in grouping of subjects.

4. At the lower secondary stage, study of subjects will gain in rigour and depth.

5. At the higher primary stage, the curriculum will broaden and deepen, teaching methods will become more systematic, and standards of attainment more specific.

6. At the lower primary stage, the curriculum should be simple with reduced load of formal subjects and emphasis on language, elementary mathematics and environmental studies.

7. Standards of attainment should be clearly defined at the end of each substage.

8. The formation of Subject Teachers Associations in different school-subjects will help to stimulate experimental and in the upgrading of curricula. SISE and NCERT should help them in co-ordination.

9. Ordinary and advanced curricula should be prepared by State Board of Education in all subjects and introduced in a phased manner in schools which fulfil certain conditions of staff and facilities.

10. School curricula should be upgraded through research in curriculum development undertaken by University Departments of Education, Training Colleges, State Institutes of Education, and Board of School Education by periodical revision based on such research; preparation of text books and teaching-learning materials; and orientation of teachers to the revised curricula through

in-service education.

11. Schools should be given the freedom to devise and experiment with new curricula suited to their needs. A lead should be given in the matter by training colleges and universities through their experimental schools.

Evaluation

Aiming to provide national education for national development, the recommendations of the Kothaari Commission are a beacon and source of inspiration in the long history of development of education in India promising fulfillment of individual, social and direction may be felt ion following manner:

1. National Policy - The Commission recommended development and evaluation of national education policy as it was against fragmentation of education by putting it on the Concurrent list.

2. Autonomy of Colleges - Universities must respect the autonomy and freedom of the colleges in the same manner as they would crave for their own. Degrees issued by the universities established under the provisions of the Constitution would be mutually acceptable and recognised as equal for all intent and purpose.

3. Two levels of Syllabus - The Commissions had recommended two levels of syllabus in science, mathematics and social sciences. One type of syllabus was to be taught during the first 10 years to the average students, and the other to those having special aptitude and wanted to go for further study and research. The Government accepted the suggestion of compulsory teaching of science and mathematics at the school leaving level, in conformity with the existing policy on science and technology since Independence.

4. New Education Pattern - The Commission suggested a new pattern of 10 ×2×3 which, with initial reluctance

and reservation, has been a great success since its introduction in 1975. However, its industry-orientation and self-employment approach did not quite make it because of lack of coordination and opportunities.

5. Social, Moral and Spiritual Values - Modernisation does not end up with getting rid of all that is traditional. Tradition is the root, modernisation is the roof. Educational system should, therefore, preserve what is ancient year relevant to the Indian ethoes and psyche. A value-structure reigns deep into our culture and morality, and any educational system worth its name, should delve upon inculcating social, moral and spiritual values so that India does not lose its identity and originality. Modernisation and values must go hand in hand.

6. Modernisation of Education - Though the Indian society is rooted in great culture but so as to fit with the current trends it should go in for modernisation in an appropriate measures to take up cudgels with national reconstruction and international reckoning. The Commission, therefore, recommended that six more universities of international standard may be opened.

7. Social and National Integration - As national integration can be achieved through culture and moral education, the Commission suggested the following steps:

a. Developing all Indian languages and to enrich Hindi so as to make it function effectively as the national language.

b. Making social and national service as integral part of education at all stages.

c. Common school system of education.

8. Education and Productivity - Education should be linked with productivity, and the Commission, therefore, suggested implementing following programs:

a. Work- experience as integral part of general education specially at the secondary school level to meet the need of industry, agriculture and trade. It was in view of this that the Commission envisaged vocationalisation of secondary education as a means of self-employment and job-creation.

b. Science as basic component of education and culture.

9. Education and Social Change - Education is the most effective instrument of social change. As such, the Commission recommended a national policy on education which will not only sharpen the intellect but also develop desirable attitudes and outlook.

10. Population Explosion - Due to population explosion, the avowed aim of equalisation of opportunities is in the doldrums due to wide socio-economic gaps and narrow loyalties and angularities foraging into various programs of national reconstruction as envisaged by the Commission.

11. Education as a Complete Unit - The Commission considered education as a complete unit from pre-primary upto higher stage. It is a king of an edifice with three storeys but one common staircase running through the whole structure wherein each storey is complete yet interdependent.

Comments

1. The report allows, for instance, ten years for the general adoption of an advance curriculum in class 1 to X. Experience in other countries indicates that the change over to higher standards could be much quicker. We have erred too long and too woefully through understanding the capacity of the pupils.

2. The Report does speak of teacher initiative and the freedom to experiment at all levels of education.

3. The wittiest thing in the book is the passage of Dr.

Kothari's covering letter to M.C. Changa in which he apologizes for the size of the Report. It could have been shorter he says but that would have cost more money and time and delayed action.

4. The report is something less than an encyclopedia and considerably mor than a book. In the fact, the whole report is more or less in the same idiom as the Government of India's Resolution setting up the Commission.

5. In the event, the largest of the world's democracies gave itself the largest written constitution in the world. We have now matched it with largest ever Report on Education and National Development.

6. In important respects out attitude to Commissions is different from that of the Britishers who invented them By the look of it the Kothari Commission's Report is likely to be on our conscience for a long time to come.

7. No administrator should be permitted to implement any of the recommendation until he has gone though the intellectual exercise of trying to tear the Commission's arguments to pieces and of being finally converted to the commission's point of view. If he does not agree with the commission's thinking and its recommendation on any particular point, he should be free to seek other solution.

8. Most people approached the recommendations of the Commission with certain healthy scepticism. The recommendations call for administrative action that, other things being as before, we dread. But the text of the report spells out the attitudes and the thinking behind the recommendations and, though one sometimes wishes they had not spoken in the tones of patent school master in an idiot school, the attitudes are largely reassuring.

10

HEALTH EDUCATION

The health standards are efficiently administered and maintained only when adequate knowledge and information about personal and environmental hygiene and sanitation; awareness of various diseases and their remedial treatment, at least the first aid level; available utilisation and resources, facilities and technical information at various primary health centres upward; is disseminated by means of a mass health education programme. These programs are launched to create general awareness of health and nourishment of the population at different levels and stages of the development of an individual and other contingencies, by means of health education. Health therefore, is the primary task of any government so as to harness the optimal human resources development of its masses. Health education is central to the overall progress and development of a country and should be accorded necessary and suitable priority at all levels. It is all the more important during the period of growth and development of a child.

What is Health?

1. According to Webster Collegiate Dictionary, "Health is the state of being hale and sound in he body mind and soul especially free from physical disease and pain."

2. According to World Health Organisation, "It is a state of complete physical, mental and social well being

and not merely the absence of disease."

3. According to J.F. Williams, "Health is the Quality of life that ensures the individual lives longer and serves best."

Health education is the sum total of all those experiences derived from the school and other environmental situations that influenced health habits and attitudes of an individual, community and society. As the statement implies, health education implies control of environment. It is the family, society and the school that determines this social environment. Health education helps an individual and the community to remain healthy. Based on hygiene education which is derived from Greek word Hygea. Hygea is considered as the goddess of health in Greek mythology which later developed as the science of personal and social health education.

Meaning of Health Education

Consisting of awareness programme, health education aims at improving general conditions at the individual and community levels by encouraging people to change their behavioural pattern, habits and life-style to achieve necessary standard of health. It must be remembered that physical development and maturation are essential for a child's overall growth and development in such other areas as mental, emotional and social growth and development. Healthy mind in a healthy body is the age old slogan and ideal of any civilised society. Hence, all those who are concerned with the growth and development of children should know the basis of child health and its preservation. Health education, therefore, is a vital aspects of Nursery Teacher's Training programme.

Importance of Health

Good health starts from the very infancy. It is here the protection and care is needed, so that each organ functions well, each organ develops naturally, and there are no deformities, disabilities and diseases but often the health of children remain, neglected with the result that they grow unhealthy and that affects their education as well.

A healthy child develops into a healthy adult. In case the child does not grow properly, and he remains handicapped in some way, his ill-health spoils his adult life. He cannot join any active service; he cannot be a successful professional, nor can he lives his life happily.

Health is real wealth. A healthy person is an asset to himself, to his family and to his community. On the other hand, an ailing person is a burden on all. He is a danger for coming generations because heredity plays an important part in this respect.

Health is the pivot upon which is man's whole personality and its well-being depend. An ailing and a aching body saps the enthusiasm for pursuit. Unwholesome feelings and sensations retard the pace of functional activity, economic development of spiritual uplift.

Health cannot be achieved merely by taking one or two pills everyday nor by observing a few restrictions. It can be achieved only by understating what health is, on what is depends and then applying this knowledge in every-day life. The care of the body regarding food, cleanliness, exercise, rest and protection against disease, are essential for the preservation of sound health. Life if for living, without health, life is deprived of not only much of its use fullness but also its joys and pleasure. The steam life will be rich and lasting in proportion to the sources which nourish it. These sources belong to every person. They are food, exercise, proper posture, care of bodily functions, avoidance or alcohol and tobacco and wholesome mental and emotional attitudes.

Scope of Health Education

1. School Health - School health has been great concern for a long time. The health of the nation depends on the health of its children. School health has also been a subject of international concern. The need for successful health education programme is widely acknowledge for which careful planning is being undertaken. The most important planning occurs between the teacher and the pupil, to begin with.

2. Community Health - Real wealth of a country is its human resource. A healthy and happy community wherein a healthy person is an asset to the society and a sick person is a liability, is an index of national health. Community health and social services do provide medical and counselling cover against disease and trauma, maturity and child welfare, school medical services, hospital and medical research institutions. Health and sanitation education is imparted through extension education program conducted by various government, voluntary and international agencies.

Characteristics of Positive Health

1. Cheerfulness.

2. Patience and tolerance capacity.

3. Adjustive nature.

4. Sense of cooperation.

5. Positive mental attitude.
6. Self-confidence and self-control.
7. Ability to work efficiently.
8. Sense of well being.

Promoters of Health

The following factors promote good health in children and adults-

1. Physical exercise, sport, games, athletics, gymnastics, rhythmic exercise - These help circulation of blood, stimulate of glands, strengthen the organs, development and growth and promote general health. Details about these are given in subsequent pages.

2. Bodily posture - In the case of children bodily postures are very important for maintaining health. The chile should possess own knowledge of correct postures of sitting, standing, walking, reading and writing. He should practise the same. In the absence of such practising, the bodily organs become deformed, the eyesight weakness, and the nervous system hardens. The major causes of bad postures are malnutrition, bad dress, bad furniture and bed habits. Children should be trained to have correct postures.

3. Air and sunlight - Air provides oxygen which purifies blood and activates our bodily organs. Fresh air contains more of oxygen which is needed by the body. The foul air, which contains more of carbon dioxide or nitrogen, products physical and mental fatigue heaviness and weakness. Cross ventilation of rooms helps obtaining fresh air and dispelling foul air.

It adds vigour and vitality to the body. It gives power of resistance to germs. It increase certain minerals like iron, calcium, phosphorous and iodine.

4. Nutrition and balanced diet - It provides energy for the normal working during the day. Diet provides fuel to the working machinery. It constructs tissues, builds the skeleton, helps growth and development and provides continuous replacement of blood cells, consumed in the metabolic function.

World Confederation of Teaching Profession has stated that health education in school should, as general rule, be the responsibility of the school teachers.

Health is primary and enjoys the most important place in the hierarchy of human values, which has a special role in the development of nation. In a democratic set-up human life and its prestige has been given an important privilege. Every citizen of a country is encouraged to develop his fullest potential of work and prestige so that he may contribute towards the prosperity and peace of the society. This is possible only when every individual citizen enjoys high standard of health.,

Today's youth lose their working capacity when they have low standard of health. Every person will feel happy and comfortable when his health permits him to enjoy the life at school, in the family, place of work etc. That is why it is pertinent that every person should have optimum physical, mental, and moral health conditions as to enhance the country's strength and development of prosperity.

Chid's physical and mental development is the prime responsibility of the parents. Children are the future citizen of the nation. School plays a crucial role in the over-all development of child because child spends mot of his working time in the school. Parents may not be able to provide adequate health facilities and health awareness due tot ignorance or low economic status. Health of the child therefore, should be accorded the highest priority.

Health Education and Nursery Schools

Health education at Nursery schools refers to-

1. Fix the level of health education - Health education aims at achieving the following goals in nursery schools-

a. To provide for health education, health services and health inspection.

b. Basic understanding and treatment of child diseases.

c. Knowledge of health related rules and practices.

d. To fix the lowest acceptable level of child health and care.

2. Knowledge of health education for teachers - Without the thorough knowledge of health education, the teacher would neither be able to take care of their wards nor would they be responsive to the health care of the children.

3. Health related knowledge - To provide health related information to children and teachers to protect and enhance their physical and mental by making use of the knowledge. This knowledge is given directly and or indirectly.

Scope of Health Education

Health education is very vast term. It has a wide scope. It is dependent and closely released to many other aspects, besides health. These aspects include housing, economic security, agricultural or industrial propriety etc. Normally, health education includes the following -

1. Emergency and firs aid.

2. Mental health, sex hygiene, domestic and community hygiene.

3. Various ailments and diseases. Their causes and ways and means of their prevention and cure.

4. Abnormal conditions and bad habits. Their adverse effect on the physical and mental health of an individual.

5. Water, air, light, physical exercise, recreation, rest and sleep, etc.

6. Food and its importance in the development of human body.

Aims of Health Education

1. Develop sense of civic responsibility.
2. Take curative measures.
3. Take precautionary and preventive measures.
4. Create healthy environment./
5. Arouse interest in own health care.
6. Inculcates habits of clean and heathy living.

It is evident that child education aims at developing the awareness towards the rules and practice of child health care. For the successful implementation of the school health service, the following principles are enunciated-

1. Periodic medical check up.
2. Mid-day meal.
3. Knowledge of the human body.

4. For total implementation of health care programme necessary and suitable priority should be accorded to health education by its school administration and management.

5. Simple and usable health education should consists of simple and pragmatic practices and activities.

6. Cooperation of community and parents.

7. Physical exercise.

Health Education in School

Health education, in principle and in action is and integral part of the total educational programme of the school. Its aims and objectives are in harmony with the broader aims and objectives of education. Its content and methods are also guided by understanding of the learning process. Then the development of child-centered curricula, the use of teaching units and emphasis on school community relationship are recognised and followed in health teaching also. When health is so harmonised with the total educational programme, its effective is increased and education as a whole, is also enriched.

Physical health is the pre-requisite of the education. According to the Crow and Crow, "Palatial school buildings, extensive equipment, thoroughly prepared teachers, supervisors and other school personnel, expertly constructed curriculums elaborates measurement techniques and well-organised and well-administrated programs of guidance, all fail to achieve their respective purposes unless directed towards the improvement of physical, mental and emotional health of every child adolescent or adult, who comes with their sphere of influence.

A learner is a developing individual before his mental development takes place. We must ensure his physical development and degree physical of fitness. The mastery of book material of skill is of no avail if the person master, lives a physical work.

Thus, it clear that health education greatly helps the educational process in influencing the behaviour pattern of the pupils. The health side of health education prepares the pupils physically to face the hardship of the educational process while its education side provides a basis, on which the whole educational set up can be built up very effectively.

In the end, it can be said that the goal of health education in a school is to give pupil the tools with their potential energies and social, physical, mental and emotional effectiveness can be fully realized. Decisions and actions, based on the application of such tools, become more deeply satisfying and constructive.

Programme of Health Education

Following steps should be taken to protect the health of the students-

1. Modern adjustable seats and desks - Good designed furniture specially designed for children of different age group should be available.

2. Safe and sanitary lunch room - During the recess period, children of a school generally take their lunch, but there is no separate lunch room provided in most of out schools, for girls and boys. The result is that most children sit in the open compound, grassy lawns or even in class-rooms for taking their lunch. This is quite unsafe and insanitary. There is seldom any arrangement for washing hands.

3. Safe and adequate sewage system - In India we generally lack this system in majority of our schools. Except in modern school building built in bit cities sewage disposal system is not available in other schools. However, it flush system is not possible, ever-clean latrines and good drainage systems must be provided in every school building.

4. Ample sanitary, washing and toilet facilities - A sufficient quantity of good water is also needed for sanitary, washing and toilet purposes in school. It is a pity that most of our schools, especially the elementary schools buildings do not even have latrines, urinals and bathroom attached to them. And where such arrangement does exist, little attention is paid to washing and cleanliness. Foul smell coming out of this portion of the school premisses spoils the entire school environment. It is therefore, essential that toilets and latrines etc. must be regularly washed and kept neat and clean.

5. School building, its site and location - The school building should contain a number of rooms according to the standard of the school and needs of pupils and teachers. It should be located in a quiet and pleasant environment, away from the noise and dust of the populated area of the town or village. It should have extensive lawns and play-grounds. It should serve as a big laboratory where total health may be lived, learned and remembered for future living.

6. Good refreshment and pure water - Pure water must be available in the school. If there are wells, they must be kept in perfect hygienic conditions. Sellers of fruits and other edibles should be carefully inspected and they must not be allowed to play with the health of

students by selling rotten and stale things. The school should also arrange for some refreshment in the mid day. This refreshment should consist of nutritive elements.

7. Education in physiology and hygiene - Every student should be made conversant with basic elements of physiology and hygiene. For this, at least one period of week should be devoted. Some suitable lecture by some physician or specialist at least once a month should also be arranged.

8. Health examination - Every student in the school should be medically examined atleast thrice a year. According to a prescribed programme, the result of this examination should be communicated to the concerned teachers and guardians in order that the necessary may be done for the child. The progress of health of each student should be carefully watched on the basis of the medical examination result. For this, each teacher should be required to perform his share of the responsibility, and due allowance should be given for this in assigning teaching load to him so that he may not feel overworked.

9. Arrangement for adequate light and fresh air - In the forgoing pages we have emphasised at several places the importance of sufficient light and fresh air in the school. This should be considered as one of the most important constituents of health education programme.

10. Cleanliness - The cleanliness of the school environment is the first thing to be attended to the rooms, play-ground, lavatories, urinals and other places should be kept entirely clean. It should not be difficult for any school to attend to these basic things howsoever, poor it might be financially. But many schools ignore this vital

necessity and their rooms and the total environments are full of kinds of unhygienic conditions. It hardly needs mentioning that this situation adversely affects the health of child.

Agencies of School Health Service

The school health service is provided by means of-

1. Sports Department under the charge of a qualified physical education instructor.

2. Red cross units of the school.

3. School dispensary.

4. School health education.

5. School medical department under the charge of a school doctor.

Value of Health Education

It is the sacred duty of the teacher to accord as much of emphasis of health education as on other contusion, affective and psychomotor activities. They should ensure that the classroom are appropriately ventilated and have adequate natural light. Health education, as any other type of education and training, must be put to practice. Even the parents should also be give orientation to health education. Physical growth and development is central relationship between mental retardation and physical growth and development. Therefore, in the interest of the child's overall development, due emphasis must be given to health education. A healthy mind in a healthy body is as much true today as ever before.

Components of School Health Service

The following are the essential components of an efficient school health service-

1. Records of Immunization arrangements in the school - Records of immunization given to the child should be noted on the medical proforma. Immunization campaign can be arranged in schools from time to time. Proper coordination among the doctor, the teacher and the parents should always be ensured, with the sense of moral towards the children.

2. Provision of first-aid and emergency care - Every educational institution should be equipped with the first-aid amenities from the students funds. Staff members of every school should be trained for giving emergency and first-aid help to the students when needed. First-aid boxes should be provided in all the institution. It is desirable to set apart a separate medical room for the purpose. Medicines, ointment, glucose, bandages, cotton, etc. are some of the important items for the first-aid box. In addition, a bed can be provided for the patients to lie down for sometime until the parents or the doctor comes to take charge.

3. Psychological services - Sometimes, children suffer from inferiority complex due to certain psychological problems. If psychological counseling is offered by the institutions about the mental retardedness, prevention of mental defects, development of complexes etc. will encourage the child to be alert and healthy which lead to his proper physical and mental development.

4. Role of the parents - Today's parents should have the basic knowledge of nutrition, health problems and changing physical needs of a growing child. Children these days are over-burdened with studies and mental work. Proper nutrition and exercise will help the child to be healthy.

5. Role of teacher - The teacher and other staff members must impress upon the children the primary hygienic requirements like cleaning of teeth, eyes, ears, combing, cleaning and cutting of hair, nails, wearing clean clothes etc., which should be according to the prevailing season. If any abnormal symptoms are detected then priority should be given to inform the parents promptly.

6. To keep records - Proper health records of the students should be maintained by the school. These records of the students should be discussed with the parents. A uniform proforma for health records should be made available from the National Health Council for this purpose.

Means of Child Care

1. Systematic talks - lectures, instructions on health education.

2. Time table - Time table should be such that it does not cause too much of stress on the children. The subjects that need closer attention should be kept in the earlier periods or immediately after the break.

3. Regular medical check up - The children should be regularly checked up against disease and infection. A proper record in this regard should be maintained.

4. Balance diet - Mid-day meal should be nutritious and palatable, without much of oil and species. These drills should be supervised by the teachers.

5. Furniture - School furniture need not to expensive. It should be just of the size that the children feel comfortable. Further, the furniture should be such that is encourages right postures. Right postures are manifestations of healthy child care.

6. Air and Light - Air and Light are the basic essential of child growth and development especially in these days of all kinds of environmental pollution. Children must have fresh air and adequate natural light to keep them healthy and fit.

7. Cleanliness - Educate the children about the blessing of cleanliness. The school campus must be cleaned by the staff regularly to give a healthy outlook.

8. School Environment is the basic factor of the school health. The school should give a neat and orderly look. It need not have expensive and imposing buildings and other infrastructure. Cleanliness, orderliness, and neatness should be the watch words for developing health school environment. Central schools organisation and Central Board of Secondary Education had fixed a land norm of 15 acres which had now been badly compromised due tot paucity of land. Open spaces are a must for an open mind.

11

VOCATIONALIZATION

In the changing society with reference to the concepts and beliefs of the modern age, our country lags behind other countries in terms of hundreds of years in the race for progress. We want to achieve quality of life with the developed countries, but in this process, as we move forward, the developed countries move even faster and go ahead of us. The reason for this is that our knowledge has not been related to modern science and technology. In view of this, the education commission has proposed the vocationalization of education at every level, not only at the secondary stage. Kothari Commission has sought to gave this vocationalization upon productivity. Hence, after considering the mutual relationship between education and production, it has proposed the basis of the scheme for the restructuring of education in the following terms-

1. Laying special stress upon agriculture and related sciences, scientific ad technological education at the university level should e developed.

2. Education at the secondary level should be vocationalized in order to meet the needs of industry, agriculture and trade.

3. Work experience should be an integral part of general education.

4. Science should be the basis of education and

culture.

Higher Secondary Level

At this level, The Commission has made provisions for a very large number of vocational courses.

1. Short Term Courses - These syllabi should provide training in health, trade, administration, small scale industries, etc. through courses lasting for six months to three years. At the completion of the course, students should be given diplomas or certificates. In view of the importance it has attached to the vocationalisation of secondary education. The Commission has proposed that the central government should aid the State Governments in implementing such a programme. Citing the example of the U.S.A. The Commission has thrust the entire responsibility for the vocationalisation of secondary education upon the Union Governments.

At present the exiting system of secondary education does not make provisions for vocationalization which will satisfy the needs for skilled workers in the next twenty years. At the secondary level, these schools satisfy only 3% of the need. In 1965-66 there was increase of 20%% at the lower secondary level. For the next twenty years. The Commission made provisions for the admission of 24,13,000 students to vocational schools. In the same manner the projected figures of admission to professional universities is 6,87,300 students, which is 43% of the total number of students. The Commission set for itself the target of 50 percent.

2. Minimum Qualification - The syllabi in the industrial training centres should be such that the minimum qualification for admission to them should be class 10.

3. Full Time Courses - Along with an expansion in facilities for full time study there should be provisions for part-time syllabi at the higher secondary level, though it may be through arranged industries, evening classes, part-time or correspondence courses.

Why Should Secondary Education be Vocationalized?

For vocationalizing secondary education. The Commission has considered in detail the vocationalisation at both its levels (i) the higher secondary, (ii) the lower secondary. In the Commission's view, 20 percent of the students in classes 8th to 10th should obtain vocational education. In the same way, 50 percent of the students in classes 11 and 12 should receive vocational education. The Commission clearly accepted the principle that among the most important reforms is that vocationalization of higher secondary education 50% of all students should take admissions to the vocational courses.

Lower Secondary Level

1. Domestic Science - A large number of girls get married soon after leaving schools. From them arrangement should be made to provide them general education as well as education in domestic science.

2. General and Professional Education - Most students belonging to the rural areas will work on their ancestral fields. They should be given opportunities for general education and professional skills, etc.

3. Suitable Opportunities - Students who stop studying after 7th or 8th class usually take up their family profession, while some of them hope to set up a small scale industry of trading organisation. For such

people arrangements should be made for short term or part-time syllabi so that they may be able to develop their abilities and skills. The Commission purpose that a separate department should be set up within the education department to keep in touch will youth and provide them with suitable opportunities for receiving vocational training on a part-time basis along with their general education.

4. Suitable Courses - Industrial training centres must have courses suitable to post-primary educational levels. If the age of admission to such courses is set at 14 years, the number of students entering such institutions after copulating primary education will be very large.

Work Experience: An Integral Part of Vocationalization

The Commission has suggested that work experience is essential for arousing loyalty towards the vocation. In its view, work experience can be defined as any productive activity which contributes to productive work in the school house, laboratory, fields, and factory or at any other place. The Commission has recommended that work experience should be introduced at every educational level. The concept of work experience is base on the principle that the process of generation knowledge and wealth should be co-extensive.

The reality is that work experience evolves an attitude of loyalty towards the profession. Because of this liberal attitude, it is proposed that, at the higher secondary level, a variety of specialized courses should be available. The students should be allowed to make his choice from among them according to his interests and inclinations and thus be prepared to choose a career of his liking. This will also facilitate his adjustment in life. With reference to the attitude, as regards the higher classes. The Commission has argued that in these classes, it can take the form of teaching of art which will lead to the development of the student's creative ability and technological thinking. Work experience can be imparted in the actual circumstances of real life, for instance, working in fields at the time of sowing or harvesting, or engaging in productive work in a family unit. Such situations can be exploited to the maximum possible extent.

The Commission has declared that, in the coming years, one workshop should be arranged for every school, or at least for a group of schools. At the lower secondary level, work experience can take the form of laboratory training. At the higher secondary level, where students are more mature, and they are comparatively less in number, they can be given work experience in workshops, fields, industrial and trading enterprises. Many kinds of materials are needed in school teaching. Work experience relating to the production of these materials should be available in schools and institutions. It has been students should engage in full-scale production. In some institutions the apparatus used in school and college laboratories and workshops should be produce. Some institutions should manufacture some things like furniture, etc.

The Kothari Commission has suggested the introduction or work experience at every level of education. Its aim is that the nature of education should be transformed in order to bring about social, economic and cultural transformation of Indian society. The utility of work experience was evaluated at the general and vocational levels of education. According to the Commission, we define work experience as participation in productive work in school, in the home, in a workshop, on a farm, in factory, or in any other productive situation.

Work experience has been accepted as an integral part of education. The question we now face is: why the need for such educational programs felt, soon after independence? The reason is that the system of education prevailing in the country has produced a class of educated persons who are not dependent upon themselves. Who have no faith in hard work. A nation's progress becomes impossible if the people become indifferent towards work. In view of this, the idea of work experience was developed so as to take the nation to the peak of progress and development.

The Education Commission has analyzed the country's problems, in the educational context, in the following terms - 1. Our students have made a negligible contribution to national development. 2. Our education is too bookish and inclined to take the students far away from the realities of life. 3. Our education is not job oriented. The Commission has sought to remedy these defects through the concept of work experience.

1. Real Life Conditions - The Commission has stressed the fact that the productive work should take place in conditions similar to those obtaining in real life.

2. Work Experience at All Stages - Work experience which involves participation in some form of productive work under conditions approximating to those found in real life situations should be introduced as an integral part of education at all stages.

3. Integral Part - As another programme to relate education to life and productivity we recommend that work-experience should be introduced as an integral part of all education, general or vocational.

Vocational Education at the School Level

Regarding the vocational education at the school level. The Commission has expressed the following ideas-

1. Technical Schools - The Commission recommended that the name of Junior Technical Schools should be changed to Technical High Schools. Such schools and the I.T.I. should make arrangement for production oriented training.

2. Number of Poly-techniques - At present there are 356 polytechnic institutions in which 1, 13,000 students can study.

3. Intensive Courses - As far the question of outstanding students is concerned, instead of putting them into special courses, they can be made to do intensive work within the same syllabus thus the deficiency can be made up.

4. Variety of Courses - The Central Government should introduce a variety of courses for boys and girls in 14-18 age groups. The responsibility for this should fall upon the Union Government, thus creating a parallel with the Smith Hughes Act of the U.S.A.

The Objectives of Work Experience

1. Eradication of Rich and Poor Concept - We must also lever keep before us a long-term objective. Through work experience we have to eradicate the different between the educated and the uneducated and thereby make steady progress towards our cherished goal of a

classless society a society in which difference of high and low will be unknown.

2. Contribution of Production - Its aim is to make the child conscious of the fact that whatever works an individual does at his own level contributes to the productive effort of the whole nation.

3. Choice for Profession - The purpose of work experience is not to prepare the child for a particular profession. Instead, the purpose is to develop in him those abilities which may facilitate his choice of a profession.

4. Employment World - A third objectives of work experience is to acquaint the student with the working of employment, agriculture, industry and other pecuniary activities. The student should become conscious of the fact that, in the years ahead, science and technology will play a very important part in every king of activity taking the form of employment.

5. Earning while Learning - Another objective of work experience should be that the child should be able to earn something by his own labour so that he may share the burden of his education, which his parents have to bear.

6. Dignity of Labour - The most important objective of work experience is to accustom the child to physical labour, to develop in him the ability to do physical work for sometime continuously, and to make him a participant in the country's economic development through physical labour.

Assumptions Regarding Work Experience

An important fact regarding work experience is that it is based on self-determination. Some important assumptions basic to it are the following-

1. Extra Part of Education - For the next few years, work experience must be accepted as an extra-curricular activity, and not a necessary part of the curriculum. Hence, it cannot be evaluated in terms of marks, and thus, it should also not influence a student's passage from one class to the next.

2. Local Conditions - Work experience should also be in consonance with local conditions. For example, at places where bamboos are available, the work experience should concentrate on industries producing goods from bamboos.

3. According to Age - Work experience should be in accordance with the student's age and his physical and mental capacities.

4. Income Oriented - Work experience is inalienably related to production, and so, as far as possible, work experience should also give rise to income.

5. Real Conditions - The work experience should be in accord with the actual working conditions in real life i.e. the student's activity should take place in exactly the same conditions as those obtaining in real life. In other words, the student should work in the same manner in which India's farmers and workers perform their functions.

6. Forward Looking - Work experience is forward looking i.e. it should be intimately related to the scientific, industrial and technological methods of production. Work experience should give the student not only the experience of working with his hands but also an acquaintance with the progressive techniques of production employed in the country. This principles also implies that the method of working should progress and improve continuously.

7. Problems Solving - Work experience is essential for the proper education of the child. It helps him in understanding and solving problems, and at the same time makes him aware of the productive process contributing to national development.

8. Inspiration - work experience is itself inspiring i.e., the work should itself possess some motivating elements so that students may willingly become involve in it. Work experience should not be thrust forcibly upon the student.

9. Physical Labour - In every kind of work experience, physical labour is inherent necessarily. Hence, such activities as book-keeping or working in an office do not fall within its sphere.

Vocationalization : Utility and Achievements

Many problems will come to an end with the vocationalization of secondary education, though as present, these problems have a gigantic and daunting size. The Commission has not encouraged employment, as was the case in Basic Education. It has opined that every individual should work to fulfil the needs of the country, and every aspect of his work should contribute to national development. The fruits flowing from vocationalisation will be the following-

1. Science and technology will be accepted as the foundation stones and so. In moderation, religion and work will be harmoniously blended together.

2. The vocationalisation of secondary education will make possible the best utilization of the country's resources and circumstances. In 1982, The Hunter Commission had proposed a plan of education very similar to the present one.

3. Students will be convinced that education is purposeful, and that they too are needed for the building of their nation. The Commission views this change as the most profoundly significant.

4. The Commission hopes that, in this way, every educated individual will be given a job along with his certificate.

5. The country's economic condition will improve and its manpower will be put to constructive use.

6. The individual will depend, for his livelihood, upon hill limbs rather than upon offices.

7. There will be a direct relationship between employment and education.

Scholarship and Vocationalization

The Commission has suggested that provisions for scholarships on a large scale are desirable, with a view to promote vocationalization of secondary education. It has said that in vocational colleges, there are more provisions for scholarships, and that the proportion there is greater than in general education. For future progress, the following principles should be adopted - (i) an increase in the amount of the scholarship, (ii) liberal policy in granting admission.

Guiding Principles of Work Experience

Following are guiding principles of work experience to be kept in mind while implementing it -

1. Job Oriented - Work experience should be job-oriented. The term job in this context, should be taken to refer to one complete unit of work in any occupation, for instance, varnishing of furniture, joining together various parts to produce a complete chair, carpentry,

weaving, etc.

In this report, The Steering Group of The Planning Commission has said that work experience should be of the educational programme at every stage. Student should have a knowledge of the work-a-day world. This programme can be effective by introducing students to the real conditions of work, putting them in touch with public and private producers, etc. In order to take this process a step further conditions favouring work experience should be created by creating contact with factories, farms, laboratories, workshops, etc.

2. Full Awareness - From the educational view point, it is desirable that the child should be made aware of every of every activity concerned with a particular mode of production so that may develop the capacity to produce the complete product through his own effort.

3. Family Occupation - Children who enforce facilities for obtaining work experience at home should be encouraged to learn the family occupation. If the school, college or university can assist the student in improving this occupation, it should extend its help.

4. Use of Other Source - In rural areas, where schools do not have their own land, students can obtain work experience by working on the farms of private individuals at a time when there is additional demand for labour, for instance, during the sowing and harvesting seasons.

5. Teaching of Technology - Wherever opportunity is available, the use of technological means should be taught in work experience.

6. Help from Retired Persons - In places where industrial training institutes or polytechnic institutions

are available, the retired teachers from such institutions can be made use of. With the help of these institutions, some general tool kits can be prepared for use in work experience.

7. Division of Time - The division of time in work experience will be in accordance with the nature of the activity. In agricultural activity, it will be necessary to devote 2 or 3 days continuously at the time of sowing or harvesting whereas in wood-working for instance, two periods of 90 minutes duration in the week may prove adequate.

8. No Part of Time - Work experience will not be a part of the curriculum. Hence, arrangements will have to be made in the time-table to ensure that the regular teaching time-table is not disturbed or reduced.

9. Profit - The profit from work experience should flow to those who have words of it. In other words, the cost of the raw materials involved should be deducted from the income, and the profit handed over the students.

10. Vocational Basis - Every activity indulged in, must have a vocational basis. The income or production obtained from work experience, must, in every case, be more the expenditure incurred on it, whether it be agricultural or industrial activity.

11. Less Expensive - In preparing a programme of work-experience, it must be remembered that a scheme involving vast expenditure is not to be considered. Instead, the programme must envisage only the maximum utilization of the facilities commonly available in schools.

12

EDUCATION AND MODERNIZATION

Meaning of Modernisation

Modernisation denotes a process of change-change in behaviour. The very concept of modernisation warrants redial changes-changes in the traditional society in different walks of life. Originally modernisation is marked by industralisation, urbanisation, socialisation, vocationalisation, technologisation of agriculture, economy, education, commerce, transport and communications etc. It also means rationalisation of ways of thinking and behaving. Modernisation, in real, depicts a process change-change of a traditional society into all society based on science and technology. It is felt that progressive utilisation of modern science and technology can ensure economic abundance and the material comforts that the more advanced countries enjoy.

Among the diverse models of modernisation had been the models of West Europe, North America and Japan. The Communist mode of U.S.S.R. no longer exists now-a-days. The content and the character of modernisation depends to a large extend on the complex interplay of factors like the ideology governing the use of state power.

Main Components of Modernisation

1. Scientific temper
2. Universal brotherhood

3. Respect for the dignity of the individual

4. Materialistic outlook

5. Mass education

6. Vocationalisation

7. Decentralization of power

8. Explosion of knowledge, attitudes, interest and expectations.

The following two points are important while understanding the concept of modernisation -

1. Modernisation is not westernisation - These two terms should not ne used synonymously. Modernisation does not necessary imply the adoption of western manners, habits, modes of dress, cultural and other values. Japan is a modern country. It has adopted science and technology in different areas like agriculture, commerce and industry but it still wedded to many of its past cultural values.

2. Modernisation is not wiping out all traditional values - According to Thomas, "It is true that new values are emerging as a result of the changes in society. The emerging of new values does not mean that traditional values have been wiped out.

Main Features of Modernisation

There are three main features of modernisation which are as following-

1. The Explosion of Knowledge - In a traditional society, the stock of knowledge is limited, In a modern society, on the other hand, the stock of knowledge is far greater and the pace of its growth is infinitely quicker.

2. Science- Based Technology - The most important

feature of a modern society, in contrast with a traditional one, is in its adoption of science based technology. This has helped societies to increase their production immensely.

3. Rapid Social and Cultural Changes - One of the important features of a modern society is the quick rate at which social changes take place.

Role of Education in the Modernisation of Indian Society

1. Establishing Major Universities of the excellence in the country.

2. Awakening of curiosity, the developing of proper interest, attitudes and values and the building up of such essential skills as independent study and capacity to think and judge for oneself.

3. Changing the composition of the intelligence, educating people of all strata of society.

4. Emphasizing vocational subjects, science, education and research.

5. To adopt new methods of teaching.

6. Education and equalisation of educational opportunities.

7. Education for developing a wider outlook.

8. Education for the promotion of emotional and national integration.

9. Education for the establishment of a socialistic pattern of society.

10. Education for increasing production.

11. Education for the promotion of secular ideas and ideals.

12. Education for synthesizing cultural and scientific values.

Characteristics of Modernisation

S.C. Dubey has given the following characteristics of modernisation-

1. New attitudes to wealth, work, savings and risk taking; faith in the desirability and possibility of change; economic, political and social discipline; and capacity to put off immediate and short run satisfactions for higher satisfaction in the long run. These attributes of modernisation relate to certain attitudes, motivations and values that are very essentially interlinked with the cultural and social implications of modernisation.

2. Relations Ends - means calculations. It is believed that people with high achievement motivation learn faster and work harder to reach high level goals.

3. Achievement Orientation - This refers to inner concerns that motivate and sustain economic growth.

4. 4, 5, and 6 - Interest articulation, interest aggregation and institutionalized political competition. These characteristics recognise the vital role that interest and power groups and power relations play.

5. High Participation - It indicates the increasing participation of people in social activities.

6. Mobility - It means equipping persons for rational, situational and structural choices.

7. Empathy - It implies the capacity to see ourself in the situation of others.

M. Inklets gives the following characteristics of modernisation -

1. Faith in equal justice.

2. A practical and realistic approach to the world.
3. Emphasis on the present rather than the part.
4. Adoption of new techniques and methods.
5. Curiosity for acquiring latest knowledge.
6. Acceptance of new ideas.

According to the Education Commission, "Modernisation aims, amongst other things adoption of a science based technology, keeping pace with the explosion of knowledge and quick almost breath taking rate at which social changes take place at creating as economy of plenty which will offer to every individual a larger way of life and a wide variety of choices."

According to Black Bellah, "The most distinctive features of modern society is its adoption of science and technology. On this basis, societies are increasing their productivity. Science based technology has other significant utilisation of social and cultural life and it involves fundamental social and culture changes which are broadly described as modernisation."

Obstacles in the Modernisation of Indian Society

Though our country has been making progress after achieving independence, yet there is far more to achieve. Progress is not as rapid as it should have been. There are still the following obstacles in the way of modernisation of Indian Society -

1. Narrow form of individualism.
2. Corruption in all spheres of life.
3. Narrow loyalties.
4. Narrow religious faiths and beliefs.
5. Closed type society.

6. Illiteracy of the masses.

7. Poverty of the masses.

8. Old cultural beliefs and traditions.

9. Gap between ideals and actuals.

10. Lack of political stability.

Modernisation and Science and Spiritual

According to the Education Commission , "A basic distinction between traditional and modern societies is the development and use by the latter of science-based technology which helps modernisation of agriculture and development of industries. In a traditional society, production is based largely on empirical processes and experience on trail and error rather than on science, in a modern society it is basically rooted in science."

Science based technology has other important implications for social and cultural life and it involves fundamental, social and cultural changes which are broadly described as modernisation.

While emphasizing the role of science in the modernisation of society. The Education Commission equally stresses the role of spiritual values. It states Modernisation does not mean- least of all in our national situation- are visual to recognise the importance of or to inculcate necessary moral and spiritual values and self-discipline. Modernisation, if it is to be a living force, must derive its strength from the spirit. In other words, we should learn to harness science but must also learn not to be dominated by science.

In this context, Pt, Jawahar Lal Nehru has rightly staged, "Can we combine the progress of science and technology with the progress of mind and spirit also?

We cannot be untrue to science because that represents the basic fact of life to-day. Still less can we be untrue to those essential principles for which India has stood in the part throughout the ages. Let us then pursue our path to industrial progress with our strength and vigour and at the same time remember that materials riches without toleration and compassion and wisdom may well turn to dust and ashes."

Effect of Modernisation on Economic Activities

1. Economic crisis Articles belonging to luxury become easily available and articles of necessity become costly.

2. Decline of violate industry.

3. Increasing the problems of the labourers.

4. Industrial disputes.

5. Encouragement to class distinction.

6. Capitalism.

7. Division of labour.

8. Production at a very large level.

9. Economic development.

Negative Effects of Modernisation

Modernisation has also led to some disruptive tendencies as communal disturbances, violence, provincial, regional and national conflicts and despite. It has also created many social as well as economic problems. Material values sometimes dominate spiritual values. In developing and progressive nations, in the initial phases there appears a wide gulf between the rich and the poor. It is also responsible for the explosion of frustration among many sections of society.

Education in India and Modernisation

Modernisation of Education in India cannot be envisaged without a happy and harmonious blend of science and technology with spirituality. Education in India in the context of modernisation may be envisaged as under -

1. Study of Foreign Languages - To know various important languages of the work is very important to enlarge one's outlook. It is also important for a variety of academic and practical purpose. Russian, French, German, Japanese, Spanish and Chinese besides English are important world languages of communication and for acquiring knowledge and culture.

2. Modernisation and the Teacher - The teacher's attitude and outlook, his progressive philosophy and his dynamic as well as revolutionary methods of teaching all have important place in promoting modernisation.

3. Harmony between Science and Spirituality - According to Vinoba Bhave, the present age in the age of Science and Spirituality. Actually for the real development and modernisation, material affluence and power should be harmonised with the higher values. The concept of mingling of Science and Spirituality is of special significance for Indian education.

4. Education for Social and National Integration - Social and national integration is very important for the creation of a strong and united country. It is an essential pre-condition of modernization.

5. Dynamic Methods of Teaching - In a modern society knowledged ceases to be something to be received passively. Now knowledge is provided in such

a way that the child becomes active and curious. He tries to know the facts himself. Through education he tries to explore new things. Old methods of cramming or rote memory are the talk of the past. New knowledge is something to be actively discovered. It this is rightly understood, it would involve a revolution in traditional education.

6. Development of Skilled Manpower - Out country cannot make rapid progress specially in the agricultural field unless the farmer is ready to adopt techniques that increase yields and to move out of his age-long conservatism. The same is true of industry. The skilled manpower needed for the relevant research and tis systematic application to agriculture, industry and other sector of life can only come from a development of scientific and technological education.

7. Vocationalisation of Education - In modern times only academic formal education would not do. In the curricula of most contemporary school systems particularly in the socialist countries of Europe, a place is found, for what is variously called, manual work; or work experience. At present, emphasis is being given up on vocational aspects of education, so that the citizens of the country achieve self-sufficiently and they contribute a lot in the economic progress of the country.

8. Science-Based Education - In modern world, the role of science cannot be forgotten. New discoveries of science have changed the world scenario completely. Therefore, science education must become an integral part of school education. Also some study of science should become a part of all courses in the humanities and social sciences at the university stage.

The quality of science teaching also has to be raised

considerably as to achieve its proper considerably as to achieve its proper objectives and purposes, namely to promote an ever-keeping understanding of basis principles to develope problem solving, analytical skills and the ability to apply them to the problems of the material environment and social living and to promote the spirit of enquiry and experimentation.

9. Universalisation and Mass Education - In our country, a small part of population is literate This number will have to be increased and for the rapid progress of the country, it is very essential to produce educated and skilled citizens and to train an adequate and competent intelligent to modernise society quickly.

10. Aims of Education and Modernization - In this context, Kothari Commission has stated, The very aim of education has to be viewed differently- It is no longer taken as concerned primarily with the imparting of knowledge or the preparation of finished product, but with the awakening of curiosity, the development of proper interests, attitudes and values and the building up of such essential skills as independent study and the capacity to think and judge for oneself without which it is not possible to become a responsible member of democratic society.

Universalisation of Education and Modernisation of Indian Society

The concept of universalization implies education for all, irrespective of caste, colour, creed, sex or age.

Universalisation of education relates to (i) Education of the illiterate adults between 15-35 years of age. (ii) the education of children covering age group of 6 to 14 as stipulated in Article 45 of The Commission. Universal elementary education is essential for the modernisation of society. According to J.P. Niak, "The progress of primary education in an index to the general, social and economic development of the country as a whole." It has also been observed that countries which have made proper provision for primary education are far ahead of those with inadequate provision. In a similar way, adult education plays a crucial role in the modernisation of society. It is important to note that the World Conferences of Education for all, held at in March 1990, made the World Declaration on Education for All.

13

EDUCATION AND VALUE

Meaning of Value

The dictionary meaning of the term value is something that has worth, utility and importance. Ordinarily we may define value as a thing which is good. Operationally, the concept of values may be defined as "factors which affect human behaviour."

We may define value as a "concept which is accepted by the sub-conscious mind, is understood by all and perceived by the individual. " When we talk of human behaviour, we generally refer to factors which affect human behaviour and emotional attitude.

Actually, a value is a preferences as well as the conception of the preferable. According to Kluckohn a value is a "conception of the desirable" and not something "merely desired". A conception of the desirable seems to be nothing more than a special king of preference for one end state over other end state. A value is a conception of something that is personally or socially preferable.

In the view of shower, values are standards and principles for judging worth. They are criteria by which we judge things, actions and situations to be good, worthwhile, desirable, or on the other hand, bad, worthless, despicable, or, of course, somewhere in between these extremes. We may apply our values consciously or they may function unconsciously as a part of the influence of own frame of reference, without out being aware of the standards implied by our decisions. Robin williams has also remarked that a person's values serve on the criteria or standard in terms of which evaluations are made. Shower's definition contains three key elements -

1. Values are dimensional rather than absolute categories. In other words, they are criteria for judging degrees of good and bad, right of wrong, or praise and blame. Values are not simply the presence or absence of these characteristics. They are sets of rules for rating behaviours or objects along a continuum of worth.

2. Values exist in the mind independently of self-awareness or public affirmation. A value does not have to be explicitly announced or put into practise to qualify as a value. Values often form a part of frame of judgment without man's conscious knowledge or deliberate choosing.

3. The values are concepts, not feelings. Values embody and express feelings, but they are more than feelings.

Forms of Values

According to shaver, values may be categorised into three forms-

1. Moral Values - According to Shaver, "These values are the standards, the principles, by which we judge whether aims or actions are proper." These have two following characteristics -

a. They are more than merely matters of personal taste.

b. They vary widely in their importance and applicability.

2. Instrumental Values - These values are derivatives rather than fundamental principles. Discipline and punctuality are not end but means to achieve some goals or perform some task effectively. Classroom instructional objectives may be instrumental values for long term educational goals. Instrumental values are intermediary standards designed to solve large goals.

3. Aesthetic Values - Through these values beauty is judged. If someone is appraising the beauty of an object, it is only a person taste. Aesthetic judgement is different from moral judgement. A boy wearing dirty cloths may not be immoral.

Moral values are placed on a continuum from personal preference to basic values. The value of cleanliness is the least significant moral value as it is involved in the issue of personal preference. On the other hand, the value of sanctity of human life is a most basic value as it is essential of humanity. In a democratic set-up, the basic values may be freedom of speech and justice.

Between the poles of personal preferences and basic values lie a wide range of middle level moral values. Patriotism, dedication, honesty and cooperation may be middle level values. These values do not have ground in human nature but they are important for social set-up.

These values may vary in the degree of importance and quality, but all moral values express something more than individual standard. Because of the moral values are used to justify and judge ethical decisions, and these have impact on other people, moral standards are not merely matters of personal taste. When a person is faced with a moral dilemma, he is asked what he ought to do. These values necessarily carry a basic massage of obligation. These values are of high priority in the value education than aesthetic and instrumental value.

Some Other Definition of Value

1. Johnson, "Values may be defined as a conception of standard, cultural or merely personal, by which things are compared and approved or disapproved relative to one-another-held to be relatively desirable or undesirable, more or less correct. All kinds things may be evaluated: feelings, ideas, actions, qualities, objects, persons groups goals means.

2. Kluckhohan, "A value is a conception, explicit or implicit, distinctive of an individual or characteristic of a group of the desirable which influences the selection from available modes, means and ends of action."

3. Flink, "Values are normative standards by which human beings are influenced in their choice among the alternate courses of action which they perceive."

4. R.K. Mukherjee, "Values socially approved desires and goals that are internalised through the process of conditioning, learning or socialization and that become subjective preferences, standards and aspirations."

5. J. Kane, "Values are ideals, beliefs or norms which a society or the large majority of a society members hold."

Value Oriented Education

Education is a cultural phenomenon. It means that the culture and education promote each other mutually. Each all time develops its own specific from for its development. In other words, culture creates education and all education produces culture. Thus culture and education both are important and essential for human existence.

All scholars agree that the main function of education is to promote a balanced development of physical, mental, social moral and spiritual aspects of the students in order to produce balanced citizens who strive to promote social welfare and progress. Education in the context of social changes but also to inculcate the values of humanism, democracy, socialism, secularism and national integration. This is necessary for the realization of our national objectives of building a democratic and just social order based on equality, fraternity, freedom and social justice.

Most of the scholars have stressed the need and importance of promoting values through education which is facing the crisis of character in different spheres of life. According to Radhakrishnan Commission, In addition to the search for truth through scientific and scholarly, pursuits an important task of education is a concern with values. Kothari Commission with its emphasis on education's role in national development includes among the functions of higher education cultivation of right interests, attitudes, moral and intellectual values. The National Policy of Education observes, The growing concern over the erosion of essential values and an increasing cynicism in society has brought to focus the need for re-adjustments in the curriculum in order to make education a forceful tool for the cultivation of social and moral values.

The inseparable link between education and values is evident in the nature and aim of education. The primary task of education is the creative extension of knowledge, but it is not the total task. Actually, the educator's task is a wholistic task and one can not say to the students that he will take care only of their minds. Young people of their school and university should be given an understanding of moral and spiritual values. It is the business of education to impart an integrated view of life.

Values may be categorize also as follows-

1. Institutional Values - Which include the political values the moral values and establishment value. Evidently both our societe and its values are rapidly changing. Modern youth questions the values of their parents. If we are to cope with these changing attitudes, it is imperative to discuss the importance of values in our school system.

Actually, there is no need to preach and teach values to the youngsters. Once they understand the basic values, the relevance of these will be self evident. The child has learnt to appreciate all that truthful, beautiful and good and discard things and behaviour which are undesirable.

2. Social Values - What is good for the society. It discuss the basis of the relationship of the individual with other people.

3. Cultural Values - Which involve the survival of the culture.

4. Personal Values - What is profitable and good for the individual.

5. Essential Values - These values involve the basic nature of man himself.

Societal Concerns

1. Protection of environment.
2. Protection of Public property.

3. Dignity and worth of human beings, universal brotherhood.

4. Developing national pride in cultural heritage.

5. Inculcation of ethical and moral values.

6. Stress on small family norm.

7. Religious tolerance, Mutual understanding.

8. Social or public goods are more important than private gains.

9. Basic equality of individuals.

10. Condemning communalism.

Personal and Social Values

1. Cooperation, Fellow feeling.

2. Good manners, Good behaviour, Responsible behaviour.

3 Self-Confidence, Self-dignity/Self-esteem.

4. Morality, Faith in God.

5. Dutifulness, Work is worship, Valuing time.

6. Simple living. High thinking.

7. Comparison, Kindness, Merciful, Sympathetic.

8. Tolerance, Patience, Forgiveness.

9. Love, Affection, Friendly attitude.

10. Punctuality, Regularity.

Modes Operandi for Inculcation of Values

1. Some specific suggestions are as the following -

a. By telling do's and dont's of good behaviour whenever and wherever needed. Value conflicts need to be resolved at the earliest occasion.

b. By observing from time to time the behaviour of students and suggesting corrective measures lovingly whenever and wherever needed.

c. Giving examples from books of proven worth.

d. Teaching values through morning assembly, co-curricular activities in the classes and outside deductions.

e. Telling stories, anecdote etc.

f. Organising plays, dramas and debates.

g. Preparing reading material in human values and making it available to teachers and students. Appropriate print material need to be prepared to teachers also.

2. The parents in general, have mentioned that they devote time towards studies and towards inculcation of moral and ethical values, however, such time span varies from 15 minutes to 2-3 hours per day, but a few parents have stated that they devote time towards their wards as and when required.

3. Though, the parents agree that values are caught at home, in neighbourhood and in schools, yet they forcefully plead that values need to be taught in school through a systematic programme of education in human values. Some books on human values need to be prepared for children and one or two periods per week for value education may be allocated in school time table.

4. Teachers and parents should be role models for students, specially the lady teachers should not be fashion models, rather they should be role models.

5. Generally, the teachers and of the opinion that values are caught by children by observing. The

behaviour of parents, teachers, elders, leaders and other personalities. However, several teachers are of the view that values may be taught in the first instance through curriculum transaction and personalized attention towards students.

Certain General Comments

1. Knowledge of all religious and respect for them facilitate perfect growth of human beings. One should strive for universal brotherhood.

2. One should take pride in the culture heritage of his/her country.

3. Values need not be inculcated by scolding or by force. Good values may be inculcated through polite means.

4. Inculcate such values that can be applied practically.

5. Value not be imposed, they should come from inner self.

6. Educational programs should comprise of courses of studies and programs of education in human values.

7. Students should be capacitated to discriminate between good values and bad behaviours.

Role of Media, Music, Art and Drama in Inculcation of Human Values

1. Some students have opined that media is neither good nor bad. It depends on how one selects media programs.

2. Whereas some students have shown preference of Indian Art, dance and Drama, several others have shown preference for western Art, Dance and Drama.

3. Though some students are of the opinion that media plays positive role to inculcate good human values, others have condemned media in this regard. They are of the opinion that media plays derogatory role in so far as it relates to inculcation of human values.

Role of Parents for Inculcation of Values in Children

The parents are required to become good role models for their children. They should not show double standard in home. The following are some suggestions regarding role of parents-

1. The should keep in touch with school teachers/ principal in the context of progress and behaviour pattern of their wards. They should also give feedback of their efforts to the teachers.

2. They should devote at least 15-20 minutes daily to tell about moral values to their wards through stories, adventures, anecdotes etc.

3. They should not generally condemn their works. Things may be got done through love and affection.

4. Parents should keep a watch on day-to-day activities of their wards. Corrective measures need to be taken whenever and wherever needed.

5. Mother is the first teacher of the child. She should discharge her duties meticulously both through words and through actions.

14

EDUCATION FROM PHILOSOPHICAL POINT OF VIEW

Before discussing historical background of education, it is necessary to analyse various issues or concepts which are related to education. Since a long time, various questions were being debated by philosophers and educators relating to concept of education. Although answers of these questions were found by the philosophers, but still even today such questions are found to be unanswered because of which various experts are engaged in exploration of these questions.

It is necessary to find out the answers of these questions as they will lead to benefit of human beings. In every age, experts try to get answers of these questions for which they analyse or take into consideration responses get earlier. Thus in changed conditions, experts analyse different issues but for this always take help of earlier responses. Such responses are taken into consideration while making all the plans for freeing the education from various drawbacks or limitations.

One of an important question regarding education is philosophy of it and it is because of this reason that philosophers of education are now recruited in almost all schools of varying standards. Questions on which these professionals concentrate have philosophical nature and they use philosophical methods for finding out their answers. An important philosophical question on which philosophers concentrated in past was who should be educated and through which method. These experts reached on the conclusion that answer of this question depends on needs of society and varieties of human talent.

Answers of such questions are also provided in present time also. In present context, answer of this question will be that all human beings should be educated. Today, question which is more urgent to answer is that how all the children should be educated. A kind of disagreement is found among educators regarding this issue. Some experts are of the opinion that similar kind of education should be provided to all the students till twelfth grade. However, a majority of experts are of the view that method which should be used to educate students should be decided in accordance with needs and interests of individual students.

By analysing various philosophical questions, it becomes easy for the experts to design educational policy. Various philosophical issues can help in identifying and clarifying basic issues relating to education. An important function of philosophy of education is to analyse the language which should be used for imparting education. Such important questions are being analysed by philosophers of education. Answers of these questions will keep on changing in accordance with context in which they are asked, but still past responses will also be used as a basis for present or future investigation.

Views of Some Experts

One of an important philosopher and educationist is

Socrates. Plato, one of his discipline, performed the function of publicising his views and opinions. One of an important achievement of Socrate was a unique educational method in which he used to impart education not through writing but by engaging students in dialogue. This method was known as Socratic method.

In Socratic method, he used to ask some very simple questions from the student. After getting answer, he further ask some complicated questions which were mean to analyse the reason for which student gave that answer. Such kind of analysing process keep on running till it is felt by him and student that issue of analysis has gone to possible extent. Method of Socrates was not merely a method of teaching but also a method of learning. His method was an outstanding way of questioning which led to critical thinking among the students. He used to begin his investigation with one simple question and after exploring it briefly move on to another question. In this way, he used to build a kind of relationship or connection in between the answers of all the questions. Socrate was interested in exploring the questions pertaining to general life. He never used his method for trivial questions. Socrate used to criticise those persons whose thinking and behaviour revealed ignorance or apparently evil intentions.

Plato

Plato was Socrates people and he gave new dimension to thinking and studies of his master. Republic is an important work of literature created by Plato in which he has discussed much about of the nature and importance of education. In Plato's views, while imparting education, one should keep in mind the abilities and capabilities of students. Only such kind of education can lead to good results. In other words, Plato was of the view that education should be tailored in accordance with the student.

This philosopher was of the view that although human beings differ from each other considerably but on basis of some common features, they can be grouped in three categories and all the people belonging to different categories require different kind of education, which arises the need to create different kinds of educational programmes. According to Plato these three categories were of workers or artisans, of soldiers and of the rulers. Persons belong to first category, namely workers, should be provided special kind of education so that they can become well versed in specific occupations. Persons belong to second category, namely soldiers, should be provided with physical and moral education as they had to fight in wars and had to save lives of other peoples. Rulers or persons belong to upper strata of society should be imparted education of complex or difficult subjects, which could widen their mental horizon.

If one go through Plato's Republic, it will be found that he was interested in creating an utopian state. He provided his model of education while keeping his objective of creating such kind of state in mind. According to him, educational programmes should be designed in such a manner that all needs require to create the best state could be fulfilled in all the respects. He was of the view that an ideal state could be developed only through a well developed educational program. Function of imparting education should be performed by efficient persons so that they could produce such qualified persons who could prove to be useful for the state and could play an important role in development of their state.

Plato believed that education helped to develop feeling of self-actualization among students and only such persons could play an important role in developmental process of the state. A truly good life could be spent only by a highly or well educated person. He was of opinion that irrespective of class or creed, all the persons and especially children should be provided with equal opportunities to get education and to develop in their life. Education policy or programme should be developed with such a view to provide equal opportunities to all the children belong to different sections of society. All the children should be provided with an equal opportunity to get education of those subjects which could help them to make progress in their life and to lead a prosperous life. It would be a matter of injustice if no such kind of opportunities were provided on equal basis to all the children.

In view of this philosopher or expert, both males and females should be provided with right to get education and education of both the sexes should consist of certain common features. As various kind of differences were found between male and female, for which educational programmes should be modified or transformed in accordance with their needs and abilities. According to him, although for proper development, one should be provided information of various subjects but there were certain subjects which must be included in the curriculum, which were literature, history, mathematics and philosophy.

Aristotle

No discussion of philosophy could be completed

without taking into consideration the views of Aristotle. Views and thoughts of Aristotle triggered rich debate during his time and even today. Through his views or opinions, Aristotle did not try to create an ideal or utopian state in any way. His views were based on reality and he used to analyse all the views critically.

Aristotle was of the view that it was must for all people to be educated, but the purpose of education should be to make people able to have their appropriate place or standing in life. With experience, every person became proficient in performing that task. All human beings possess of different kinds of virtues. Moral life grows out of practices in communities and demands which are generally make by these practices. Sometimes individual right's of citizens get eradicated by community's needs and requirements. A good citizen is one who is ready to give up his individual rights for the sake of community's welfare. Thus a person leading a highly moral life can prove to a good citizen or member of society in Aristotle's view.

On basis of Aristotle's views, models of moral education have been created by educationists. An important view of Aristotle is that morally appropriate modes of conduct should be used to train or educate children. The responsibility of inculcating right values in children rest with society and it is the society which provide a strict vigil on all the activities children perform. He was of the belief that children are not little adults because of which should not be taught the reasons of moral deeds or matters. It is only in their twenties that children become mentally able to understand such matters and to grab out the moral teachings from all the happenings. In their childhood, or immature time, children should be taught to respond ethically out of habits of good character. The ground upon which their future reasoning will be based will grow from this good character. Thus, character education was an important part of educational programme for children according to Aristotle's view.

If viewed minutely, Aristotle's views are very simple in nature, that it is first important or essential to create right kind of character in a child and only then he or she should be allowed to analyse and to question different matters. Even till now, model of moral education is based on Aristotle's views, however, it will be insufficient just simply reading about the virtues and their enactment in the lives of others. Moral values get developed only by practising them in reality. It is because of this reason that various kinds of practical activities for children have been included in school curriculum which can lead to development of moral values among them.

Rousseau

No discussion about history of education can be completed without mentioning about early Christian era and of Middle Ages. Various kinds of changes can be seen in thinking pattern of people, which led to emergence of various thinkers and philosophers one of whom was Jean Jacques Rousseau.

Rousseau was a thinker who extol primitive condition of human beings, in which they were nothing better than animals as they did not feel any kind of pressures and corruption of political state. Philosophy of Rousseau was mainly based on his views regarding nature. In his view, all human beings were born free and they could remain in such condition only in natural environment. Human beings get corrupted in some way when they have to lead a life in company of other people, as in such state, they become dependent on each other for fulfilment of their needs. In Rousseau's view, individuals with rational capacity for contract making, whom he called genuine, did exist before establishment of society or communities. Theory based on this view was called as Social Contract Theory.

Although Rousseau believed that society did impose certain kinds of restrictions on human freedom, but he recognised the fact that it was not possible for any human being to achieve his highest potential without society. He was of the view that such conditions should be prevailed in the society which were marked by qualities of self reliance, love of nature compassion. It was only in such conditions that quality of self-actualization could get develop in any human being.

According to him, education should be imparted in such a way that natural goodness could get preserve within human beings which could induce a positive sense of social responsibilities. He was of the view that as males and females differ from each other in various respects because of which different kinds of educational program should be designed for them. He was firm believer of the fact that while imparting education, it was necessary to provide students with freedom as no person could learn anything in restrictions or limits. Education should be imparted in natural surroundings and there should be an element of dependence on nature in all the educational programmes. Only such kind of educational programme could prove to consistent.

In Rousseau's view, education should be imparted without or with least possible restrains or boundations. No special kind of moral education should be imparted to students as children are good naturally right from the time of their birth. If children have to save from being getting corrupt, they should be educated in rural settings as atmosphere of urban area possess more probabilities of getting children corrupt. No abstract thoughts or early booking learning should be imposed on children. While imparting education, interest and experiences of students or children should be taken into account. Feelings should be given more importance than thoughts. The function of teacher or instructor should not be to impose heavy bundle of information on children but to answer various kinds of questions arising in their mind. In other words, teacher should act as a guide, who should attempt to direct children's interest in healthy and proper direction. Concept of open education, which is very popular in today's time is based on Rousseau's views and opinions.

Thus it can be said that Rousseau of the view that children are good right from time of their birth and they should be provided only with proper direction in accordance with their interest and abilities. Pressures to make children grow up too fast can prove to be devastating from them and can ruin them completely. It does not imply that no place should be provided to formal education in school curriculum, however, it should be provided with a limited space and only to the grown up students. Children are born with potential for both good and evil doings and transactions with educational or mis-educational environment can direct them towards one or the other. Thus, no pressure or compulsion should be created on children but they should be provided with opportunities to do functions or task in accordance with their interests, however, teacher should remain present at all times to ensure that they do not harm themselves or anyone else around them.

Another important view of Rousseau in respect of education was that all the children belonging to different age groups possess different abilities by which they could learn or understand different kinds of skills or information respectively. To make proper utilisation of appropriate opportunities, teachers should keep a strict vigil over students. Thus, importance of proper timing in educational process was first propounded by Rousseau, which is still important. Without knowing the abilities of students or about the fact that what their students are ready to learn, no teacher can impart education properly. It is only by keeping the abilities of students that a teacher should chose appropriate activities which can trigger developmental process among them. In assimilating knowledge, this fundamental structure acts as an important mechanism. Through such kind of educational pattern, children can be make able to face difficult situations and even to find solutions of different kinds of problems.

In addition to thinkers mentioned above, there are various philosophers who provide their views regarding education in modern time. One of an important such thinker was John Dewey, whose contribution in literary field is very extensive. Some of the books written by him reveal his interest in evolutionary themes and his passion to make use of evolutionary metaphors. Dewey in his life-time raised some special kinds of questions or issues which even still interest modern man.

Dewey had lots of beliefs and recommendations concerning students and their role in their own education. It was because of his views on education that Dewey prove to be enormously influential in domains of philosophical and educational thoughts. He was a firm believer that students should be provided with an opportunity to participate in their educational planning. Often he is criticised by some people to infect the students or educational institutions with feelings of moral relativism and for substituting socialization with true education. It was his odd beliefs that a large number of critics can be found of him. However, there is a large number of people and especially students who are of the belief that Dewey contributions to educational thoughts are considerably and it is not reasonable to ignore his work in any way.

An important feature of Dewey was that he used to sought explanation of all the matters in terms of natural phenomena. He did not favour any kind of explanations that involve sources other than nature ones. He used to apply method of science in all the spheres of human activities. It is because of his naturalistic orientation that his work contains various evolutionary themes and issues.

Dewey's philosophical education was based on the belief that only mind was real and human thoughts progress toward a pre-ordained ideal by a dialectic process of resolving opposites through synthesis. However, in comparison to pre-ordained ideal process, he used to believe more firmly on dialectical process. While talking about education, he compared old and new pattern of education. However while doing so, he did not endure the new educational pattern. He pinpointed both the positive and negative points found in both kinds of educational patterns. By doing this, he tried to create a revised vision of education, which in some expert's opinion was an entirely a new creation.

To clarify his thoughts and to move on to a new level of planning and acting, a dialectical method was employed by Dewey, however, he never claimed that new level found by him was final position as he believed that various kinds of scrutiny or modifications were possible on that position also. Dewey considered philosophy of education to be the most fundamental and important branch of philosophy as it was the base upon which all other branches of philosophy depend. Dewey was of the view that philosophy of education was in reality philosophy of life. Dewey rejected concept of transcendent entirely. He never posited unobservable, underlying mechanisms of mind to explain what was accessible to all kinds of observations.

In Dewey view, there did not exist any kind of difference between concept of education and growth. An important biological metaphore which he employed was end growth of the human being. However, majority of people do not satisfy with the aim of education just as growth, and especially in today's modern and complex world. According to Dewey growth is its own end and any question asked about growth towards what is not consistent in any way. Growth leads to continuous process of growth and it is neither possible nor desirable to specify its direction which only make this concept rigid.

Dewey was of the view that the fundamental aim of a human being is to live more life. Likewise, process of growth gets developed by preliminary growth. Aim of education should be to provide a direction to future life of students. It should not be concerned merely with present interest and purposes of students. All kinds of experiences can be considered educative only if they lead to process of growth in any way. It seems that Dewey did not intend that growth should serve as a fully operational definition or purpose of education.

The sense in which Dewey made use of concept of growth was in such a manner that could help us to think more deeply about connection between present and future. Some experts are of the view that concept of growth defined by Dewey is vague in nature. However, based on his view it can be said that according to Dewey, aim of education should be to have more education. In this way, it is both as an end and means that education should function. He was of the view that all the activities included in educational curriculum should have some specific aim which jointly make aim of education. According to him, in reality, aims of education is not fixed or rigid in nature. Both students and teachers play important role in educational process, but they do not perform different kinds of activities with specific aims. All activities have different aims and all aims are retained till they guide that activity. Human beings abandon such aims which do not give any kind of guidance and substitute them with other kinds of aims. Thus according to him, aims function in means-end planning and human beings decide to make use of new and different kinds of means if present means do not fulfil or help in getting desired end.

An important dimension of Dewey's view regarding education is that right to participate in educational process should not be provided only to teachers, but to students also. As teachers are empowered to decide or set goals for which they perform different activities, students should be provided with such power to set objectives of their own educational process. Dewey's insistence that students, as active organisms, must be involved in the establishment of objectives for their own learning underscores his belief in the connection found between purpose and activity.

According to Dewey, tendency to imitate is found very strongly among the children however, this concept is quite complex in nature. Children do not imitate all the activities or actions performed by elders, but they chose certain out of them. While imitating their actions, they adopt certain specific modes of behaviour for their own individual purposes. Imitation is a real work of childhood and should not be considered just as mocked one.

From his minute observations, Dewey found that children possess four kinds of interest, which included:

- construction or making new things,
- inquiry, or finding out
- expressing themselves, and
- communicating their ideas or views.

To create a rich and healthy elementary school curriculum, all of the above mentioned interests or activities should be taken into account. A great deal of information or things can be learnt by children about traditional disciplines in course of pursuing their own interests which can happen only if teachers arrange proper experiences for them in a systematic manner.

A model of thinking or problem solving was also

created by Dewey, which is still influential. According to him, a person starts thinking when he senses feeling of problem or unsettlement. A hypothesis is yield by initial exploration which should be tested or analysed properly. Then thinker makes a plan which is a set of means to test hypothesis. Different kinds of alternatives are being considered in each stage of exploration. It is only after this that plan is enacted in reality. Outcomes of previous decisions are analysed by the thinker and then he evaluates them systematically. Continuous thinking is done by the careful thinkers. They not only keep their eyes on present results but also future outcomes also.

Another contribution made by Dewey in education was method for analysing one's experiences and its place in educational process. Dewey did not consider an experience merely an exposure or passive undergoing but something which have a specific meaning to activity perform by person. Another important feature of notion of experience considered by Dewey was that experience must have a social and cultural nature. Thus concept of experience used by Dewey in context of education possess personal meaning and social inter-action.

According to Dewey, the most desirable manner in which education should be imparted is to provide different kinds of experiences and then to establish a connection among them. Human beings get developed by different kinds of experiences, thus teachers should analyse the level of development led by experience provided by him. A kind of continuity should be established in the educational experiences. For this reason, it is very necessary for the teachers to have thorough information of prior experiences of their students. It is only on basis of their past experiences that future experiences should be planned out by the teachers. While preparing the subject matter, teachers should take into account student's level of experiences and their future needs.

Educational experiences should be meaningful and there should be a kind of continuity in them. A direct interaction should be there in between objects of the study and students. An important drawback found in old educational pattern was lack of such interaction. Level of confidence and interest goes down when students are forced to plod through material with which they are not really engaged for some obscure future ends. In such situation, they even lose faith from importance of education.

Thus it can be said that it is because of Dewey's views and believes which led to emergence of concept of what is called child-centred education. He insisted on appropriate attention to both internal and external aspects of a learning experience. He did not approve use of only those activities which provide pleasure or entertainment to children and did not have any kind of purpose. He did not recommend passive kind of educational pattern but such kind of programme in which students also find opportunities to get actively involved.

According to Dewey, knowledge is much more bigger than truth. In his view, knowledge is properly construed as that body of information which one applies intelligently to inquiry. In the process of testing hypothesis, some of the materials can be discarded or modified. Truth is the end product of all inquiries. As naturalistic, Dewey wanted to avoid any kind of dependence on unobservable entities to which no clearly observable effects could be traced out. He preferred knowing in place of knowledge as it is a systematic process of inquiry. Knowledge in his view was just a material used to guide inquiry.

Dewey was of the view that only right kind of proposition or material is used by human beings to guide inquiry. All misleading or false propositions are being deleted from information by human beings as soon as they come to terms with reality. Such wrong or false propositions could not be considered as knowledge as they were not used to guide inquiry in any way. While trying to collect knowledge in some stable form, generally human beings escape the difficulties. In such condition, human beings move away from a noun-interpretation of knowledge to a verb-form.

An important feature of Dewey's theory of knowledge is that human beings at every stage of maturity, make use of material from prior experiences which guide them in making present enquiry. As it has real effects, thus it is knowledge in the pragmatic sense and it is this that explains the function or task of person making inquiry. Growth is represented by control over one's own procedural processes.

Social and political philosophies have remained important subjects in which Dewey directed his efforts. According to him, democracy was a form of associated living which was consonant with various methods of science. Dewey wanted to analyse relationship existing between democracy and education. He considered human beings as social animals. Impetus for construction of common values is get arise because a desire to communicate with other exists among human beings. While discussing about values cherished by human beings, Dewey took into account general biological conditions. It was because of his naturalistic view that he had quite a different perspective to education from majority of experts. In his view, impulse to communicate was important trait that preceded creation of culture. Through social interactions, various kinds of qualities get arise in human beings. Human beings are not born with certain common values however they are being made by them. It is on his this belief that Dewey argue that schools or educational institutions need not prepare students for eventual communication by pouring into them the specific values and knowledge of culture, whereas, children should be encouraged in all possible ways to communicate and to construct common values themselves.

15

EDUCATIONAL POLICIES FOR EMERGING INDIAN EDUCATIONAL SOCIETY

A need to formulate national policy of education was felt by the Indian government but it was not an easy task to formulate educational policy for such a wide nation, where people living in different regions have different life style, different religious practices and even different languages. Before formulation of such policy, various prominent educationists were invited to provide their suggestions and views regarding such policy. For formulation of national policy of education, a nation wide debate got developed in which number of seminars were organised at national and international levels. Various state governments were invited to provide their recommendations for such act.

All the recommendations and suggestions provided by different persons and authorities were analysed in detail by education ministry, on the basis of which a revised document was being brought out by Ministry of Human Resource Development in the year 1986, which was known as National Policy of Education-A Presentation. At the meeting of State Ministers of Education, National Development Council and Central Advisory Board of Education discussed the document and in the light of these discussions, it was revised and a finally a Draft National Policy on Education was put forward in the Parliament by ministry of Education in Parliament House.

In this policy, all the issues relating to Indian education were touched upon and discussed at length. It is not possible for us to discuss all the subjects in length, but some light have been thrown on all the subjects in brief in manner in which they appear in the policy.

In the beginning, policy states that education has continued to evolve, diversity and extends its coverage since dawn of human history. In this complex and dynamic growth process, action of education need to be planned with greater sensitivity. It was also stated in the policy that education is necessary for all the people belonging to different strata of the society as without it no human being can think of getting developed. An acculturating role is being played by the education and by it a person becomes independent, physically, mentally as well as spiritually. For different levels of economy, manpower is being developed by the education. The basis on which functions of research and development gets developed is education and it develops the quality of self-reliance in human beings.

When we talk about National System of Education, we imply that upto a specific level, all the persons should be provided right to get educated irrespective of their caste, creed and sex. Thus, a common educational structure is being envisaged by national system of education. Basis of such national system of education should be national curricular framework. All secular values will be comply with while imparting education. For each stage of education, minimum levels of learning should be laid down. One of an important objective of educational process is providing conditions in which students can get education through maximum possible extent.

A lot of importance was being assigned to all acts which could help in removal of social and economic inequalities found in the nation. Education was considered as an agent of basic change which could bring about a change in the status of women in society. Provision of providing various kinds of encouragement was made in the policy by which general public could come forward and could participate in programme of eradicating illiteracy from the nation.

In the policy it was made clear that without adopting a sympathetic and encouraging attitude, no children could be attracted to attend schools. Programmes of early childhood care and education should be child oriented and should be designed on basis of individual differences and interests of the children. No formal methods of teaching should be used by teachers at primary level. At primary stage, the need to adopt a child centred and activity based process of learning was emphasised in the policy. To improve quality of education at primary level, an operation known as Operation Blackboard should be implemented, under which there should be provision of atleast one blackboard in each class room for students of different levels and standards. Provision of allowing free education could be made in school if teachers found any student talented but who is unable to bear expenses of his or her studies. For re-organisation of education, various vocational educational programmes should be implemented at school level. Education at higher level should be of such nature should be prepare students to understand and reflect critically on various cultural, social and moral issues.

Professional education should be imparted in the schools and educational institutions, under which provision of adequate number of computers should be made in the schools and children should be provided with adequate information relating to operation of it. Although it is essential to provide education in a serious kind of atmosphere, but still students should be provided with adequate freedom, as without it, they will not be able to make use of their creative abilities and mind. Teachers should engage themselves only in the function of imparting education and all students should be make ready to get education from inside.

Various steps or measures should be taken to avoid de culturalisation at school level. Such education should be imparted to students by which they can get attracted towards technological developments, but can keep themselves tied with their traditional values and norms. Such qualities should be tried to develop in the students by which they can be made willing to live a peaceful life by maintaining unity with people of other religions. Only through such education incidences of violence and fatalism could be checked properly. Appropriate environment should be developed in the schools. For checking the educational abilities of the students and to bring about qualitative improvement in education, examinations should be employed.

Socio-cultural ethics of the society get reflected by the status of teachers, thus teachers should be paid due importance and place in the educational system. Functions performed by teachers are continuous in nature for which proper attention should be paid to it's pre-service and in-service components. High priority should be paid to system of planning and management of education. Need to invest large amount of national income for promotion and development of education was mentioned in the policy.

Programme of Action for the implementation was being announced by Ministry of Human Resource Development, which was done after declaration of National Policy of Education. Such a follow up programme was prepared in India for the first time, which make it a remarkable event in educational history of the nation. Total twenty three task forces were being prepared and each of them was being assigned specific topic which was being covered by the policy. With these task forces, various eminent people of the nation were associated. Situation in respect of subject assigned to task forces were being analysed in detail and on basis of their analysis, broad lines were being indicated by them. In a series of meetings convened by Minister of Human Resource Development, reports of the task forces were being discussed. These reports were again taken into consideration in conference of Education Secretaries of State Government and Union Territories. A vast gamut of the important educational parameters were being covered by the Programme of Action. Educational position of the country was being analysed minutely and various strategies to implement recommendations provided in the policy were prepared. Various aspects of the education were being discussed in the policy. Various educationists and thinkers did hard labour to produce Programme of Action and it provided the valuable information relating to various issues relating to Indian education, because of which it is considered an important document in educational system of the nation.

As various kinds of changes took place in different areas in our nation, because of which it became necessary to bring about some special kinds of modifications in the National Policy were made in 1992, which was set up in the year 1986. Implementation of points mentioned in the policy were reviewed by two committees, which were known as Ramamurti Committee and Janardhana Committee.

A new para was being introduced in the revised national policy in which need to produce skill manpower resources of kind and number required by society was being felt. To meet the requirement, it was felt to introduce such vocational courses in the curriculum which could make students self-dependent and self employed. Need to introduce more and more skill based programmes was mentioned in the new or in revised National Educational Policy.

It was found that in all parts of the country, educational structure of 10+2+3 was being accepted. In new educational policy, more importance was paid to the measures by which problem of children dropping out of the school could be sort out. It was also attempted to adopt an array of meticulously formulated strategies which were based on micro planning and could be applied at fundamental level all over the nation which could ensure retention of students at schools. Proper co-operation of non formal education would be taken for this purpose.

Provision of providing five years of schooling to all the children in the age group of eleven was also made in the policy. For achievement of this goal, provision of launching a national mission was made clearly in the policy. Need to include more vocational courses in the school curriculum at higher secondary level was felt and was being mentioned in the revised policy. Courses which were being offered in the curriculum should be reviewed properly and timely. To encourage diversification at the secondary level, it was made important for the government to review its recruitment policy.

Educational development should be provided an important place in scheme of national development and survival for which a large funds should be allocated for this purpose. Need to find out additional sources from where funds for the programmes laid down in the policy could be found, was mentioned in this policy. On the basis of monitoring and review, actual requirements should be computed from time to time, however, greater provision of utilising large portion of national income for promotion of education should be done.

Thus, while keeping needs and requirements of the nation, Indian Government keep on bringing about various kinds of modifications in the National Policy of Education. This function is performed by Ministry of Human Development and is being performed at an interval of five years, when five year plans are being announced by the government of India.

It is not an easy task to modify national policy of education, for which various kinds of investigations and analyses are required to be performed. However, the proportion of national income which is supposed to be expected for promotion and development of education has remained lower than mentioned in the policy, but still share invested for this purpose has increased in the past and now almost in every part of the nation, atleast one school has been set up, as a result of which, number of literate persons in the India has increased to a considerable extent by which our nation has got recognition in international society because an educational society is the perfect recognition of any nation's pride and identity.

PART-II
EDUCATION IN EMERGING INDIAN SOCIETY

1

SOCIETY AND EDUCATION

Introduction

Man forms a society, because he cannot do without it. When some persons come in contact with others, and for protecting their interests indulge in natural give and take, they form a society. A group of persons alone cannot be called a society. For a society it is necessary that its members feel a sense of unity and mutual relationship. When various persons of a community feels interested in each other and consider themselves bound with some feelings they bind themselves in a society.

There is no limit to the dimension of a society. Within its size there may be only two persons or all the persons of the entire world. Within a big society there may be several small units and a certain person may be a member of several societies. In the world society there are several nations, within a nation there are several nations, within the nation there are several provinces, within a province there are many cities, in a district several village, in cities several mohallas, associations, committees and many other social units.

A society has its own ideals. Every member considers his duty to safeguard them. The organisation of a society is such that its members may look after the social interests along with protecting their own individual personalities. A person being a medical doctor, an engineer, a teacher or a musician can observe the social ideals in his particular field of activity. The purpose of a society is quite comprehensive and permanent. It includes all the aspects of an individual's life.

Society Responsible for Education of the Child

There is a close relationship between society and individual. It is the individual who forms the society but he is all the time being influenced by society. After becoming a member of the society the individual becomes so much concerned with its ideals and traditions that if he happens to ignore any of them, he is concerned and regarded as immoral. Only that person is regarded as educated who is very well rooted in the social ideals of society. Family, school and State are different types of social institutions and all these leave undeniable imprints on the development of the child. The child learns many things unconsciously to his environment. So those responsible for the development of the child must try to organise the environment in such a manner that it does not adversely affect the child's development. Really speaking, it is our duty to make the child social.

But the process of his socialization should be such that the experiences no difficulty in the same. In some social system the State shoulders the entire responsibility of the growth of the child. This situation is particularly true of a communistic state. In a democratic set-up everyone tries to fulfill his duties regarding the child. In a democracy the various units of the society arrange for education of the child in their own particular sphere. But these units are responsible to the State for education of the child. In other words, in a way, even in a democracy the state undertakes the responsibility of child's education, but at the same time the society also cannot free itself from the same.

Definition of Society

Society is defined in various ways and the various definitions may be quite appropriate in their particular contexts. In this chapter by the term society we shall understand a group of individuals of a particular geographical entity which shares some common experiences and follow a certain culture. For the interest of all concerned this community recognise some institutions and some local unity. Some consciousness is always present in it . For the fulfillment of some social purpose this group works as a unit.

Individual and Society

The child is the future citizen of the society. Therefore, the welfare of the society rests on the proper education of the child. The society should shoulder this responsibility very sincerely. It should organise the environment in such a manner that the child can himself build up his personality in an ideal manner. In its attempt to make each individual social, sometimes, the society crosses its limits. Then it is seen that many persons come under the pressure of some old social traditions and customs. As a result, their growth is blocked. If under this situation someone crosses the social sanctions, he is given some punishment.

In our country many people are afraid of social boycott. So they do not dare to go against social sanctions. Adherence to social sanctions must not simply that one should not rise against social evils. If social evils are not eradicated the growth of society will be blocked. The social environment should remain so open that everyone feels free to reach his maximum development. It is for the interests of the individual and society both that they maintain mutual co-operation and adjustment and each regards the development of the other as its own development. Thus the individual and society are interdependent.

Some Educational Duties of the Society

In the modern days of democracy, it is very necessary to bring the school near the society. But at the same time it becomes imperative on the society to perform certain educational duties. These duties are related with the all-round development of the individual's personality. Thus each social institution in same way or other will act as a centre of education. Then in the general life of the individual the process of education will ever be on.

The society establishes the school in order to ensure the mental development of the child. Similarly, the society should be careful about the other sides of child development. It should open gymnasium, and provide playgrounds, parks, garden, and hospitals. The society must see that adequate provisions are made for distributing pure milk and other food articles and necessities of life at reasonable rates to all. Such as a provision is not be for children alone but for all- adult, old, men and women irrespective of their vocations.

The society should make arrangements for vocational education of children. If this is done everyone will be able to earn his living and the problem of unemployment will be solved in due course.

The society should see that every one is permitted to enjoy freedom of speech. Any idea or doctrine must not be imposed on anyone. Everyone should be made free to follow his own ideals of life as long as he does not interfere with the rights of others. For encouraging freedom of speech, reading rooms, libraries, radio and T.V. sets should be provided in order that people may become well informed about the various national and international happenings. Suitable arrangement should also be made by society for adult education. In fact, to educate the huger illiterate masses is a sacred educational duty of the society in our country.

The society should also look after the moral development of its citizens. It is on morality alone that the permanence of society exists. So attempts should made for the maintenance of discipline in society. Fostering of liberal attitude and spirit of co-operation, tolerance, dutifulness, politeness and patience are necessary for moral development of the society. Black-marketing and dishonesty on the part of some shopkeepers and businessmen prevail only when the society tolerates it. The state laws cannot eradicate these evils unless the society also comes forward and takes suitable measures to stop these vicious practices. So it is the responsibility of society to maintain a moral environment. If the society is able to perform these duties the individual will automatically get education for developing good character.

The society must keep its ideals very high in order that it may not fall. High ideals of society ensures honesty, dignity of labour, self-respect and self-reliance in its citizens.

It is the duty of society to promote aesthetic senses in children. This may be possible through education in fine arts, painting, vocal music and dancing. If an individual forms the habit of being aesthetic in all his activities, then he will not tolerate any filth in his home, village and society. Thus a healthy environment will be maintained in society and all will be happy.

Regarding religion, the society has a special duty. It must see that every citizen feels free to practise his faith without interfering with others beliefs. The society must teach its citizens that all religions are equal and based on love, sympathy and compassion. There should be no strives and dissensions in name of religion.

Co-operation between School and Society

The co-operation between the society and its various units is very necessary. If there is lack of co-operation between family and school and between society and school, no suitable environment for the child will be possible. The problem of co-operation between the society and school is not so complex as between the school and family. Sometimes the gulf between the school and family becomes so wide that the child has to fact two types of environments resulting into lack of harmony in his behaviour. Similarly, there should be no gulf between the school and society. The school has to serve the interests of society. In other words, the school should represent the society. It is in this sense that John Dewey has remarked that the school is a society. In the activities of the school the shape of the society should be clearly seen.

School cannot be separated from society, because the school is a necessary organ for the development of society. The students and teachers are members of the society and through their personalities they bring to school various social problems. The parents also bring pressure on the school through their demand expectations. Even then there appears to be a gulf between the school and society, because the environment of the school has become artificial. Whatever is done in the school does not appear to be related with the demands of society.

So after completing his education, an individual is facing unemployment and cannot stand on his own legs. By bringing the school near the society, self-confidence and self-reliance may be created in the individual. Therefore the school must be related to the social demands. It has been suggested by some educationists that parents should be invited to participate in school functions and they should be made conversant with the various activities of the school. Sometimes the teachers should visit homes of students and should talk to parents about their children's difficulties. By these measures the parents will feel that the school is paying due respects to them and it is sincerely interested in the growth of their children. The experts in the field of education have also stated that the teacher should take the responsibility of cultural development of the nearby society. For this the teachers should organise some appropriate activities in the society. Thus the school will be influencing the society in a healthy manner, and in a way it will become a centre of social life.

Socialisation of the Child

The sole purpose of education is to soicialise the child. The family is the first school of the child for this purpose. Then come the neighbours and companions. The child learns many modes of behaviour consciously and unconsciously through imitation of his elders and companions. So the elders and others who come in contact with the child must be very careful in their behaviour. Their behaviour should be ideal before children. When the child starts going to school, he faces a new world and revolutionary changes occur in his behaviour. He regards the teacher as his ideal. So the teacher must present himself as an ideal individual before him. It is through socialization that the child picks up the social ideals, traditions and customers to be followed in order to win the approval of his elders. Needless to say society and its various units have to play a very important role in the socialization of the child.

Steps to be Taken for Co-operation between the Society and the School

From the above discussion it is quite clear that for the healthy development of the child co-operation between the society and school is very necessary. The society must take keen interest in the activities of the school. The school is fulfilling only some essential functions of the society. Therefore the society and its various units must always be prepared to help the school whenever necessary. The parents must never doubt the sincerity of the school and they must never interfere in its activities. They should provide all that the school demands for the education of their wards.

It is not possible for any society to provide opportunities for the development of all. Hence mutual co-operation between the society and various schools is very necessary. The schools of urban or rural areas should sever as social centres for education and recreation of adults. In the social centres local problems of industries and general occupations may be discussed for finding out acceptable solutions.

We should keep in mind the following points for establishing a close relationship between society and school-

1. The curriculum should be so flexible that changes may be introduced in it according to the needs of various individuals.

2. It is just possible that everything cannot be taught through the school programme. So the students should be given a list of literature in order that they learn something on their own.

3. Each one should be given the knowledge of reading, writing and arithmetic.

4. The students should be given all facilities to form their own programmes.

5. It will not be useful to teach everything. The children should be acquainted with only some local experiences. Then alone they will learn something useful.

6. The society should be the starting point in any aspect of the curriculum.

7. The services of all available social institutions in the state should be utilized as far as possible.

8. Community resources should be found out. The teachers should try to find the numbers of workers engaged in the local agricultural fields, factories, shops, gardens and laboratories.

9. The needs of the local people should be as ascertained. As far as possible, the school should try to meet them.

2

EDUCATION AS AN INSTRUMENT OF SOCIAL CHANGE

Introduction

Education is one of the most complex of all social institutions. Its complexity increases as the social change becomes more complex and variegated. Few of man's social institutions are more sensitive and responsive to the society than education. Hence, the slightest change in the sociological forces outside would call for an adequate adjustment on in the part of the education. This may be considered as social determinism in the field of education.

What goes on in the world generally and in a particulars country specifically affects its public education, change in the form of government leading to significant changes in the economic and social structures of the country, welfare demands of the various social and religious groups, cultural reorientations, peoples aspirations etc., there can be numerous sociological forces and trends which may influence the organisation and processes of education. Contrarily, education may also modify socio-cultural conditions of the society.

The process of education does not go in a vacuum; it occurs in a society which is above with all kinds of its peculiarities, problems and process. All these constitute sociological basis of education. Education is basically the product of the society and a reflection of that which the society genuinely desires to have. The whole of the educational process is shaped by the culture, the groups it serves, the family and the values of the people in general. No educational enterprise can operate completely out of touch with the social set up in which it is installed.

While many functions of the school are dictated by the social structure, the school in turn helps to determine the nature of the social structure and to help individuals to relate themselves to that structure in the most positive way possible. The community as a whole provide the climate for education. Its educational level, occupational pattern, population composition, social tempo and economic conditions, all determine the shape and process of its education. In turn all these factors too are determined by the educational programme the community happens to have. Education can never he deaf to the voice of the society, and at the same time should never be quite when the direction and the future of the society which supports it are being determined.

Meaning

Derived from Latin schools, meaning leisure, school is an organisation that provides necessary opportunities for self-development and self-sufficiency to its wards over a prolonged period. It is the centre of social development and change, and is the most powerful instrument to mould and prepare future citizens to suit designated socio-political designs. As individuality develops in a social environment where it can feed on common interests and activities, the educational process needs socialisation, in accordance with the nature of society in which it takes place. School, therefore, is a social system presenting an epitome study by diversification of social life.

Comments

School, or education, is a means of socialisation and social control that brings the individual and society closer in a spirit of mutual need, respect and fulfillment. Socialisation is central to this process as it makes one fit for social living within a prescribed framework, wherein any change has to be mutually acceptable and desirable, affecting abilities, attitudes, adjustment, all summed up as social effectiveness of education, so very vital for affecting change.

Educational Sociology

The close interrelation of education and society led to the emergence of new concept- educational sociology. Educational sociology is the study of the inter-relation of education and social institutions, working in a close proximity for mutual development and satisfaction. Society fixes the norms, targets and aims of education in consistence with its socio-economic, political and cultural heritage and aspirations, whereas school works out ways and means to fulfil and achieve these ideals to the best of the satisfaction of the society. The feedback loop helps to evaluate this inter-relation.

The proximity of the outcomes of the aims would justify the functional performance of the school. Any major deviation will have to be mutually sorted out or, augmented. However, the school being a more active agent has more positive influence in this process, and is, therefore, considered central to any change in society.

It is one single instrument of social change that mirrors and manifests, controls and directs any such measures that the society may prescribe in the process of its evolution and growth.

Social Process

Education is not merely a process but is a social process encouraging and envisaging interaction amongst children and their environment, eventually leading to socialisation of the child. As a matter of fact, education is socialisation. In the absence of the joint family system, this responsibility devolves upon school, socialisation is always in a group, and the school provides this facility, as group life is a psycho-social life.

Education as an social process may help eliminate social aberrations, and perpetuate desirable institutions, group activities, and attain for society the ideals and standards that it aims to achieve. Social process should be conducive for attainment of social objectives, aims and goals.

Social Structure

Social structure consists of-

1. Power Structure - It refers to pressure groups and various centres where power actually resides. Fears of powers structure may lead to nationalisation of education. In India, education was initially restricted as a function of a state government, but now is upgraded to the Concurrent list where the respective state governments and the central government assume its functions and responsibility, suggesting centres of power. Social structure, therefore, forms the basic structure of society and all socialisation revolves around it.

2. Social Status - It consists of education for masses, heterogeneity of student population, child's social status and school administration.

3. Cultural Structure - It is based on religion, region and topographically exclusive races.

4. Social Stratification and Social Hierarchy - It is based on caste, social classification, residence, constitutional, occupational, social hierarchy and cultural environment.

Social Control

School exercise social control by performing the following functions-

1. Critical - School is both creature and creator of society. It keeps an eye on the desirability and acceptance of such social norms thrown up form time to time, and takes on overall critical overview. These measures and means of control may be direct or indirect, suggestive or prescriptive, but are definitely normative in nature.

2. Creative - Evolving a new social setup is not merely adjustment and adaptation but needs of vital creative force for pushing back areas of social injustice and for building a new social infrastructure. Education helps break new grounds to open up new vistas, horizons and frontiers- provide a new vision in an overall national outlook and work-culture.

3. Conservative- Social control is not merely a question of adopting man to a certain given level of development but of producing individuals capable of developing of the existing form of society beyond itself to a further stage. Conservative function is essential as it prevents discarding of the old order for simply being

old. It retains values and ideas on merit and efficacy.

Social Change

Social changes imply changes in the social structure and in the functions of its various units. It consists of shaping of new functions and emergence of new values and systems. Breaking of joint family system, urbanisation, mechanisation and such other changes in socio-economic patterns cause corresponding changes in social functions. Similarly, advancement in technical culture affecting the leisure and pleasure principle, supersede old values had give birth to new order. Social changes indicate the growth and development of a social system, and represent the growing needs and aspirations of a people. It is the most operative component of socialisation.

Education and Social Change

Social changes are the changes that occur in various components of socialisation above for whatever reasons and circumstances. We have also observed that social change is the most operative aspect of the society.

Definition

Social change is a term use to describe variation in or modification of any aspects of social processes, social interactions or social organizations, and are variations from accepted modes of life existing in a society from time to time. Society is dynamic, it grows and it grows through social change caused by various circumstances and reasons over a period of time. Social change is in fact, a variation in perception between generations separated by time and space. But, does it not make social change as good as cultural change? Are social changes and cultural changes not integrally related? In short could there be any social change without corresponding culture change, and vice versa?

Determinants of Social Change

We have already made passing reference in a proceeding section to some of the factors that influence and cause social change. These are called the determinants of social changes and are structural in nature as they may effect the social structure of a setup. These are-

1. Inter-dynamics.
2. Scientific and Technological Advancement.
3. Physical Environment.

Concept of Social Change

According to Brown, there is no difference between social change and culture change, the latter being more operative and instrumental within the process. Ogburn shares the same views, any distinction between social change and culture change. He, however, denominates two forms of culture- material and non-material. Materiel culture generally refers to civilisation and to such items that man has created for his comfort, efficacy and happiness, causing structural changes in the social system. Non-material culture refers to ideas, attitudes, values, habits, customary with each other to avoid any social imbalances.

According to Spencer, social change and social evolution are identical, prompted by the painful to comfortable. He, therefore, also falls in line with Brown and Orburn. Lister Ward, however, vies it differently, as he considers social change related to changes in social aims and aspirations- mechanical, and related to individual according to this own perception of aims and objectives.

Comments

According to Orburn, social change first occurs in the material culture and then in the non-material culture. But Ottaways holds that these culture changes do not take place one after the other, but it is product of the inter-dynamics of the two Ottaways has clearly stated that social or cultural change occurs because of the interaction of technological researches or scientific inventions and the ideals, values and aims of society. In other words, social change occurs through the interaction of technological techniques and social values. Both the elements are essential. Anyone of them without the other will not bring about any social change. As these factors namely technology, techniques and values play an essential role in any social change, it is necessary to understand the meaning and significance of these words. Technology is that branch of science which develops various techniques. Techniques are the means which fulfil various basic needs of human beings in a society. In the end values are those objectives; beliefs, thoughts and abstract concepts which make human life dynamic, successful and purposeful.

It may, therefore, be observed that neither technological advancements alone nor the values in themselves bring about any real social change. It can also be not determined definitely that which one of he above two has a greater share in achieving social change. In fact when technology changes, it effects change in values and when values change, they bring out the corresponding change in technology. In this way technological advancements as well as values are both the essential basis of social change. Both are equally important and essential. Both actively interact and bring about social change.

Educational and Social Change

1. Inculcates spirit of reform and social welfare to conceptualise and promote change.

2. Increases depth and variety of knowledge to appreciate change.

3. Prepares enlightened public opinion by removing the resisting factors and obstacles to social change.

4. Spreads the message by word of mouth, print and electronic media.

5. Helps maintain human and social relation by keeping the structural equation and balance.

6. Promotes unity and total integration which fosters social change at a mass scale.

7. Education is a means of conserving and transmitting culture from generation to generation facilitating social changes at appropriate time.

8. Prepare ground for social change by generating public opinion.

9. Education determines the desirability and efficacy of the social changes by continuous and critical evaluation.

10. Helps understand and accept the emerging social change smoothly and willingly.

11. Education helps perpetualise, stabilise and consolidate some eternal values by many of its programmes and application thus inculcating faith in social change.

Factors Resisting Social Change

The following factors resist social change-

1. Degree of Isolation - Some sections of society remain isolated and insulated, with hardly any outside contacts with progressive groups, and deny themselves the benefits of social change.

2. Vested Interests - These interests suit a privileged

section of the society who are powerful and influential to toward any change.

3. Fear of the New - People stick to traditional routine life for fear of the new elements that may turn harmful and injurious. Believing in status quo, such people are contented with the existing socio-economic order.

4. Cultural Inertia - Cultural inertia refers to such blind beliefs, superstitions, customs, taboos, traditions, etc. which are passed down form generation to generation, and are considered sacred and inviolable.

Social Factors Determining Educational Policy

Generally education leads to social change but at times social changes also determine

3

EDUCATION AND IDEALISM

Introduction

Over against the philosophy of progressive education, with its main props in pragmatism, reconstructionism, and romantic naturalism, stands that of essentialism or traditionalism. In the midst of the welter of change and diversity the essentialists believe that there are some points of the educational compass which are more or less fixed. Life is not all that fickle and lucid, it has substance and permanence which act as the needle of the compass and gives direction, stability and significance. Essentialism has several philosophical props, one of the principle being Indianalism. Accredited with high regard for individuality and freedom in education, its activity programmes are voluntaristic and development, and there is a measure of absolutism in the idealistic philosophy of education that brings it closer to the essentialists. Absolute is essential, remains constant in the midst of the welter of change, and should, therefore, be the object of meaningful educative process or activity. What is the nature and extent of the absolute may have to be understood and resolved in advance. According to Rusk, Idealism contends that the material and physical universe known to science is an incomplete expression of reality, that it exits but to sub-serve, and requires to compliment it a higher type of reality, a spiritual universe. In this manner, idealism is an advancement over realism by giving it a higher type of reality, over and above the plane of subservience and convenience it is essential and is for its own sake.

Definition

According to Brubacher, idealists point out that it is mine that is central to understanding the world nothing gives a greater sense of reality than the activity of mind engaged in trying to comprehend its world.

Idealistic philosophy takes many and varied forms, but the postulate underlying all this is the mind or spirit is the essential world-stuff, that the true reality is of a mental character. This is in direct contrast with the materialists who consider matter to be the stuff of which the external world is made.

Idealistic educational philosophy refers to a branch of thought which considers the ultimate reality as idealistic, hence mental and spiritual in character wherein the ultimate reality is not only monistic and absolute, unchanging and eternal, infinite and limitless, but also inherently essential and conscious. Hence, it is the essential and the absolute that should constitute education of a child. Idealism, therefore, considers are ultimate, fixed and eternal values and, unfoldment of a child in accordance therewith.

As man is the embodiment of the Real, a lot of attention is focussed in idealism on the status of man as he could not be considered the creature of his environment in the sense in which that term is applied to any other animal men emerges in the course of evolution he sets about to question, to inquire and to strive after something better than the given. Idealistic philosophy of education, therefore, considers human personality of supreme value and constituting the noblest work of God.

Chief Exponents

A long chain of great leaders of mind find its culmination in the wide delta of idealism where names such as Socrates, Plato, Descartes, Spinoza, Berkeley, Kant, Hegel, Richte, Schelling, Schopenhave, Gentle and other amongst the westerners and a host of India thinkers finding inspiration form the Vedas and the Upanishads, shine like bright stars in a dark sky cutting across the barriers of space and time, region and religion, obsessed and possessed by a common bond of spiritualism.

Essential Features

1. Life is essentially spiritual.

2. Ability of man to control and manipulate the physical environment through his spiritual, cultural and moral possessions.

3. Ideals do not happen, they exist, i.e. ideals are not the outcome of experience but are its very condition and man simply discovers them.

4. As man is supreme, education should aim at study of mind.

5. Higher rating to moral and cultural endowments.

6. Ultimate aim is to achieve the three absolute values- Truth, Beauty and Goodness, which, in fact, are the comminution of the three domains for mind-cognitive, affective and, conative.

7. Realisation of higher values of life.

8. Spirit and intellect take precedence over physical matter.

9. Emancipation of spirit, as reality is spiritual and man is its manifestation.

10. Ideas are ultimate cosmic significance.

Bearing on Education

If the ideas conditioning the very pattern of the world in which the child lives are in fixed and final form, they must necessarily constitute the essentials of his education. Hence, the aim of education should over around total development of a child's spiritual nature which is universal, unchanging and eternal admitting, of course, the individual differences. As such, the idea or ideal toward which his mind matures must potentially exist within the child before he starts to learn. Education therefore, should be unfolding of what is already in child, is bringing out and not pouring in, and should make definite what formerly was inchoate. As man is a spark of the divine, education should help him achieve that wherein its objective is to strive to realize itself, to become what is was meant to be.

1. Character building and development of versatile interests.

2. Develop Intelligences and Rationality - There is purpose in the natural phenomena. Education should help one understand this purpose and help man manipulate and recognise experience. A highly developed mind and intelligence can perceive and understand this all-pervading force. In all things there reigns an eternal law an eternal unity, God. Education should lead and guide man to face with nature and to unite with God.

3. Preparation for Holy Life - Education should create conducive environment and situations in which one

may be able to concentrate on spiritual development and self-realisation. The object of education is the realization of a faithful, pure, inviolable and hence, holy life.

4. Sublimation of Innate Nature - The emphasis one ideals should not be the cost of man's innate nature which should be developed and sublimated into spiritual qualities and values. There should not be any repression and suppression in this regard.

5. Cultural Heritage - Education performs a three-fold function in conserving, promoting and transmitting cultural heritage of a people. As such, education should acquaint children with cultural values and national heritage.

6. Truth, Beauty, Goodness - The educative process should be so designed that it helps one in realisation of the ultimate values of life by developing his moral and spiritual aspects.

7. Health and Fitness - The aspect of physical health and fitness of body receives due attention in idealistic education for without such health and fitness the pursuit of spiritual values is seriously handicapped.

8. Spiritual Development - Adam interpreted idealism in the form that universe is nothing more than a though process- it is rational, cosmos rather than chaos. As such, attainment of rationality in universe should be the aim of education and should enable mankind through its culture to enter more and more fully into the spiritual realm, and also enlarge the boundaries of spiritual realm.

9. Self-realisation - Therefore, is the ultimate aim of idealistic education. According to Ross the aim of education specially associated with idealism is the

exhalation of personality, or self-realization, making actual or real the highest potentialities of the self.

Meaning of Idealism

Both out of Plato's theory of ideas, wherein ideas are of ultimate cosmic significance, but they are not merely mental states as suggested by the term idea. In fact, they are the archetypes that gives form to the cosmos, and are the immaterial moulds into which all matter is cast. In the matter-mind/content from controversy, idealism upholds the supremacy of ideas which act as ideals whereby acts of the senses, which concern matter, are judged.

They are the standards- eternal and unchanging, which give form to the content presented by senses. Accepting the matter-content and mind-form equation, idealism gives credence to mind-form for its durability and universality. According to Ross, 'idealistic philosophy takes many and varied forms, but the postulate underlying all is that mind or spirit is the essential world-stuff, that the true reality is of mental character. If reality is mental, could man be far being in the race for top honours because of his inherent intellectual endowments, sense of discrimination and facility of manipulation of situations, circumstances and environment thus giving him an edge over the physical, and a peep into the spiritual and is an account of man finding himself as an integral part of a universe of mind.

Deduction of Fundamental Principles

The following fundamental principles of idealism may be deduced from the above-

1. Unity in Diversity - Idealism reduces all diversities into divine consciousness which imparts

spirituality of all natural entities, howsoever different they all may seem to be. The Ultimate of this process is the fulfillment of man in universal consciousness, and is called self-realisation. All diversities of body-mind and matter-from get resolved in the Divinity of God.

2. Importance of Personality Development - We had discussed somewhere that aims and goals of education would differ with the meaning and significance one ascribes to self. Idealism considers man to be spiritual and as a manifestation of the divine. Man, therefore, should develop toward perfection of his true self which consists in approximation to the ultimate. Not only that, self-realisation is possible in a social context. As such, man should develop qualities of head and heart, such as love, sympathy, mutual well-being, cooperation and goodwill toward one and all. This emphasis on total development of man is characteristic of idealism. The grandeur of worth of human at its best are emphasised by idealism. Human personality is of supreme value and constitutes the noblest work of God.

3. Faith in Spiritual Values - Spirituality is an essence of divinity. Man, therefore, has a spark of divinity in him. Education should, therefore, help harness and realise the totality of mind on his way of self-realisation. Goodness, truth and beauty are seen to be absolutes, each existing in its own right and entirely desirable in itself. However, that beauty and truth could exist harmoniously without goodness is as debatable as existence of goodness without truth and beauty- the three are integrally related, so that what is beautiful is inherently true and good, and vice versa. Idealism is marked by its faith in primordial values which are spiritual.

4. Man Over Nature - Idealism considers man superior to nature as he has intellectual prowess to manipulate and control nature to his advantage. Man is not limited to experience alone but has ability to reorganize and recreate nature in order to create his own world of virtue and value. Spirituality is not a derivative of the physical, and Rusk rightly says that the spiritual or cultural environment is an environment of man's own making- it is a product of man's creative activity.

5. Ideas More Important - Ideas are ultimate whereas material objects are ephemeral. In fact, all objects of material world are embedded in ideas. Ideas are of the ultimate cosmic significance are rather the essence which gives form to cosmos are eternal and unchanging.

6. Two Forms of Existence - Idealism believes in two forms of existence, spiritual and material. Nevertheless, it gives precedence to spiritual world which is real and ultimate and wherein the material world is transitory and finite. According to Horne, "idealism holds that the order of the world is due to the manifestation, in space and time, of an eternal and spiritual reality and we would have never found it there if the nature of mind had not pre-imposed it is the very act of knowing it.

Herbart and Curriculum

Method

Idealism did not cut much ice with methodology of teaching-learning. As such, it sticks to the old traditional and formal method of teaching which is generally verbose. Whereas idealism has fixed, specific and definite aims of education, as well as the corresponding curriculum, it does not have a definite method of teaching. Everything is fixed. It only has to be transmitted in a manner conceived best by respective thinkers except that an authoritative approach to teaching-learning is central as idealism considers classrooms as temples of learning wherein learning is intrinsic and not instrumental. Teaching-learning, therefore, is a formal, intellectual and autocratic pursuit wherein teacher and content take supremacy over the child. Teaching methods as advocated by some of the idealists are as under-

Teacher

A teacher should be a role model inspiring pupils to cultivate values in life. He should be morally high, intellectually developed, and culturally advanced, and be an impeccable source of inspiration. According to Ross, "the education constitutes the special environmental factor whose function is to lead the child nearer reality, and to guide him towards his outmost possible perfection.

Discipline

Freedom is the soul of discipline wherein both should live in harmony. Education, therefore, should lead to freedom but this freedom should be curtailed and restrained- it should not be licence, and should be an attitude of mind wherein a child is disciplined internally and not through extraneous means and consideration, Freedom, therefore, should guide and help in cultivating a disciplined mind engaged in the pursuit of the three highest values of life. Idealism believes in impressionistic discipline wherein teacher should be king and sympathetic.

Broad Division of Educational Content and Process

1. Plato distinguishes between the world of intellect and the world of senses, the world views which are qualitatively different. Intellect further is of two kinds, reason and understanding; Of these, he considers reasons as of a higher kind for its purity of ideas and dialectic methodology. Understanding is the kind of intellect which is applied it is inferior to reason in that it uses hypotheses which it can not test. Hence, not self-sufficient, whereas reason in all its purity and extent is based on the laws of self-sufficiency. Even Kant and Hegal rated it higher tan senses and understanding which operate at the level of empirical reality and creates objects out of Nature or, in fact, creates Natures hence having limited use and import.

2. Philosophy for Plato is a king of vision, the vision of truth. It is not purely intellectual and it is not mere wisdom- it is love of wisdom.

3. Plato's philosophy rests on the distinction between really and appearances, with a religious overtone. He was an idealist giving his own theory of ideas which went for depth and gravity. According to him, "opinion is of the world presented to the senses, whereas knowledge is of super-sensible eternal world,"] with fixed ideas and concepts. Idealism is a special gift of Plato to mankind.

4. Education is divided in Two Parts -

a. Music, which means everything in the field of muses, fine arts, literature, general information about natural and social sciences, etc. culminating in culturised man.

b. Gymnastics, mans everything concerned with physical training and fitness, generally called athletic. So, Plato believed in a healthy mind in a healthy body and aimed at cultivating gravity, decorum and courage through his educative process, with strict control on the type of information/experience that the young may have access to in the early years.

Plato drew the line to only what was authorised. There was no poetry in his educational regimen hence no Homer and Hesiod for their poor portrayal of gods at times behaving in an unbecoming manner contrary to the general belief in their eternal goodness. God is the author of only good things and this position cannot be compromised under any amount of stress and emotion. Secondly, there should be no fear of death as sometimes suggested by Homer and Hesiod. Plato considered death as the reward of the brave. Thirdly, Plato lays stress on decorum and propriety. Any reference to or mention to the contrary is viewed as unbecoming of a gentlemen. Fourthly, moderation in behaviour and conduct is the key to social grace, creating a desirable moral environment wherein lust, greed and cowardice have no place. The young one should see no ugliness or vice, but may be exposed to enchantments, both in the shape of terror that must not terrify and of bad pleasures that must not reduce the will. How tough and demanding rituals that one had to quality before designated as gentlemen.

Thus, the two divisions of education in Plato produced men with clarity and depth of perception and thought and nerves of steel and courage.

Plato

According to Rusk, "it is to Greek thought that we turn when we wish to consider any of the problems of ethics, education or politics, Greek thought has in addition to its originality, a surprising universality. Plato was the foremost of the Greek philosophers and educationists, so much so, that even Rousseau said that, "if you wish to know what is meant by public education, read Plato's Republic. It is the finest treatise on education ever written. What a tribute!! Plato and Aristotle were the two most influential of all western philosophers, ancient, medieval, or modern; and of the two, it was Plato who had the greater effect upon subsequent ages. I say it for two reasons; first, that Aristotle himself is an outcome of Plato; second that Christian theology and philosophy was much more Platonic that Aristotelian. In Plato's Utopia, "the first thing to be considered is education divided in two parts, each having a wider meaning than at present, and aiming at turning men into gentlemen as understood in high society today, all over the world.

Curriculum

1. Philosophy - Plato gave maximum importance to the study of philosophy for total comprehension of truth in all its forms. He was, as such, a rationalist. He, however, based study of philosophy on diathetic, and knowledge of other natural and physical sciences.

2. Curriculum for Higher Education - For the education of higher classes Plato has prescribed higher Mathematics, Geometry, Mathematical Music, Astronomy, Philosophy etc. Plato has praised Mathematics a lot. He has also showered a lot of praises on those who are good at Mathematics. After Philosophy, it is the Mathematics that he considers most important. He has himself said, "Have you further observed that those who have natural talent for calculation are generally quick at every other kind of knowledge and avoid delay if they have had Arithmetical training

although they may derive no other advantage from it always become quicker than they would otherwise have been".

Similarly, he has praised Geometry when he says, "In all departments of knowledge an experience proves, anyone who has studied Geometry is infinitely quicker of apprehension than one who has not. Plato has prescribed teaching of Astronomy for the farmers, sailors, and he has also suggested teaching of Mathematical music for them, perhaps, from the point of view of their utility in life.

3. Teaching of Mathematics and Geometry -Plato has also prescribed for the teaching of Mathematics and Geometry for early education. He believes that the teaching of these subjects leads to exactness in the children. He also suggested teaching of those subjects that lead to the formation of the background of philosophy. He had also suggested timely examinations in order to test the knowledge acquired by the children.

4. Music and Physical Training - During infancy or early years of childhood, Plato has suggested that music and physical training must be taught. He was of the view that education should begin with music and then should come the physical training. This will lead to harmonious development of the body as well as soul. He has himself said, "and, therefore, music training is a more potent instrument than any other, because rhythm and harmony find their way into the inward places of the soul, on which they rightly fasten imparting grace.

An regards the physical training, he remarked, "Now my belief is not that the good body by any bodily existence improves the soul, but on the contrary that the good soul by her own excellence improves the body as far as this may be possible.

5. Plato rejects that perception is knowledge. He unlike Socrates, says that we receive knowledge through sense organs rather than with them, and further, that some of our knowledge is not even connected with any sense organ, as mind "contemplates some things through its own instrumentality, other through its bodily faculties. We experience hard and soft through touch, but it is the mind that judges that they exist and that they are contraries. Knowledge transcends perception, and consists in reflection. Here again he is emphasizing the element of purity is knowledge to determine its origin, nature and extent, as later advocated by kant when he spoke of empirical and pure knowledge, giving almost similar examples of number at both levels. Number is pure and a priori, but is known only through perception of things around, such as ten fingers. Number, as such are eternal, immutable, but at the same time are logical fictions, and can be known only through experience.

Contribution of Plato to the Field of Education

1. Plato was one of the greatest Greeks who really understood the requirements of human body and soul. He understood the importance of education as well as Philosophy and presented if before the world in a very skilful and nice manner. It was this exposition that forced Rousseau to remark, if you wish to know what is meant by public education, read Plato's Republic it is the finest treatise on education ever written.

2. He believed in the balanced and proper development of the personality and has, therefore, prescribed for the educational of the body as well as soul. In this regard, he has given a psychological foundation

to education which is considered important even today. He gave importance to the study of philosophy as well as Mathematics. He also prescribed for the teaching of moral values and religious concepts. He thought that these things would bring about the development of virtues in man.

If men are virtuous they create a virtuous society free form evils. According to him, preparation of ideal citizens is the real aim of education. The aim is still very valuable for all such countries that are wedded to democracy and democratic way of life. To create love for the absolute truth and democratic way of life. To create love for absolute truth, beauty and goodness was also an aim of his education. He had this aim in view because he thought that this love can bring about the development of the social faculties of the child.

3. Plato was one of the greatest philosophers of democracy and he has propounded democracy in its best form. He also believed that the government of the people, for the people, and by the people in the best government. This government can be successful only when the citizens are well equipped to live up the standard of democracy. They should be guided by reasons and have a balanced personality. According to Plato, democracy should provide equal opportunities but he also believed that the government should and abilities but he also believed that the government should be run by better people. He did not believe that four heads, even if they are dull, can surpass one head of a philosopher.

Views of Education

According to Plato, 'education consists of giving to the body and the souls all the perfection of which they are susceptible. Plato, therefore, is a perfectionist and views education to perform this function. It, therefore, has the following aims-

1. Self-realisation.

2. Inculcate feeling of appreciation for beauty, which is one of the eternal aims of life.

3. Provide vision of truth which is one of the absolutes the other two being beauty and goodness. Plato, in this sense is an absolutist and an essentialist.

4. Development of body as well as soul- advocates the concept of healthy mind in a healthy body.

5. Inculcating the idea of good citizenship and virtues.

Socrates

Socrates was born at Athens in Greece in 469 B.C. His parents were very poor. His mother was a nurse and father was sculptor. Socrates could not receive systematic education. He learnt reading and writing and could not receive education in music which was taught to most of Greek boys during those days. He was not interested in father's vocation and he had to travel beyond Athens thrice as he was in the army of Athens. Thereafter he started teaching. He was not attached with any school. He wandered and taught.

Socrates used to put questions, problems to the youth on public places and when they were unable to answer his questions, he himself told them. He put series of questions and generally youth were found to be perplexed over the questions. He put several auxiliary questions to the main question. This way he held the discussions on various issues.

Sophists made man the centre of philosophical

equity. Socrates was also having the same view. But he emphasized moral questions more. He concentrated on universals instead of particulars. Socrates was father of concepts.

Socrates based the questions of good on intellect. To him Knowledge is Virtue. This knowledge can be achieved through knowing oneself. So he said Know Thyself. To him the outer beauty was not enough. He paid attention to the beauty of soul.

According to Socrates, the aim of education is the attainment of knowledge. The virtuous of life is impossible in ignorance of virtue. Socratic Method of Teaching is a kind of dialogue with the students and teachers. Teachers puts questions and students answer them. Again the teacher puts another question and the student answers it. This process goes on continuously. This Socratic method is based on serosity, activity and students participation. It is a psychological method of teaching. The progress gave birth to Inductive Method. The impact of Socrates on educational theory and practice is felt even now-a-days.

Merits

1. By encouraging impressionistic discipline, idealism makes a child realise the nature, need and meaning of self-discipline in the process of self-advancement wherein discipline is intrinsic and internal and very much integral to self-actualisation as virtues and values are perceived by a disciplined mind only. Discipline, therefore, is a means of self-control and self-development.

2. By encouraging personality development of a child, idealism shows difference toward his individuality and stimulates his creativity and appreciation.

Universality of educative process is subject to one's individual interest, ability, aptitude, needs and aspirations.

3. Teacher acts as an inspiring role model by his kind, sympathetic and encouraging behaviour and leads and guides the child through the maze and instricacies of self-development. He is not a bye-stander but is fully involved with and seized of his responsibility toward his wards in the process of their overall growth and development.

4. Aims at universal education in order to help self-realisation which is by one's own efforts and diligence.

5. Pursuit of the ultimate, eternal and universal values of Truth, Beauty of Good will help one inculcate the best in him both morally and spiritually, in fact, the total development of all the domains of mind.

6. Indialism makes a salutary contribution toward the aims of education by giving an exhaustive account and description of what education should help an child achieve in the process of his overall development.

Limitations

1. Reduces science subjects to a secondary level in tis curriculum.

2. Formal and stereotyped methods of teaching laying more emphasis on rote and cramming./

3. The focus of attention shifts to the teacher curriculum who becomes more central to the educative process, whereas child psychology stresses that the educative process should be child centre keeping in conformity with his needs, interests and capabilities.

4. The concept of immortal values may be a dent

into individual freedom and enterprise wherein one may evolve one's own sets of values depending on experience, needs and social interaction.

5. More emphasis on intellectual development and strengths;.

6. Avoids the realities, troubles of the day top day living, whereas education should make one capable to solve problems and thereby live a happy and contended life.

7. It is a abstract and vague doctrine laying more emphasis on preparation for the next world rather than for the world here and now.

Comments

The limitations mentioned above are not the demerits but reflect only the inadequacies of the doctrine which takes a side look at the educative process which points forward to the absolute rather than the mundane, howsoever relevant and useful it might be.

By emphasizing the eternal and unchanging laws of nature, accepting a purpose behind all creation and by highlighting the innate and inborn capacities of man, idealism makes man the centre of existence wherein he moves toward self-actualisation and seeks his identify with the ultimate by sheer dint of his own irritative, effort and diligence at home, school and in society. It runs counter to blatant greed and material outlook and zeroes on the ideal and spiritual nature, needs and essence of man. Man is divine; man is power. These power and their products are peculiar to man, and differentiate him from other animals; they lie beyond the range of the positive sciences and raise problems which only philosophy can hope to solve, and make it the only satisfactory basis of education.

4

COMMUNICATION IN EDUCATIONAL ADMINISTRATION

Introduction

Communication can be considered as a personal process that involves the transfer of information and some behavioural input. Communication is something people do. It does not exist without people taking some form of action. It has all to do with relationships between people and can be complex or simple; formal or informal, depending on the nature of the message to be passed, and on the relationship between the sender and the receiver.

It consists of the transfer of information and understanding between parts and people in an organisation, and the various modes and media involved in communication interchanges. Effective communication, therefore, is critical to the success of an organisation.

Some of the common answers to the question of why communicate/ are as follows:

1. It helps people to understand the need for change- how they should manage it; how to reduce resistance to change.

2. It makes the better relationship and understanding between boss and subordinate; amongst colleagues; and among people within the organisation

and outside it.

3. It gets people involved with the organisation and increases motivation to perform well; increases commitment to the organisation.

4. It keeps people in the picture.

5. It leads to greater effectiveness.

There also needs to be a clear massage, which must be understood by the recipient. A headmaster might say to a teacher : Well, I wonder if you'd like to look at your style of teaching, it's a bit more complex. This is rather ambiguous, but if he were to say, Mr. Janardhan, your style of teaching needs improvement in the field of eliciting examples and illustrations, then there would be no doubt in the teacher's mind what his superior means.

Interpersonal Communication

The word communication is not easy to define. One way of looking at it is as an interpersonal process of sending and receiving symbols with meanings attached to them. It is therefore supposed to results in the exchange of information and shared understanding between people. So a measure of the effective management of interpersonal communication is that information is passed, and relationship are built.

The success of information passing depends very much on the nature and quality of the information received which in turn depends on the nature and quality of the relationship between the persons involved. People tend to experience personal satisfaction when communicating and interacting with friends, relatives and others they know well, in fact, with people with whom they feel comfortable. They do not feel the need to be guarded because of the smooth way they manage their relationships with each other.

They can speak openly and honestly, and joke about serious matters. Personal abuse is a form of comradeship. But the headmaster frequently have to work with others with whom they have not developed close relationships in order to achieve organisational and educational objectives. Misunderstandings may occur, leading to disagreement and conflict, or often the avoidance of conflict and the development of mistrust. Out of this can develop lack of cooperation and an unhealthy work climate. People are polite to each other, and apparently genuinely cooperative. But because the underlying interpersonal problems have not been faced, the quality of interpersonal communication is poor.

People are different, and we need to understand the nature of those differences so as to modify our interpersonal behaviour to cope with them. An individual, may have a consistent view of the world, his organisation and his job, but he has to work in an environment consisting of other people. That is his dilemma. In reality, one of his greatest challenges, as a manage, or superior, is that others people are different from him. Two of the basic differences between people are personality and perception. These differently toward others in different situations, and cause communication problems.

Managers and Communication

One of the classic managerial dilemmas is that of balancing the pressure of short-term results with the need to take a long-term view, as in problem-solving and making decisions versus planning, forecasting, etc. Managers have to work within the reality of their organisations and to recognise that they need to build power bases in order to influence others. This means that they have to (a) be able to communicate with and influence other managers (b) develop credibility for their personal and professional expertise.

When you consider the nature and purpose of the communication which managers have to carry out, the topic takes on a whole new dimension. The audience might be public or private, requiring adjustments of style. Among the numerous purposes of communication will be the following;

1. Trying to influence those over whom you have no power.

2. Building up networks to obtain real information which may be given freely or concealed- which means you need to ask the right questions, or else you will find yourself drowned in data but starved of information.

3. Evaluating communications - are they fact, opinions, gossips?

4. Working in different roles - as chairman, leader, analyst, subordinate, colleague.

5. Using both formal communication - meetings, reports, proposals, notices; and informal communication: counselling, advising, talking to other employees.

6. Talking to different levels within the hierarchy-to individuals, to groups, to departments, and extremely to parents, inspectors, public at large and educationists.

7. Seeking of receiving information, allocating blame, encouragement, control, seeking proposal, confrontation.

The headmaster and other superiors in an educational institute need to be effective communicators to achieve positive results.

Communication Process

To communicate well, we need to know ourselves and our frames of reference and to be able to assess other people. Only then can we hope to find the best ways in which to communicate effectively with them, both to pass information and build relationships. Some of the reasons we do not assess other people well, are given below: the reasons we do not assess other people well, are given below:

1. We are not sufficiently interested in, or pay enough attention to, other people.

2. We make constant errors because of own limited frames of references and self-concept.

3. We are too influenced by apparent negative point, e.g., if someone is not very good at short-term decision-making, we might assume that he/she is not going to be good and long-term planning either.

4. We are positively influenced whether we have common characteristics with other people, e.g., same school, same function, etc.

5. We try too hare to put everyone into consistent categories.

6. We assume that they are going to behave the same way in every situation.

All of the above can cause us considerable problems in the communication process which consists of basically four phases :

1. accepting.

2. understanding.
3. receiving.
4. sending.

There is always noise, or barriers to communication, every time the process is conducted. If you are turning in to an FM radio station, you know that you have to tune in to the right frequency or you will simply hear random noise or a distorted signal. So it is in interpersonal communication where the barriers consist of such factors.

Status effects can occur when one person is considerably higher in hierarchy than the other.

Semantic problems occur when people use either the same word in different ways, or different words in the same way. Do you know that there are 15 different meanings of the word charge in the English language? They also occur when people use jargon or professional shorthand which they expect others to understand, or language which is outside the other's vocabulary.

Perceptual distortions can be caused by having a poor self-concept of self-understanding, or a poor understanding of others.

Culture differences affect communication between people from different departments in the organisation, e.g., between staff room and administrative room. The staff room has a long time horizon with long-term goals regarding growth and development of the pupils: while the administrative room is more concerned with keeping discipline and ensuring submission of fees and completion of other necessary records. They also occur frequently between people who have experienced different social and religious environment.

In England an invitation for dinner at 8 p.m. would see most guest arrive at about 8.15; in India even later - if all! In most parts of the world nodding your head means agreement, shaking your head means, no-except in some parts of India, where the reverse is true. Communication can be very difficult at times!

Physical distractions cause a lot of noise, often literally- insufficiently insulated rooms with traffic noises filtering through poor lighting, a typewriter clattering away in the nearby office; and such things are frequent movement of body posture, fiddling with a pen in the hand, even the arrival of coffee at a critical stage of the communication.

Poor choice of communication channels - Of you want immediate action form the receiver, you would not send a lengthy discussion report, you would probably pick up the telephone or go to this office to tell him what to do. Remember also that one picture is worth a thousand words', and in this age of computer graphics the information can be produced more quickly in this way too.

No feedback - Although one-way communication is quicker, two-way communication is more accurate. In complex situations it helps both sender and receiver to measure their understanding and it improve their joint commitment to the task. It enables both parties to pick up and correct misunderstandings, leading to a high quality of reception and acceptance.

Total Communication

One of the major problems in communicating with other people is that it occurs through different channels and at different levels. Personal beliefs, values and frames of reference influence the ways in which we send and receive messages. They causes us to communicate through four separate channels:

1. Opinions - Attitudes taken about in one's own positive way in a given situation; views that are subjective, not objective.

2. Values - Fairly unchanging beliefs about oneself, the society and culture.

3. Feelings - The reactions on an emotional plane in a specific situation.

4. Facts - What are perceived to be facts, based on own experiences.

Management Style and Communication

A headmaster should try to get things done through other people. This means that he manages people and the resources he requires to get the task done. The management of people can be called leadership, and all of us have our own preferred leadership styles which affect the ways in which we communicate with others, especially our staff.

There is, however, no one magic style which will make us effective leaders. We have to work at it, to develop different styles which are most appropriate to the three elements in every leadership situation.

Only by understanding and analysis these three elements can you choose the right style for any given situation. There are four basic leadership styles:

1. Delegating
2. Supporting
3. Coaching
4. Directing

Each of these is appropriate, in the right direction but we all have our preferred styles and often find it difficult to change it even when we need do. Directing is most appropriate when a complex task has to be performed and your staff is not experienced or motivated to do it; or when you are under time pressure for completion. You explain what needs to be done, and tell them what to do. In such a situation, you can fall into the trap of over-communicating-excessive explanation and confuse and waste time.

Coaching is appropriate when the subordinating staff is more motivated and is becoming more experienced in coping with the task. Here they should be explained in more detail and help them to understand by spending time building up a good relationship with them.

Supporting works when people are familiar with the techniques required and have further developed their relationship with the superior. The headmaster should take time to talk to them, to involve them more in work decisions, to listen to their suggestions for improving performance.

Delegating is right when the staff is thoroughly conversant and efficient in the performance of the task, and they can be simply let to get on with it. People of experience do not take kindly to a manager sitting on their shoulders and interfering with every aspect of their work. However, the superior still needs to keep an eye on their performance to ensure that the required standards are being maintained.

Of the four basic leadership styles are combined with the characteristics and the experience of the people being managed, the superior can identify which is most appropriate style of leadership in a particular situation-he will be using situational leadership to become effective in choosing the right style of leadership- in other words, to change the style to meet the needs of the situations- which is needed to develop three specific skills:

1. Communication Skill - To explain the need of varying the leadership style in different situations to the individual subordinates concerned. Each person's experience and motivation to perform certain tasks will be different. People being managed in a delegating style would react adversely to a directing style if the superior is not capable of communicating effectively to them the reason that a different style was being used because the task they were being asked to perform was of a nature completely unfamiliar to them.

Most people whom you manage are likely to fall into the medium experience, medium motivation categories. So the two styles supporting, and coaching- will work for most of the time. But, if the superior sticks to these styles, to paraphrase Abraham Lincoln, You can managed 80% of your people effectively for 100% of the time, or 100% of you people for 805 of the time, but you can't manage 100% of your people effectively for 100% of the time.

The superior will need to use all four styles at some time or the other, and so he will need to developed the following communication skills:

1. How to explain why he is behaving differently as a leader in a particular situation- why, in effect, he is being consistent in his inconsistency.

2. How do delegate effectively, so that there is a clear understanding of what problems people should bring up.

3. How to share problems with them, and listen to their ideas and feelings.

4. How to build relationships with the staff.

5. How to encourage people when work is well done.

6. Hoe to tell people what to do and how to do it.

7. How to explain clearly, and concisely, the nature of the task.

Organisational Communication

Communication in organisations uses two basic channels - formal and informal. Both are important and both carry massages- sometimes reinforcing, sometimes conflicting-throughout the organisation.

Formal channels are the ones which have been set up by the organisation. Messages flow in three directions: downwards, upwards and sideways. The downwards messages consists primarily of information which is necessary for any staff to carry out their work, such as policies and procedures, orders and requests which are passed down to the appropriate level in the hierarchy. Upwards messages are reports, requests, opinions, complaints. Sideways massages are between different departments, functions or people at the same level in the organisation.

There tend to be strict rules about the use of these formal channels. For communication to be effective, all three channels need to be opened and unblocked at all times. The upward channel is the one which blocks most easily, and when this happens it is an indicator that an organisation's policies, procedures and employes relations need to be review.

Informal channels spring up by virtue of common

interests between people in organizations- these interests may be caused by work, social or outside relationships. Informal channels often become the only means of communication when formal channels become blocked or break down.

So for communicating effectively, you must get to understand both formal and informal channels in the network- what the are, how they work and how to use both channels to send and receive messages.

Active Listening

Active listening requires definite commitment and personal discipline. You prepare yourself deliberately to concentrate and not be influenced by external influences. It is time-consuming and you need to pay attention to the other person on three different levels. As managers, it is critical to effectiveness, to listen to other people. But we all make conscious decisions on whether to listen, to half-listen, or to ignore communications from them. If the information confirms our current needs and beliefs, and if it helps us to satisfy our current needs, we are likely to listen intently. Information that conflicts with either or both is likely to be rejected - try telling your boss that his department is not running efficiently.

We have to be careful not to discard important information as irrelevant noise. We make choices about listening- you may train a cat to listen to a melody on a piano. Introduce a mouse, and the cat shuts out the melody to concentrate on catching the mouse. People have the same ability. However, the more skilful we are at listening, the better we are likely to be at communicating generally.

Formal channels are the ones which have been set

up by the organisation. Massages flow in three directions: downwards, upwards and sideways. The downwards message consist primary of information which is necessary for any staff to carry out their work, such as policies and procedures, orders and requests which are passed down to the appropriate level in the hierarchy. Upwards messages are reports, requests, opinions, complaints. Sideways messages are between different departments, functions or people at the same level in the organisation.

There tend to be strict rules about the use of these formal channels. For communication to be effective, all three channels need to be opened and unblocked at all times. The upward channel is the one which blocks most easily, and when this happens it is an indicator that an organisation's policies, procedures and employee relations need to be reviewed.

Informal channels spring up by virtue of common interests between people in organisations- these interests may be caused by work, social or outside relationships. Informal channels often become the only means of communication when formal channels become blocked or break down.

So for communicating effectively, you must get to understand both formal and informal channels in the network- what they are, how they work and how to use both channels to send and receive messages.

The Approach to Communication Training

When we are to trying to develop effective organisational communication and individual communication skills, the questions raised by the four basic components become even more important. Organisations need to use a development approach to training. By adopting this approach, organisations are more likely to develop these skills which can be used effectively to improve individual and organisational performance.

Managerial Work and Communication

Managers work in a stimulus-reactive environmental. The nature of their work is typically varied, spasmodic and brief, and they do a great quantity of work at an unrelenting pace. In general, they prefer to deal with specific issues, prefer verbal media, and to control to some degree their own activities. However, it is likely that managers will carry out their work, even in very similar jobs, in different ways, dependent on their choices concerning what to do and how to do it. These choices are influenced by the managers own perceptions, preferences and personal characteristics.

Within their personal work contexts, managers work in three clearly identifiable roles which change rapidly from one to another because of the episodic nature of their work. These roles can be classified as interpersonal, informational, and decisional. However, to make effective decisions managers need to collect relevant information, and to collect information they require effective formal and informal communication with bosses, colleagues, subordinates, and contacts external to the organisation.

So, to the effective managers, skilled in decision-making on which they are most frequently judged and appraised for salary and promotion, they need to be effective communicators. But as they make choices regarding their approached to individual jobs, the specific communication skills they need will vary from manager to manager, from job to job.

Assertiveness

How can you impress another person without necessarily upsetting him/her? How can you be forceful yet sufficiently sensitive to the other's feeling? The answer is, by being assertive. Each of us has our own personal space, both physical and psychological.

The size of this personal space is influenced by our values, emotions, ideas, and views about the world. People have a right to those values and do not thank others for encroaching on their personal territory. Assertiveness is a means of making an impact on other individuals without encroaching on their personal arena- it is a means of influencing others without demanding your interpersonal relationships.

Assertiveness lies between submissive and aggressive behaviour. When you are submissive, you are unwilling or unable to express honest feelings. You let other people violet your personal space and crush your rights. When you are aggressive, you tend to walk on other people. You impose your point of view and values on them and express your feelings at the expense of theirs. You are likely to generate resistance in others by blocking their demands or views, and have difficulty in getting them to make commitments.

Being assertive lets you say what you want, without overwhelming or abusing other people. You are clear about your own position and let other people know this, but can also accept that they may have other views and so may wish to negotiate their position accordingly.

Assertiveness training is a critical element in developing communication skills. It helps in all the following ways:

1. Protecting yourself from being taken advantage of by other people.

2. Recognising that you have certain rights and your own personal values system.

3. Making more decisions and free choices.

4. Taking responsibility for what happens in your life- at home, as well as at work.

5. Learning social skills that form close interpersonal relationships.

6. Getting more of your needs accepted.

7. Learning to relax and reduce anxiety.

8. Open, honest communication.

Assertive behaviour is more likely to alter someone else's behaviour and less likely to violate his or her personal space; there is little risk of damaging existing relationships or reducing the other's self-esteem; and there is less likelihood to demotivate, or risk uncontrolled defensive behaviour.

To improve the likelihood of success in an assertive approach, the following procedure should be adopted:

1. Focus on the solution.

2. Recycle the process, if necessary.

3. Listen actively and reflectively to the defensive response.

4. Send your assertive message.

5. Prepare thoroughly beforehand.

The superiors in an educational set up are like managers who need to develop assertiveness skills to become effective communicators.

Giving and Receiving Feedback

These are skills which we tend to overlook as we feel generally that we are pretty good in these areas. However, generally we are not. To establish and build on relationships we need to obey certain rules in our social interactions which will help us to improve. Most people find both giving and receiving feedback, handling praise and criticism, equally difficult- the result is that we only hear and listen when there is a real problem.

Here are some hints for improving the provision of feedback:

1. Refusing Requests - Ask for more time to decide if you need it, Ask for more information if you need it, Do not apologics profusely, Give reasons if you want to, but do not invent excuses, Keep your reply short, do not ramble on justifying yourself, Evaluate its accuracy and potential value to you, Do not show over-reaction to a feedback, Ask for clarification/examples, Check your perception of what your hear, Paraphrase what you hear, Note down areas of question/disagreement, Try not to let hackles rise, your defences built, Listen carefully. Active listening and feedback go hand in hand. They help to give and receive massages of greater clarity and understanding.

2. Disagree with Others - The superior should follow the advice : Recognise that others may have different points of view from those of yours, Give reasons for your disagreement, Be willing to change your opinion if more facts emerge, Be doubtful in a constructive way the difficulty I see is, how can we get round the constraints, State your disagreement clearly No. I disagree with.

3. Give Criticism - The people should not be put down

in front of others when the facts have been described; the solutions should be sought jointly with the others person in private.

4. Give Praise - Genuine praise is more likely to be accepted if it is for better-than-normal performance and if it is given straight to the performer, rather than beating about the bush.

5. Concentrate on Behaviour which can be Changed - The superior should concentrate on the behaviour which is within the control of the other person, rather than making personal comments about the individual.

6. Give Reasons for the Comments - Giving reasons for the comments can be an effective method of involving the subordinate and making him share the viewpoint.

7. Comment on Specific Actions - The superior should say you sorted out that awkward problem very well instead of you are good with difficult problems.

Listening

We have discussed listening, especially active listening in the preceding paragraphs, If we do not listen, we receive distorted of garbled messages. The information on which we make decisions is, therefore, of minor value to us, and affects our effectiveness. We need to learn to listen for all cues, verbal and non-verbal, which, interpreted accurately, will give use complete understanding of messages being sent.

Solving Problems

Solving problems is all about trying to find some form of mutual agreement about decisions and actions to be taken in problem situations. The superior or headmaster, and manager, may have all the facts and resources at his disposal and may be therefore able to solve the problem with any discussion with other persons. This is not always the case.

He may have to share with others the problem, the facts, the feelings in the situation, so that he can make a high quality decision. It may also be necessary to gain the total commitment of others to the decision so that it will be implemented successfully. He will not necessarily achieve this if he makes the decision by himself.

The process of involving other people, especially the subordinates or colleagues, is simple:

1. Agree to a solution which meets these criteria most closely, and which is appropriate to the situation rather than to any one person in particular.

2. Evaluate those solutions against the criteria which have been agreed upon and are necessary for a positive outcome.

3. Identify all possible solutions.

4. Explore the situation from all points of view, seeking inputs from the others involved.

5. Share facts, feelings, values and opinions about the problem/situation with those who can contribute to a positive outcome.

This sharing process, genuinely involving other people, means that everyone has the opportunity to influence the decision and they are thus, likely to be committed to it. This style is, however, time-consuming. It needs to balance the time and cost involved in the process against the quality of the decision required and the degree of commitment and motivation it procedures.

Resolving Conflict

Conflicts, tensions, problems with individuals or groups are inevitable in organisations. People are different: they have their own views on issues, and their own approaches to solving problems. Interpersonal conflict arises just as much because of the manner in which discussions take place as from disagreement on specific issues. People can end up still disliking each other even after they have agreed on an issue, simply because of the way in which the negotiations were constructed. Leaving question whether they will do what they have agreed upon, still open. Are they committed to doing it? If not, this will eventually lead to further conflict.

To gain greater collaboration and commitment, the superior should consider these approaches to conflict situations:

1. Identify and appraise carefully the actions for the parties:

a. Identify areas of potential future conflict and try to agree joint approaches to them now.

b. Make sure you have a commitment for implementing the agreements; by whom, when and how?

c. Assess the consequences of these actions for both parties.

2. Concentrate on issues:

a. When you have reached agreement on one issue, consider how you can build on this reach agreement on others.

b. Break down large issues into smaller workable units, then deal with each problem separately.

c. Gather facts.

d. Do not increase interpersonal tensions by criticism or negative feedback.

3. Reduce communication blockages between the parties:

a. Do not make false judgements, e.g., confusing opinions with facts.

b. Do not try to dominate, to be aggressive, or to threaten.

4. Use assertiveness skills:

a. To maintain their commitment to implement the agreed solution.

b. To make a powerful impact on others.

5. Use active and reflective listening:

a. To generate trust so that you can be open and honest with each other.

b. To improve understanding of each other's positions and views of the situation/problem.

Communication at School Level

All school activities are interrelated and the classroom communication is a part of communication at school level. The teachers employ various media of communication in the classroom interaction to facilitate teaching-learning situation by using overhead projector for still picture, motion pictures or, the computer assisted/aided instruction and, computer managed instructions. Various kinds of media help the headmaster in selection of appropriate means for use in different scenarios. It is in the role of headmaster that media of communication assist in supervision and in directing the classroom teaching, laboratory practical work, etc. All classroom activities, use of communication media and audio visual aids can also be observed by the headmaster sitting in his room with the help of video camera set fitted in every classroom, laboratory and library. The headmaster can supervise and direct the teacher as well as students. He can guide the teacher for his instructional procedure.

It is not possible for the headmaster to go around in the school campus for supervising the school activities. Generally the headmasters employ the oral medium in communication in his administration and organisation but the use of communication devices brings efficiency in his working. He renders his responsibility and accountability. In supervision, communication devices play significant role in school organisation. The oral communication is inadequate in personal situation of schools. In prayers, assembly, playground, cultural programme, there is required mike and speaker system because oral communication is not adequate for large gathering of students unless simplified. Intercom and video system should be available in each room, so that the headmaster can observe a specific class and provide instruction to all classes by sitting in his room. The headmaster thus, directs the teachers activities. This type of system is used for supervising, monitoring and controlling the school functioning.

Media and Method

Media and method are often used interchangeably in education, but they are quite different from one another. The media and method are not contradictory to one another but they are complementary and supplementary to one another. A method can be made effective by using an appropriate media of communication. These can be differentiated in the following manner:

Instruction has two components : a. instruction

time, b. instructional space. The instructional space is covered by radio and television. A teacher can reach interior parts of the country and can knock at the door of students. The media is essential for instructional space.

We can distinguish between media and method in another way. Method is an abstract entity which is determined by the nature of the content. Information through lecture, facts through story-telling or dramatisation method, concepts through experiment, are taught to students. The mode of message communication is known as media. The media is a concrete entity which is determined by the mode of communication. In information through radio, facts are communicated to the students. The media of communications are: radio, television, video-tape and tape-recorder, etc. and mode of communication through various media are speaking-listening, writing-reading and visualising-observing.

The communication must be kept open, as only then the teacher and pupils are able to communicate clearly without interference of understanding and ensuring appreciation. But unfortunately many interferences and communication barriers arise which impede the smooth flow of communication between the teacher and his pupils in the classroom, e.g., advertisements and entertainment media.

The basic communication model involves an informational or interpretive process in which massages, information reaction to information, travel from the initiator to receiver through the route called communication channel. The message conveyed by the teacher or the educational media may be verbal or visual and the receiver may listen or see and react in other ways. The communication channel in the classroom should ideally carry both massages and counter-messages; it involves initiation, reception and response which serve as feedback.

Need of Communication in Educational Administration

The headmaster of an institution has to play several roles and perform various duties. A headmaster can use the media of communication in his various functioning of the institution. The following are the major areas in which communication media is used:

The teaching process is dependent on two major components: Content and Communication. The former determines method and the latter decides the media. An effective presentation or interaction phase of teaching, depends upon the communication media which helps in achieving the learning objectives formulated at planning stage. In organising teaching, main problem is to take decision about an appropriate communication media. It becomes essential to understand the term media, theory of communication and communication channels.

Overcoming Barriers of Communication in Educational Institutions

The communication devices are very useful in educational administration and supervision wherein they facilitate the performance of the headmaster. The application of communication methods brings efficiency in the administration but there are various barriers to their usage, such as the following:

1. The teacher and students have negative attitude towards the communication system.

2. In this case, these communication sets require generator to operate which ultimately requires funds for the purchase of operate which ultimately expense for oil upkeep.

3. Another barrier in the use of communication devices is that these generally operate by electricity which is often not regular.

4. If funds are available, the communication equipment can be purchased, but another problem is that of maintenance. There are instances when the communication set has been installed but could not be maintained properly for want of guidance or maintenance staff.

5. In using the communication devices, the availability of funds is a major factor. There are several aided and government schools which do not have funds and resources to purchase communication devices for school.

Modern Devices of Communication

There are several types of communication devices which can be used in schools depending on the resources available with school the management. The following are the major devices of communication which can be used for communication in educational administration.

a. Video camera and audio-camera.

b. Telephone and fax, e-mail.

c. Still picture and other audio-visual aids.

d. Overhead projector.

e. Multi-media approach and packages.

f. Mike and speaker system.

g. Library internet system.

5

MANAGEMENTS OF SCHOOLS (ACTIVITIES AND APPROACHES)

Concept of an Ideal School

There is hardly any doubt that schools play an important role in the life of individuals, in the life of an nation and in the life of mankind. An ideal school must make itself responsible for equipping its students adequately with civic as well as vocational efficiency-, and the qualities of character that go with it-so that they may be able to play their part worthily and competently in the improvement of national life. They would not then emerge as helpless individuals who do not know what to do with themselves and can only think of crowding the colleges- which for the majority- area a last land reluctant resort, take up some clerical or teaching job which they have not natural inclination for. A school must address itself to the training of competent personnel for the ever expanding scope of opportunities. Such a school must incorporate certain features whose discussion we shall start now.

The school should provide a richly varied pattern of activities to cater to the development of its children's entire personality. The first concern of the school should be to provide for its pupils a rich, pleasant and stimulating environment which will evoke their manifold interests and make life a matter of joyful experience. It must formulate a scheme of hobbies, occupations and projects that will appeal to draw out the powers of children of varying temperaments and aptitudes.

The school must become an activity school because activity has an irresistible appeal for every normal child and is a natural path to the goal of knowledge and culture. The Secondary Commission observed in this context that the entire programme of schools will be visualised as a unity and inspired by a psychologically congenial and stimulating approach, the so-called work "being characterized by the feeling of joy and self-expression usually associated with play and hobbies and these later having something of the meaning- fullness and purpose which are normally considered a special feature of academic work." Thus, by planning a coherent programme of these different activities, rich in stimuli, the school will not be frittering away either the time or the energy of the pupils but will be heightening their intellectual powers also side-by-side with training them in other fine qualities.

Scope of School Management

Everything concerned with the education of the child through the agency of the school, will be included in educational management.

1. Supervise schoolwork.

2. Providing the material equipment such as building, furniture, farms, laboratories, library, museum, art gallery, etc.

3. Provide various auxiliary services like mid-day meals, school uniform, textbooks, etc.

4. Prepare timetable.

5. Prepare curriculum for the different classes.

6. Organise library, museum, hostel, etc.

7. Organise health and physical education.

8. Organise a systematic co-curricular programme.

9. Organise guidance service.

10. Co-operate with departmental authorities and implementing the orders of the higher educational authorities.

Characteristics of School Management

For a school management to be successful, it should have the following characteristics which we have discussed in the preceding chapter pertaining to educational management:

1. Professional Approach.
2. Flcxibility.
3. Factor of production.
4. Social process.
5. Successful achievement of the desired results.
6. Goal-oriented.
7. Conformity to the social and political philosophy of the country.
8. System of authority.
9. Needed at all levels of organisation.
10. Science as well as art.

Functions of School Management

The chief functions of school management are as follows:

1. Supervision.
2. Recording and Reporting.
3. Evaluation.
4. Coordination.
5. Control.
6. Motivation.

7. Organisation.
8. Planning.
9. Decision-making.
10. Forecasting.

Institution of Democratic School Management

Democracy in educational institutions finds manifestation through various school institutions which show the king of democracy prevalent in the schools. These, in brief, are:

1. Social Service Groups - Such type of groups can render service in the form of laying roads, arranging committees, functions, cleanliness campaigns in the neighbourhood, collection of national defence fund, literary campaigns, helping the sick, looking after the families of the martyed soldiers and other patriots, and so on.

2. Special Committee of Pupils - In addition to the student council, special committees should be formed, duly elected by the pupils to carry out specific duties and organise special activities for maintaining discipline, organising debates, dramatics, exhibitions, flower shows, literary societies, music concerts and other school activities.

3. Staff Meetings - Periodic meetings of the staff should be called to discuss different matters and the staff should have the idea that whatever has been decided upon is mainly their work.

4. Student's Council - A student council consisting of Secretaries and student office bearers from difference houses, associations and clubs should form a student's council with the aim of giving the students training in self-government. The student councils can be guided and assisted by a staff advisor.

5. Staff Council - The aim of the staff council should be to plan all-important matters of the school. Senior members of the staff should constitute the staff council. The staff council may be further split up into committees to plan and execute specific tasks. Meetings of the staff council should be held frequently to discuss all important issues.

Principle of Democratic School Management

India has achieved independence after a long period of alien rule and has now adopted a democratic pattern. It is necessary for the protection of out young democracy that every individual of the country moves out of the narrow grooves of traditional thought and develops the feeling of universal brotherhood. Our country has a number of problems and their solution depends on the citizens, who are still suffering from inadequacy and deprivation. Our democracy will be looked at with an eye of suspicion till the citizens develop the capacity to think independently and to understand the import of personal and public good. For democracy to succeed, education is very necessary.

If we are able to introduce in the educational system, the reforms in conformity with the democratic ideals, our democratic experiment will certainly prove successful. Only through education will the individuals become capable of clear thinking and of working out solutions to their personal problems, and learn to keep control over their feeling, and discharge their duties towards society. Democratic education is not much in evidence in our country, for democracy in economic and educational, and is confined only to the political sphere.

In the democratic pattern of education all the

methods of education should be based on some psychological factors. These methods should be employed in shaping the children as lovers of freedom, independent thinkers, and dutiful and heathy citizens. It is through these that the personality of children is developed in accordance with their inclinations and abilities. In this system the students and the teachers cooperate with each other. The student tries to achieve his goal by his capacity for thinking through some action. The teacher is only to give some guidance. It is the child who is the prime doer.

In the present day educational organisation the school is regarded as a society in miniature. It is the responsibility of the school to make the students proficient in all those social activities which he will need in his later life. In this educational pattern the teacher, the public and the government all have collective responsibility. Education is supposed to extend over the entire field of life from the beginning to the end. The individual proclivity of the child and his ability as also the good of the society should be kept in view while planning out the educational pattern. The educational pattern should be made child-centred in such a way that the individual while satisfying his private ends may also be able to discharge his social obligations.

All the subjects should be taught in a correlated manner and the general knowledge of the students should be increased. The entire field should be well controlled, and discipline should be related to their inner self and not imposed through punishment and fear.

The following principles should be taken into consideration while managing schools:

1. Students- Centred - The student is the focal point of education. The purpose of all educational endeavour is the well being of the student. All educational management must be largely student-centred. This flesh and blood should never be lost sight of in the midst of facts, figurers and files. Whatever is done in school should be of the students, by the students and for the students. Enough opportunities must be provided for the wholesome development of the students.

2. Freedom - The power of critical thinking is an important requisite of democracy, and it can only be cultivated by individuals in an atmosphere of freedom. Enough freedom should be given to all to exercise their powers and talents. The headmaster should give due recognition to any signs of display of resourcefulness on the part of teachers. They should be free to question, offer constructive suggestions, conduct fresh experiments and bring about healthy changes. The pupils should able be allowed enough freedom to rise to the full stature of their abilities. Democracy can become real only through its educational institutions, which will teach its children the democratic way of life. There must pervade an atmosphere of justice, freedom and cooperation in the educational institutions, only then good training in leadership and followership can be given.

3. Democratic Philosophy of Education - If a philosophy is necessary for general administration, it is all the more so for education suited to the needs and aspirations of modern India. In an educational institution in a democracy, the administrator is not a small dictator, but a friend and a guide; he consults his colleagues, honours their opinions, confers with them in staff meetings, meets them informally in gatherings and clubs- he is first among the equals. He recognizes

the worth of each individual child, finds out his potentialities and gives him help and guidance according to his potentialities and gives him help and guidance according to his requirement. Thus, the total administration becomes a joint show of the headmaster, teachers and pupils. Everyone has a clear consciousness and realisation of the purpose of democratic philosophy with which the school is administered.

4. The management must be Flexible, Adaptable and Stable - The school management should hold fast to the good, change what requires changing and be fertile in considering individual differences in all personalities involved.

Nature of Educational Planning

Educational planning is the exercise of foresight in determining the policy, priorities and costs of an educational system. Having due regard for economic and political realities, for the system's potential for growth, and for the needs of the country and of the pupils. Educational planning encompasses the provision of information necessary for framing and implementing appropriate policies in the short, medium and long term, with regard to the numbers of pupils and students in each branch of education, and the adjustment of the outflow of persons from each branch of education in accordance with economic and social needs.

It is concerned with orientations of flow of pupils into and within the educational system in accordance with economic and social needs. It is concerned with orientation of flow of pupils into and within the educational system in accordance, as far as possible, with individual desires and the principle of equality and efficiency. It includes, the main policy problems involved in creating a supply of teachers of various types, sufficient to ensure that pupils and students are adequately instructed. It is concerned with ensuring that adequate buildings and equipments are available and that they are used in an economically efficient way. The educational planner is required also to estimate the expenditure necessary to carry out the proposed programme, to investigate possible sources of finance and to promote the efficient utilisation of financial resources.

The education division of the Planning Commission is headed by a chief of education or adviser. Sometimes there have been two chiefs of equal status. They receive work from a number of functionaries who are educational planners. They are drawn from the world of eduction. At the base of the pyramid are, as usual, a number of staff comprising technical assistants, general assistants, clerks, messengers, etc.,

The central ministry of education also has a branch for planning work and for monitoring the plan. It is attached to a joint educational advisor or joint or director who works under the Union Minister of Education, under the overall guidance of the secretary to the ministry.

Every state government has a separate department for planning development headed by a secretary, who is a member of the Indian Administrative Service. This department is responsible for coordinating the secretarial plans and attending to all items of overall planning in the state government. The educational planning work is done in the education department under the charge of the directors of education and/or the education is a continuous process involving a number of interdependent steps. These should include:

1. Evaluation and adjustment of the plan.

2. Implementation of the plan and its monitoring.

3. Preparation of the plan.

4. Consideration of possible alternatives and deciding upon the one to be followed.

5. Analysis of the recent trends and the present situation.

6. Determination of educational objectives and priorities.

The objectives of planning are defined by the Constitution of India, policy resolution and statements of the Government, the election manifesto of the ruling party and recommendations of commissions and committees which might have been accepted by the government.

The educational system also has an intimate bearing on the attainment of the general objectives of the plan in as much as it largely determines the quality of the manpower and the social climate of the community. The general objectives provide implications for the educational plan too. For instance, the quality of opportunity requires universalisation of elementary education, provision of remedial teaching, and incentives like mid-day meals, free stationery and clothing; and scholarships for the weaker sections of society. The demand for increased productivity calls for:

a. Emphasis on inculcating an innovative spirit and the habit of cooperation and team work among students.

b. Introduction of science, mathematics and technologies in the curriculum.

c. Teaching of skills as an essential part of the curriculum.

The objective of full employment necessitates the introduction of work experience or socially useful productive work and vocationalisation at appropriate stages of education.

The educational machinery will have to be geared for the specific tasks which the nation set itself through the plan so as to make available in the various fields personnel of suitable quality at the required rate. In a democratic set-up, the role of education becomes crucial, since it can function effectively only if there is an intelligent participation of the masses in the affairs of the country. The success of planning in a democracy depends also on the growth of the spirit people, and on the degree to which it becomes possible to evoke public enthusiasm and build up local leadership. It is essential for the successful implementation of the plan that the educational programme helps to train the people to place responsibility before rights and to keep the self-regarding outlook and the force of the acquisitive instinct within legitimate bounds. The educational system should also satisfy cultural needs, which is essential for the healthy growth of a nation.

The system should stimulate the growth of the creative faculties, increase the capacity for enjoyment and develop a spirit of critical appreciation of arts, literature and other creative activities. The fulfillment of the objectives mentioned above will lead to the development of a personality in the individual which should be the first and foremost aim of any system of education. The procedure of educational planning as it has developed in India involves a number of steps. The educational planner does the initial exercises in drafting national plan with its priorities, broad physical targets, and financial requirements.

Stephen J. Knezevich, in his book Administration of Public Education, has mentioned the following points explaining the meaning and nature of planning.

1. Complexity Resolution - Educational planning is interpreted as a means of coping with complexity or coordination of facts of such projects. It is complexity resolution, a process for coordination and control.

2. Management of change - Educational planning provides a mechanism, a model or a tool for achieving specific objectives of an organisation. It is a part of organisation renewal. Various forecasting techniques are part of the process of educational planning.

3. Problem Prevention - educational planning should minimise the magnitude of an educational problem likely to be encountered at some future point in time. It should spell out the procedures to be followed if some crises or contingency arise. It is a king of contingency anticipation or problem-prevention.

4. Operations Optimisation - Educational planning is operations optimisation or performance improvement. It is for the enhancement of existing conditions rather than for those that exist in the uncertain future. It must result into standard operating procedures, operations manuals, administrative guidelines or system polices.

5. Decision-Making - While educational administration is mostly decision- making, planning in education is only the other side of it. It is preparation or precursor in the decision-making process. It is to help determine the optimal decision or choice rendered.

6. Goals and Objectives - Educational planning is a means of generating relevant present or future goals and objectives for the organisation.

7. Interpretation - Educational planning should cell the interpretation of future's data and its translation into competencies or operational capabilities demanded to maintain effectiveness under the conditions anticipated.

8. Forecasting - Educational planning implies forecasting or projections of important factors in education such as number and type of students and expansion of facilities needed for them and describe or defines or determines events, conditions and needs of some future point in time.

Planning of School Activities

A plan is conceptualised as a predetermined strategy, detailed scheme or, programme of action related to the accomplishment of an objective. It implies some king of mental activity during the course of analysing or, laying out a method of achieving something. It focuses on what, why and how. An educational plan refers to efforts on planned and deliberate change to be brought about in the system for achieving identified relevant objectives. Visualised in relation to objectives, these changes have to be coordinated in relation to objectives and conditions in other related aspects. They have to be systematically planned. Educational planning means the process of setting out in advance a pattern of action to bring about overall changes as viewed by national policies by closest possible articulation of means and ends.

A considerable amount of pressure from both the donors of aids and international organisation, made adoption of some form of planning unavoidable. According to Harlan L. Hagman and Alfred Schwartz, in their book Administration in Profile for School Executives, "Planning selects among alternatives, explores routes before travel begins and identifies possible or probable outcomes of action before the executive and his organisation is committed to any." Educational planning has been one of the early instruments of independent governments. Resources have to used as effectively and systematically as possible.

The complexities of modern technology in society have given rise to the need for planning in education. Today, educational planning is an absolute requirement. Increasing populations, man-power needs, ecology, decreasing natural resources and haphazard application of scientific developments require educational planning. To meet these problems, educational planning becomes a necessity and planning competence becomes mandatory. F.W. Baghrt and Albert Trull, Jr., in his book Educational Planning say, "Educational planning is a process utilized by an administrator while performing the role of a leader, decision-making, change-agent and so on. It is a basic management task. It is a means of achieving higher levels of effectiveness. It is unavoidable for bringing about a desirable change in the educational organisations for promoting the organisational health-its effectiveness and functional efficiency."

Creating Resources

Generally, there are two approaches adopted in the preparation of plans for national development. However, the main objective of each approach is to get the most and best educational results for the effort expended and to maximise education's contribution to each individual and to the whole society. The first of these approaches is dominated mainly by educational considerations, and the second by financial limitations. The ultimate solutions of the problem would have to be sought in a realistic and wise compromise between these two approaches and that, in order to provide a good educational system of Asian countries in the near future, educationists and economists would have to work together. In the process, educationists would become increasingly conscious of the new but significant science of the economics of education and the economists, in their turn, would become increasingly conscious of the significance of education in economic development. The following are the two main interlinked and inseparable approaches which determine the allocation of resource.

1. Role in Public Relation - The headmaster of the institution has prove himself to be a successful public relations officer. He has to maintain his relationship and contact with various agencies.

a. Relationship with the Community - The school is a society in miniature. It is established in conformity with the needs and ideals of the society. It is an agency to bring about the activities that lead to the fulfillment of the needs and the requirement of the society. That is why it is said to that headmaster of the institution is not only the leader of the school but also the leader of the society. He should, therefore, try to maintain a proper and courteous relationship with the community at large. He may organise social service camps and community work with the help of the students and the teachers in order to bring about proper upliftment of the society.

b. Relationship with the Guardians - The headmaster should try to maintain a liaison with the guardians. This shall be helpful for the discipline in the school as well as the proper education of the students. There may be certain difficulties with the child that may be tackled only at home. He should try to seek the cooperation of the guardians in the task of remedial education. He may invite the guardians off and on to the school and discuss with them the various problems concerning the students. He should be courteous and good to them during their visit.

c. Relationship with the Students - The headmaster should generally try to come in personal contact with the students. He should be sympathetic toward the students and listen to their difficulties and problems in a sympathetic manner. On the other hand, he should see to it that the students carry out their day-to-day work in a proper and diligent manner. He should set some time apart when the students may see him and pot forward their viewpoints and difficulties.

d. Relationship with the Teachers - The teachers are the first to come in contact with the headmaster. He should deal with them in a democratic manner and have a cordial relation with them. Without it, the atmosphere of the school will become vitiated and cannot be congenial for the all-round development of the child. On the other hand, the headmaster should not be so mild as to listen to all the demands of the teachers.

He should be capable of handling the situation himself. In the words of Professor K.G. Saiyidain, "To my mind, a good Headmaster is one who can inspire and infuse his colleagues without dominating over them like a hard task master." In other words, the behaviour of the headmaster should be sympathetic, democratic and friendly but disciplined and dignified.

2. Rof in Guidance, Motivation and Conflicts - The

students and teachers should be able to confide in the headmaster and seek his guidance on various topics including academic, curriculum selection, career options and so on. He should be able to give a piece of his vast experience with conviction with welfare wrought in every stage. Guidance function of the headmaster is of recent origin. He is expected to provide the following educational and vocational guidance:

a. He should be able to help the higher authorities in matters of curriculum, textbooks, school organisation, framing of educational policies and other educational problems.

b. He should be able to help the parents in supervision the education of their wards, in planning their education according to their abilities and aptitudes.

c. He should be able to help the teachers in organising teaching and other activities, in making a deeper study of their subjects, and in solving specific problems of discipline, backwardness, teaching, etc.

e. He should be able to help the students in their day-to-day activities and instructional work.

f. He should be able to help the students in the selection of subjects at the secondary stage, leading to suitable vocations after the school leaving stage.

Out of all these tasks, educational and vocational guidance is of outmost necessity, although it is neglected so far. The headmaster must reconvene meetings of the staff for purposes of planning educational guidance and organising a full-fledged guidance programme. He should start a guidance unit in the school and appoint necessary staff for guidance.

The guidance unit must provide not only curricular

and vocational guidance but also personal guidance to those young children who lack adjustment. For this purpose he may have to seek help from the psychologists and other organisations. The headmaster shall have to act as a liaison between the school guidance unit and the State guidance Bureau, employment officers and other organisations.

Every headmaster has to extract work from his colleagues. He cannot do it smoothly hand effectively through autocratic attitude. He has to motivate his subordinates to work conscientiously and enthusiastically. The headmaster has to create motivating situations. For this purpose, he is expected to possess human skill, besides technical skill. The human skill will mean ability to motivate others to work, judgement to evaluate their work, understanding of the sources of behaviour of others and patience to deal with different situations.

Many situations in the organisation, particularly decision-making situations, produce inter-personal conflicts for educational managers; selecting an unqualified teacher from amongst several well-qualified ones for promotion or award or doing some important prestigious job. This administrative act may generate a conflicting situation between or among the teachers which the manager has to face. A large number of such interpersonal conflicts are likely to occur in every educational organisation among teachers, students, administrators, parents and other employees as well between them in a variety of situational combination. Many of these conflicts may be trivial, but some might be serious having long histories, and thus, create crises in management.

3. Role of the Headmaster in Teaching :

a. Clear and Fluent Expression - The headmaster should have a clear and fluent expression as it is a means of imparting knowledge. If the teacher's expression is dull and vague, it is not likely to create an impression on the students. He should be able to forcefully put forward his ideas and views in a clear and fluent manner before the students. Expression, in order to be clear and fluent, should have the following requisites:

(i) Proper Expression - The teacher should be able to put forward the facts systematically before the students. If the facts are not put forward systematically in the classroom, the students are likely to be confused and teaching may be a failure. The expression should be interesting as well and punctuated with humour, as and when required. It is much true of the headmaster, he being a teacher himself.

(ii) Clear Intonation and Correct Pronunciation - Clear intonation and correct pronunciation are the essentials of good teaching. These things are all the more important in the teaching of a language. A successful teacher should speak out words clearly and pronounce them correctly. Correct pronunciation and clear intonation go a long way in creating a good impression on the students. If these things are lacking, the teacher may not be able to carry the students with him. The headmaster, in the role of a teacher, should be able to carry the students with him. Besides, he has to address the students off and on and unless he has these refinements of speech, he is likely to create a bad impression.

(iii) Clear Articulation - The teacher should be able to speak out in a way which is clear and possible for the students to understand. The speech should be clear as faltering articulation or tethering spoils the teaching.

b. Mastery and Specialisation of his Subject - The headmaster should be the specialist and master of the subject that he has to teach. He should have not only authentic grounding in the subject but also a through knowledge of it. In order to achieve this, he may take the following steps:

(i) Habit of Reasoning - Knowledge can be stable only when it is based on reason and understanding. Simply because something has been put down in the book should not be accepted as true. The headmaster should have the habit of reasoning, in order to convince the students about the things that are written in the book.

(ii) Knowledge of the References - It is necessary for a good teacher to be able to furnish referential knowledge to the student, while teaching a particular thing or subject. He has to quote parallels and references. The headmaster, in order to be a successful teacher, should take this step as well. He should acquire knowledge of the references.

(iii) Home work - A good teacher always has to prepare the lesson at home, same is the case for the headmaster. He has to devote a good deal of time to studies. He should also have curiosity to acquire further knowledge.

Approaches to Management

Management approach to teaching is an indirect approach that stimulates verbal participation by students and discloses student's perception of the situation of the teacher. It emphasises social skills of communication that are involved in accepting, clarifying and making use of the ideas and feelings of students. Based on direction and criticism, it focuses on flexibility as a means of facilitating teacher-behaviour. The emphasis on performance necessarily leads to efficiency, accountably and results. Productivity is the key work in the suggested scheme which elevates teaching to a purposeful and meaningful educational activity that involves teachers and pupils in an enterprise of mutual benefit. Productivity is the ratio between time and product.

Different consideration and frames of references are used for taking decisions which finally constitute the plan while preparing educational plans. Planning is a sort of strategy-building for achieving a central goal. It involves setting of targets, ,making assumptions and choices and finally preparing a comprehensive plan or a programme of action based on priorities. In the field of education these choices and decisions may be required to be made on the basis of several viewpoints. The central point around which planning is done provides a particular model or approach for planning. There is no one single approach to educational planning. Over the years, in many countries various approaches to educational planning have been developed. The chief ones can be said to be are:

1. Social justice approach.
2. Social demand approach.
3. Cost benefit approach.
4. Man power approach.

Each of these models, however, has its own premises, a procedural logic and methodology, but these approaches are not mutually exclusive.

1. Social Justice Approach - This approach is also known as social planning or planning for social development. Social justice broadly means providing facilities and equal opportunities for development to all the people of a country. Articles 45 of the Indian Constitution urges the state to provide for free and compulsory education for all children up to the age of fourteen is a step towards social justice, and it has now been recognised as a right too. Similarly, making special provisions for the education of children for economically and socially backward communities is an attempt at rendering the needed justice to this section of society. Weaker sections of society do need special support from the government for their social and economic development. Education is shaped, to a great extent, by social or national goals of a country. The national policies and the constitutions broadly describe these goals of social development. Many of these goals are expected to be achieved through education. Hence, education and social development get linked up. It becomes essential for the educational system to contribute to the achievement of these goals. Hence, educational planning inevitably take into consideration these expected goals of social development likely to be achieved trough education.

Social justice is an important goals of social development. Making provision for achieving this goal while planning for education of the people of the country, would amount to social justice approach to educational planning. Social Planning approach to education may also mean devising a system of education through which such social changes can be brought about that are conducive to economic and social development of all people of the society. It may also mean providing various kinds of social services which may improve the quality of human life. Social justice approaches to educational planning seems to be just one aspect of the school development approaches to educational planning.

For the balanced development of the whole society, it is essential to make such special provisions while planning programs in the field of education. Making such considerations at the time of educational planning means adopting social justice approaches to educational planning,

Besides the above there can be most frequently used approaches to educational planning there can be other approaches too, depending upon what the focus of educational planning is, which major considerations guide the decision-making involved in planning. Therefore, we can also include the following three approaches in our study.

2. School Mapping Approach - The school mapping approach resembles much to the ingredients of the demographic approach, but is extends into a larger area taking a number of other variables into account in determining the optimal location of schools. Sometimes referred to as micro-planning the school map strategy has been important vehicle for moving educational planning from a largely national frame of reference to more detailed concerns with regional and local conditions and constraints in educational development, including concerns with the distributions of educational opportunities across national and regional entities. By constructing rather detailed maps of the actual or projected catchment areas of schools in terms of their demographic, geographic, social and transportation characteristics, an attempt is made to identify physical

locations that would maximise access of a school for a given population.

In the end it may be said that none of these approaches provides an adequate basis by itself for educational planning. A synthesis of all these is needed. An integrated approach is workable in planning. Mark Blaugh and J.A. Lauwerys point out in the Yearbook of the Education, "Each is only an index, guide-certainly not an exclusive guide- to the formulation of educational policy. In one sense they are not even indices of the same thing, gut rather different views of the nature of education."

3. Demographic Projection Approach - Demographic projection forms a part of virtually all approaches to educational planning in one form or the other, in that they provide the most basic parameters for estimating the population that a future educational system is required to serve. Estimations of the size of the age cohort to be served by a certain level of the educational system at a specific future point in time lead, of course, directly to some future projections of the intra-educational kinds, as it happens in case of estimating and adjusting future needs of teachers. Even the most limited intra-educational projection is, to some extent, dependent on some rough indication of the size and the age composition of demographic developments has become a source of planning criteria in its own right. Given that, in most societies the size of cohort is rather reliably known at least five of six years before secondary and tertiary institutions are attended. The major sources of error in this approach of educational planning have to do with points in the educational system where members of an age group can make choices between different educational options such as vocational or academic

forms of schooling. Hence, previous patterns of choice serve as an approximate basis for extrapolation.

4. Intra-Education Extrapolation Approach - The intra-education extrapolation approached is relatively simple to understand. It consists of estimating the quantitative implications for the system as a whole. It signifies setting targets for one particular characteristic of the educational system. Thus, the education planners would extrapolate from this dictum the ways in which the supply of teachers, construction of new buildings, production of new textbooks, and the like would need to be scheduled to ensure that the target will be reached. Statistics of various kinds become an important tool for this kind of analysis. This can become particularly involved and complicated when an attempt is made to take various sub-national situations into account.

5. Social Demand Approach - Social demand for education has a way of growing faster than manpower requirement, leading, on some occasions, to unemployment of the educated. The number of students trying to enter in schools or trying to stay in and go for further studies reflects society's social demand for education. This is not the same as society's manpower requirement for economic and social development. These may interact. Yet they behave quite independently. Educational aspirations of parents and children, and population explosion account for rapidly rising social demand for education in most countries of the world since the end of the World War II. The crucial relationship between social demand and educational system's capacity to satisfy it, is a key point in planning for education.

There are different strategies an educational system

can use to deal with the demand-supply gap. It can, at one extreme, throw open its doors, let everyone be in who wishes, allow them to stay in for as long as they like, and go as far as they wish. It may lead to bulging enrolments, crowded classrooms and probably a sharp dip in quality. This strategy may satisfy social demand or at least appear to do so, but at the price of a storm of protest about high drop-out rates, poor quality, and the waste of public resources. The gap between the desire for education and actual participation in the process of education may lead to several kinds of problems-economic, social and political.

India has been facing this problem since long. At the opposite extreme from this, there is a "wide-open" system where the policy is to give everyone a chance for a primary education, but a severely selective process governs who goes on from there. The social demand approach to planning in education emphasises that all those who wish to take admission to a particular class or courses should be accommodated and provided with all educational facilities, if they possess required qualifications, ability and attainment. This approach is preferred in those countries which are people oriented or welfare states. They have more permissive social order and people there play a dominant role in decision-making. India is also one of those countries where social demand for education has always greatly influenced educational planning and policies.

This is the policy of competitive selectivity and promotion based on individual's academic performance. The strategy produces "educated elite" considered necessary for nation's essential leadership. Social demand approach to educational planning emphasises that educational facilities should be extended in proportion to the degree they are demanded by people. But, this does not mean that there should be no limit to educational expansion. Social demand approach is not the only consideration that should guide educational planning and determine its parameters. Social demand for education may be unrealistic and an artifact of socio-cultural environment. In that case, educational planning should bot be wholly guided by this approached.

In a country like India where people live in a democratic set-up, social demand for facilities, up to a certain stage of education, has to be met. But, this need not be overdone. If social demand for education is given whole of weightage, it will lead to unemployment and widespread under-employment of the educated, which in turn, may threaten the social and political stability. Both the strategies, if not judiciously used, may land us in deep trouble. Hence, educational planning is required to take special care so that a balance between the two is maintained.

Ever since the independence of India, there has been a tremendous increase in the demand for education. Educational planning in India has taken this factor into consideration. Educational planning in India has failed to strike a balance between the need-planning in education. Many a time, restricted admission to higher education has been vehemently advocated by experts and educationists, but government has failed to check swelling crowds at the doors of educational institutions. Inability to incorporate an element of rationality in the social demand approach to educational planning in India, has resulted in lowering of educational standards.

6. Cost Benefit Approach - The cost benefit approach

or rate of return approach is favoured by yet anther group of economists. Cost benefit analysis implies a systematic comparison of the magnitude of the costs and benefits of some fort of investment. All forms of investment involve a sacrifice of present consumption in order to secure future benefits in the form of higher level of output or income. Cost benefit analysis provides as means of apprising these future benefits in the light of costs that must be incurred in the present.

a. The level of earnings of educated people must be higher to these of the people who are not educated, confirming that return on education is positive.

b. The pupil must acquire a productive capacity, be in a position to add to the sum-total production, should do much more than what he was doing without education. The variation between the two should be called productivity ascribed to education.

It is common experience in India that graduate clerk earns less than a middle pass semi-skilled worker. Education is expected to be beneficial to both the individuals. Parents want more education for him. More education and higher earnings are supposed to be positively related. This is way people want more education. But, positive investment is not always the case. Theoretically, investment in education, both at the level of an individual as well as the level of the nation, is bound to be positive so long there is no unemployment of the educated. Positive investment depends upon a closer relationship between education and manpower requirements of a country. If other correlated factors are not meaningfully taken into consideration, return on education may be poor or low. That is the case in India. In India, return on education is quite low. The relationship between education and the earnings of the educated people, is very poor; perhaps, it is on a negative scale. It is therefore obvious that we recognise our educational system with a view that gives it more productivity and work-oriented form.

Rate of return on education approach to educational planning emphasises that change in educational system should be so planned that both the individual citizens and the nation are benefited by the education of the people in this country. Educational planning has to take note of this and develop a proper perspective for bringing about changes in the system of education. In other words, it means that educational planning should provide for increase in the earning of the individuals with more education and also for greater contribution of such people to the economic and social growth of the country.

This approach requires working out the costs of various types and stages of education and comparing them with expected returns in the form of benefits to the individuals as well as to the society. Additionally, it ignores the non-economic benefits and indirect returns of education; personal satisfaction and cultural growth of the individual and the society. This approach has certain difficulties in actual planning. Measurement of return is not easy. They have developed certain criteria no doubt. But, these criteria are not comprehensive enough. It is diifficult to obtain data on cost-benefit or cost-effectiveness.

This approach is presently at its experimental stage of development and tells us more about the past than about the future. However, this approach, when applied to education, suffers from two handicaps-availability and estimation of adequate cost data, and the calculation of future benefits.

7. Manpower Approach - This approach in educational management planning is also known as the human resources development approach. Human resources is as important as other kinds of resources. Since this is possible only through education, it should be considered to be the most important function of educational planning. When this forms the focus of educational planning, there is said to be manpower or, human resources development approach of planning.

It implies that the social system, for its efficient functioning and operation, needs educated and trained people who have certain well-defined knowledge, attitudes and skills. It also assumes that the demand for such people, i.e., manpower is variable and changes with the technical, economic and social developments. Education, training and development of such people is considered as the human resources development for maintaining modernisation of country. This orientation in educational planning emphasises that educational system should be so designed or changes in educational system should be so planned that it should fulfil the country's manpower requirement. It should, in other words, produce as many educated and trained people of different categories such as doctors, engineers, teachers, graduates, postgraduates, etc., as are required by the country for its various services. Short production or over production of these will be a defect of planning or failure of planning technology.

A dearth of competent and trained manpower is now felt in nearly every branch of national life, and is probably one of the biggest bottlenecks to progress. It will be worthwhile to remember Whitehead's warning, "In the modern world the rule is absolute-any race which does not valued trained intelligence is doomed"

If India is to achieve its targets of economic growth, it must have an adequate supply of educated specialists for each category of job to be performed. We believe that estimates of future manpower needs form a useful basis for regulating enrolment patterns above the primary level. No comprehensive programme of educational development can ever be put across unless it involves every educational institution and all the human factors connected with it- its teacher, students and the local community- and unless it provides the necessary inducements to make them put in their best efforts. For various reasons, this involvements does not take place and lack of motivation fails to create these factors which have a large share in determining standards.

Harbinson holds that we should visualise all kinds of educational institutions as skill-generating centres. Educational planning in India has failed to adopt this approach as there is fast increasing unemployment in every field of manpower production in education. A large number of engineers, doctors, teachers, graduates and postgraduates are unemployed. This effects national development adversely which educational planning and human resource development should essentially be contributing to national development. The linkage between such centres is analogous to transmission lines. The manpower problems such as unemployed and skill shortage may be attributable to power failure in particular generating centre. Manpower planning approach focuses on solving such problems and tries to keep the manpower needs of the country in the centre of all considerations and choices. Manpower planning approach assumes that education has to place in the economy of the country and positively contributes to the nation's growth. Hence, from this point of view, education if regarded as skill-intensive and need-based. It emphasises that education should be linked with jobs. The approach supports vocationalisation of education, multi-purpose educational courses, trade courses and selective higher education.

Human resource development approach to planning in education assumes a still greater importance if education is regarded as a factor of economic development of a country. New ideas, new techniques and new knowledge of production determine the rate at which the economy of a country can advance on the whole. This is the contribution which education makes to the country's economic development, as it is from higher education and research establishments that the new ideas and techniques flow. Skills, which individuals acquire through education and training, are a result of formal education. Every country, therefore, builds up a system of education to fulfil these needs for trained, skilled and efficient manpower. Educational planning, in certain countries, focuses on this perspective.

Preparation of a Plan

We think it proper to set out the outline of a plan at the outset with the definition for its clear understanding. A programme of development and improvement prepared by an educational institution on the basis of its felt needs and the resources available or likely to be available, with a view to improving the school programme and school practices, constitutes a plan for an institution. The plan may be for a longer or a shorter duration.

An educational plan concerns itself with the programme of improvement based on the felt need of the institution. It is to be framed taking into account the available material and human resources. Efforts are made not to involve any financial expenditure. The plan may be for a longer or a shorter duration depending upon its nature., In this regard E.W. Franklin has said, "Instructional Planning is a milestone in the journey towards the improvement of education. The teacher is the kingpin in any educational effort. It is for the first time that the teaching community is being asked to act as planner and executor of educational improvement.

The Kothari Education Commission has also mentioned about the need of planning in view of the great need to improve standards of education at the school stage.

Characteristics of an Educational Plan

Professor M.B. Buch has listed the following characteristics of a good educational plan:

1. As a district has a large number of institutions, an institutional plan forms the basis of the district land.

2. A good institutional plan, besides bringing about improvement in the working of school, helps in its development. An institutional plan has to consider the pace of development and, plan for it.

3. Democratic procedure should be followed at all stages of the plan. All the persons connected with it should discuss all matters thoroughly.

4. An institutional plan is not a one-man job. It is a cooperative venture of all those concerned with education. Thus, the supervising staff, the headmaster of the institution, the teachers, the students and the

members of the community, should cooperate for the success of the plan.

5. The plan should be based on the felt needs of the school. Thus different schools will have different lands according to their needs. The needs of the school be identified by teachers, students and their parents.

6. A plan can be prepared for a certain institution only. It cannot be launched in another institution in exactly the same form. It is because no two institutions have the same problems, the same material and human resources.

7. An instructional plan inspires everybody to work hard and with enthusiasm. The staff, the students and the community have a better motivation because of the plan.

8. Optimum use should be made both of material and human resources available in the school. Moreover, the resource available in the community should also be used to the maximum.

9. The plan should lead to better understanding to the community and a greater rapport with it. Most of our institutions, especially the government ones, do not make use of the resources available in the community. A good institutional plan would help in this direction.

10. An institutional plan should be continuously developing in tune with the changes taking place in the environment. The plan cannot be rigid or fixed. It has to be modified in the light of new experiences.

11. The plan must have well-defined goals and objectives. It should lead to some definite and important aspect of school improvement.

Objectives of an Educational Plan

Institutional planning leads to enrich and better instruction. Thus, the students take more interest in studies. According to J.P. Naik, the following four objectives of institutional planning are important:

1. To emphasise what can be done here and now by mobilising our existing resources than waiting for the impossible to happen.

2. To involve every teacher in the formation and implementation of plans.

3. To make a teacher effective.

4. To give freedom to the teacher.

The head of the institution should be an efficient supervisor. He should supervise most of the activities of the school. Professor W.M. Ryborn has rightly remarked, Supervision should be comprehensive; its scope covers all the activities of the school. There is no branch of the school life that should escape the headmaster's notice, for the contributes to the making or unmaking of the pupil. Not only teaching alone is to be considered, but the occupation out of the school, the games, the hostel's life, the pupils sleep and diets, and the school work he does at home, not only from the stand-point of intellectual development but from that of his physical and moral development, all come within the ambit of his supervision.

School Plan and its Preparation

The major steps in preparation of the institutional plan for the improvement and development of a school are:

1. To Evaluate the Plan - The periodical evaluation will make the running of the school in a systematic manner. Every instructional plan should be put to

rigorous evaluation at fixed intervals and in the process of evaluation of those who are involved in its preparation should be associated in one form or another.

2. To Execute of the Plan - After preparation of a plan, it should be executed within resources and with maximum of efforts. The head of the institution should observe that it starts making progress in the right direction.

3. To Prepare the Plan - The instructional plan should be prepared taking into consideration the needs of a school and available resources and local, district, state and national plans. The following points should be considered at the stage of preparing the plan.

a. Decision about managing committee and other officials.

b. The detailed budged showing the likely financial resources and expenditure.

c. Duration of plan.

4. To Assess the Resources - We can collect information in respect of the problems of the school by the help of a survey. The next step is to find out ways to collect information about the resources available or which are likely to be available. Assessing the different resources can help in the progress of institutional plan.

5. To survey the Felt Needs of a School - It is essential to undertake a survey in order to find out the problems of the school before the preparation of plan. It will help to undertake programme of action for the improvement of the school in a planned way. By the help of a survey, needs of the school in respect of buildings, equipment, staff, strength of students, laboratory, library facilities, etc. can be studied.

Private/Public Schools

The main aim of sending a child to school should be to teach him to get along in the world. The responsibility for a child's school performance, or lack of it, is therefore shared by the teacher, the parents, and the institution in equal proportion. A little introspection is required of these care-givers with regard to their attitudes towards education and school work. The child is a unique individual with independent needs, feelings, abilities, and limitations, who has to face a world full for uncertainly and change. He has the natural ability to adapt, to expand his knowledge, and to solve new problems. He can do all this on his own, given enough time, necessary experience and a suitable environment. It should be the task of the school, the teachers and the parents to provide such environment and experience. Informal methods of teaching that foster transformation and evaluation of knowledge should be combined with goal directed play and leisure.

The concept of public school own its origin in Britain. Public schools anywhere are the schools set up by private bodies and organisations. Although confined to the better-off sections of society, the children in these schools have invariably shown better standards of achievement in academic, physical and personality development sphere.

A managing committee is needed to properly carry on the work of the school. In private schools the managing committee looks after all the work and is held responsible for the best management of the affairs. According to the Education Code, every private school must have a managing committee which is to be responsible for the management of the school. The school should have an independent committee consisting of the guardians, donors to the school establishment and eminent educationists. Some membership fee should be fixed for this. The members of the school managing committee should elect the members of the managing body.

The committee should be constituted in such a way that the working of the school may be conducted smoothly in the best possible manner. It is needles to point out that an ideal committee will be constituted if representation is given to people of all categories. Persons interested in the affairs of the school and belonging to different classes should be on his committee. In this committee the old students of the school, guardians, representatives of the teachers, headmaster, financial supporters of the school and educationists should be included in proper ratio.

From time to time, the members of the managing committee elect the president, vice-president, secretary, joint secretary and treasurer of the committee. The president of the committee will work as the manager of the school. The function of the manager will be to render assistance and co-operation to the headmaster.

The members of the managing committee themselves should elect the president who very often functions as the manager. It is sometimes seen that a conflict arises between the headmaster and the management committee due to certain differences. Hence, it is necessary that the committee should prescribe the sphere of activity for the headmaster and the manager. There should be no scope for any unpleasant situation. The school is a temple of learning. So, it should be the function of the managing committee to keep its atmosphere healthy. It is the duty of all members of the committee to take full interest in the affairs of the school. The manager should be an educated and trained person. In this way he will be able to understand to problems of the teachers. He will also know the needs of the school and will try to meet them.

The manager and the members of the committee can take part in various functions of the school and thereby help the teachers. If any member or the manager is interested in literacy activities, he can encourage the students to organise various contests such as anatakshri, debates, kavi Sammelans, Mushairas, music competitions, one act plays, etc. If he is interested in Red Cross and Scout activities, he may encourage such activities. In other works, the manager and the members should participate in some activities of the school according to their interests, and abilities.

The responsibility of the managing committee is to look to the all-round development and progress of the school. It is the duty of the committee to fulfil the need and requirements of the school and to help it achieve its aims. The manager should get from the headmaster the various information regarding the school building the furniture and the library. He should always try to fulfil the needs of the school.

6

TEACHER'S EDUCATION: OBJECTIVES

Introduction

In all societies, from least to most civilized, the teacher plays a critical role. Whatever his status in the social hierarchy, there is no doubt that his responsibility as one of the chief moulders of the future citizens is profound. Yet, widespread awareness of the magnitude of his responsibility tragically has not been translated into his efforts to make carcful instructional decisions. It in not surprising that most of the teachers are relatively unsophisticated regarding the instructional process and the act of teaching as the majority of them have been trained through the used of approaches that border on mystical. Most of the training approaches consist of traditionally designed programs aimed, at best, to foster a form of imitative behaviour in student-teachers, offer a series of abstruse principles or, a number of common-sense and obtuse suggestions for classroom practice, and load them with philosophical, sociological and psychological foundations spread over the entire expanse of recorded history, without caring to establish any functional relationship with their classroom relevance and import. There has been no consistent approach aiming at identifying and developing requisite skills amongst student-teachers at initial stages to enable them perform efficiently in actual classroom situations. The theory and practice of teaching were never so distant.

Happily, the situation is changing. We are becoming increasingly aware of the intricacies of instruction and it is now considered desirable and pragmatic to transmit such tangible competencies to student-teachers that would help them in their professional calling.

However, the present system of teacher training has lost the confidence and respect of much of the public. Attacked by critics, lacking practitioner support, and plagued with fatal deficiencies, teacher preparation programs cannot continue in their present form as they do not directly address to developing requisite teaching skills in the prospective teachers so as the give them total control on concept and process resulting in a significantly high profile class-room performance.

Teacher education refers to all those programs, strategies and appropriate tactics that would help a pupil-teacher transmit learning by generating learning structures during interactive classroom situation. Teacher-education has travelled a long way from a deadpan, hackneyed, conservative and outdated situation to emancipative, progressive and pragmatic outlook that makes teacher-education central to any meaningful educational enterprise.

Need of Teacher- Education

It has been aptly remarked. "If you educate a boy, you educate individual. If you educate a girl, you educated the whole family and if educate a teacher, you educate the whole community."

The Education Commission said, "A sound programme of professional educational of teachers is essential for the qualitative improvement of education.

Investment in teacher education can yield very rich dividends against the resulting improvements in the education of millions."

Teacher education is not teaching the teacher how to teach. It is to kindle host initiative, to keep it alive, to minimise the evils of the hit and miss process; and to save time, energy, money and trouble of the teacher and the taught. The necessity of the teacher to perceive that the course in Teacher Education would help him minimise his trouble, and to appreciate that it would save the children from much of the painful process through which he has himself passed. Teacher education is needed for developing a purpose and for formation of positive attitude for the profession.

Objectives of Teacher Education

1. Undertake action research and investigatory project.

2. Keep abreast of the latest knowledge of the subject matter he is teaching and the techniques of teaching the same.

3. Develop communication and psychomotor skills and abilities conductive to human relations for interacting with the children in order to promote learning inside and outside the classroom.

4. Develop competence to teach on the basis of the accepted principles of teaching and learning.

5. Develop understanding, interests, attitudes and skills which would enable him to foster all-round growth and development of the children under his care.

6. Develop- an understanding of the objectives of school education in the Indian context and awareness of the role of the school in achieving the goals of building

up a democratic, secular and socialist society.

7. Possess warm and positive attitude toward children and their academic, socio-emotional and personal problems, and skills to guide and counsel them.

8. Help in the conservation of environmental resources and preservation of historical monuments and other culture heritage.

9. Act as a liaison between the school and the community and employ suitable ways and means for integrating community life and resources with school work.

10. Perceive his role not only as a leader of the children but also that of a guide to the community.

11. Perceive his role as an agent of social change in the community.

12. Develop Gandhian values of education such as non-violence, truthfulness, self-discipline, self-reliance and dignity of labour.

Importance of Teacher-Education

That good teachers are born is no longer true. The advancement in the field of educational technology, that raises the level of teaching to that of a science, upholds that good teachers could be produced in the same manner as good doctors and engineers are produced. Further, even if good teachers were born, they would be in short supply and the shortfall would have to be augmented by such resourceful teacher-preparation programs so that good teachers could as well be produced out of sheer necessity. The shift from the theoretical and character approach to skills and competence, paves way for it.

A teacher may no longer be idolized as a blessed tool of knowledge-transmission conceived in some seventh heaven, as he is very much a product of behavioural interaction and strategies. However, inborn potential and aptitude would, perhaps, help and be a bonus. Teacher education, therefore, is the basic premise of any fruitful classroom interactive learning experience as it would train situations and contingencies leading to optimal learning. Sending one to teach without training would be, perhaps, as much risky as sending one to drive a car without any prior knowledge of its operations and controls. Teacher-education programs are designed to prepare teachers by providing theoretical awareness of the act of teaching; developing teaching competencies by acquiring useful skills that may help one further the cause of teaching as well as to put up a high profile classroom performance; and creating interest toward teaching in the prospective-teachers so that they would address themselves profitably with diligence and ingenuity.

Though most of human learning does not come by design yet the classroom in unique because it is a structured educational experience, and entails upon professional educators and industrial and military trainers the task of envisaging ways and means to make it a gainful experience. The process, therefore, stands in need to a thorough analysis in search of specific requirements or desired objectives, as well as the alternate approaches to achieve them. Any worthwhile teacher-education programme, therefore, must generate alternate approaches to learning in a manner that the prospective-teachers learn their ropes, under the watchful eye of the teacher-educators, and make teaching-learning a mutually gainful experience as well as to make teaching a happy and satisfying enterprise.

Management Development

Management forms the nexus of an enterprise whose success depends on the diligent application of its polices and programs. As management is all-pervasive, it must fall in line with the socio-economic demands and aspirations of a society in which it operates. A major portion of management function relates to futuristic growth and, therefore, depends on sound judgements and anticipation which can be developed in the management-incumbents through exposure to carefully and appropriately designed programs. This emphasis on management development became more pronounced in the second half of the last century when more and more business enterprises were concentrating on this concept by making it integral to their programs and personal training.

Besides, management developed consultancy services rendered by various trade associations, managements bureaus, productivity councils, and a host of other consultancy firms and agencies, has given a great spurt to this aspect of management and some sort of exposure in this regard is considered essential to inculcate necessary skills, competencies and attitudes amongst the incumbents to ensure more predictable performance. Management development is a reality which has come to stay as a vital organ of any management programme, making it more realistic and viable.

Management development is restricted not only to industry and business, but has found ingress into civil and defence services, nationalised banks, Life and General Insurance, medical and engineering services, church and school where the executives are put through a series of compact package programs at various levels. Though the emphasis is on designing own management development programme by such establishments, some enterprising counselling agencies also render cover thus adding to the expertise available in this field. The realisation that has come to stay is that, as in other fields, necessary management development is vital for prospective leaders of industry, services, commerce and various other essential services so as to inculcate relevant competencies amongst their incumbents.

Pre-Service Teacher -Preparation

It was a common norm at every stage of social evolution that, since a teacher had a sacred trust and deep social obligation and accountability for the performance and progress of his wards, and as such, teaching was a professional activity, a prospective teacher, by sheer force of necessity, needs an exposure to foundational ground-work in this regard so as to enable him do his job with satisfaction and elan. This activity was referred to by various names but what is basically meant was that a prospective teacher needs to be prepared before he takes up his professional calling. Pre-service teacher-preparation, therefore, became a professional requirement. The nature and extent of teacher preparation might vary but it did not gloss over the basic principles irrespective of the form or philosophy of a preparatory programme.

A quick glance around the educational sense reveals that these programs generally varied in refinement, experiential richness, sophistication, depth and orientation, as they advanced upward on a scale of knowledge-skill-attitude, making a teacher grow along behavioural and attitudinal cordinals. However, these programs are at post-graduate level.

Starting as a Licentiate in teaching, a teacher passed through the stage of awareness and training. Since training deals at a lower intellectual level, it was considered that a teacher needs to be educated wherein he interacts at a higher cognitive, behavioural, intellectual and emotional level. However, the latest trends transcend even this approach and proclaim about teacher-development which is a far more inclusive and befitting term, especially in view of the managerial role that a teacher has acquired of late. Teacher-Development is presently the ultimate pre-service teacher-preparation.

Objectives of Secondary Teacher Education

Objective -1 : Possesses competency to teach subject of his specialisation and accepted principles of teaching and learning in the context of new school curriculum.

(i) Possesses the skills to teach.

(ii) Appreciates the rationale of 10+2 curriculum.

(iii) Understands the concept of work experience.

(iv) Knows the ways through which adolescent learns.

(v) Deficiencies, shortfalls and errors committed by an author. Suggests solutions for overcoming the falls and observes deficiency and pitfalls.

(vi) Makes an internal and external judgement of the quality of an article through ideal or principles against a criterion.

(vii) Depth of understanding of the concepts pertaining to his discipline.

Objective -2 : Understands action research, experimental research, projects or investigatory projects, to improve his own teaching effectiveness and in enabling children to develop their optimal capacities.

In-service teacher education refers to that education which a teacher receives after entering the teaching profession subsequent to passing out from a teacher's college. As such, it is subsequent education regarding his profession so that he remains on track and updated. This education, therefore, includes all such social, educational or other programs in which a teacher participates actively and willingly for his professional advancement, polishing and success, by enlarging his experience and vision, it, sort of releasing him refresher courses, seminars, workshops, extension lectures, conferences, travels and visits to places related with his profession. In short, it is continued education of teachers.

Objective - 3: Understands the role of school and teacher in changing the society.

Objective - 4 : Understand the role of school, home and peer groups in shaping the personality of the child, and in developing a relationship between school and home.

Objective - 5 : Develops skill in guiding and counselling the learners in academic vocational subjects as well as in their academic and personal problems.

(i) Applies experimental behavioural treatment and detect, its effect by finding out the magnitude to improvement.

(ii) Elites cooperation form institutional, personal,

community, experts for personality data.

(iii) Organises a guidance clinic;

(iv) Applies guidance and counselling techniques on problematic children deficient in their academic achievement in relation to their intelligence.

(v) Understands the concept of guidance and counselling.

Objective - 6: Develops skill in identifying selecting innovation and organising learning experience pertaining to the subject of his specialisation.

(i) Subjects to the situation evoking their initiative, voluntary effective participation, ego involvement and raising the level of aspiration.

(ii) Presents the learning experience in a logical and psychological sequence.

(iii) Conceiving activities which may develop the specific behaviour.

(iv) Developing specific objectives of teaching units.

(v) Analysing the learning content into its elements.

Objective - 6: Possesses sufficient theoretical and practical knowledge about an adolescent's health and physical education programme, work experience and recreational activities.

(i) Applies first aid.

(ii) He is able to make a healthy guess about the nature of bodily disorder and the type of treatment it may require.

(iii) Knows about the role physical education, games and recreational activity on the health of an adolescent and is able to detect causes showing health disorders.

(iv) Knows about the systems causing infections and contagious disease.

(v) Knows the structure and functioning of various bodily systems.

(vi) Know the sources at school, home, neighbourhood and other local institution which influence health.

Objective- 7 : Develops understanding, skills, interests and attitude which would enable him to foster to all could growth of the child.

(i) Conference with the adolescent.

(ii) Organisation of socio-culture functions and excursions.

(iii) Manifests his psychomotor sides is formal and informal institutional situations.

(iv) Understands the significance of enabling the child to make wholesome personality development.

(v) Understands the total concept of personality.

(vi) Knows the various techniques through which total personality development.

(vii) Intrinsic and extrinsic readings pertaining to adolescent growth, problems and needs.

(viii) Possesses communication, mental and social skills to interact with pupils.

Objectives- 8 : Possesses competency to teach subject of his specialisation and accepted principles of teaching and learning in the context of new school curriculum.

(i) Possesses the skills to teach.

(ii) Appreciates the rationale of 10+2 curriculum.

(iii) Understands the concept of work experience.

(iv) Knows the ways through which adolescent learns.

(vi) Suggests solutions for overcoming the falls and observes deficiency and pitfalls.

(vii) Deficiencies, shortfalls and errors committed by an author.

(viii) Makes an internal and external judgement of the quality of an article through ideal or principles against a criterion.

(ix) Depth of understanding of the concepts pertaining to his discipline.

Teacher Development

Building on the conclusions of the preceding section, a suggestion is made to usher in similar development programs for teachers. Teacher development is the ultimate goal. Why a similar development approach be not applied to management of classroom teaching? Why not apply management training to classroom teaching so as to provide right type of job experience, skills and attitudes to student-teachers? Why not develop teachers? Why should management development be not the fore-runner of teacher development?

Teacher development is a self development programme designed to inculcate right type of knowledge, skills and attitudes among prospective teachers by providing necessary exposure under controlled conditions. It helps an individual develop his abilities to the fullest and the farthest thus enabling him perform more satisfactorily in relation with a body of students. It is a performance based programme aiming at narrowing down the gap between performance and performance-objectives by means of appraisal and scientific observation.

Importance

1. The hallmark of a good teacher is that he is himself always learning and developing his knowledge and understanding of the children and the young people.

2. I prefer that my students should drink from a running stream rather than a stagnant pool.

3. A teacher can never truly teach, unless he is still learning himself. A lamp can never light another lamp unless it continues to burn its own flame.

In fact, a teacher should be a better person who, because of his attitude to knowledge, ideas, to his fellows and to life generally, is better educated than he is today. That education is a continuous process could, perhaps, never be more true than in the case of teacher education. It saves him from stagnation, disillusionment, dissatisfaction and isolation. It helps him hold his flag high and firm. However, in-service education should not be left to a teacher's own initiative and ingenuity: opportunities should be created to involve him in such forward moving activities by means of advancement, incentives and status. It is in this sense that in-service teacher education is referred to as a cooperative enterprise.

Improvements in Teacher-education suggested by Kothari Commission

1. Increasing the number of working days.

2. Increasing the physical facilities of the training institutions.

3. Improving the academic and professional qualification of teacher educators.

4. Making post-graduate courses in education flexible.

5. Developing new professional courses to orientate headmasters, teacher-educators, educational administrators, etc.

6. Undertaking surveys of the curricula and initiating revision of courses for teachers training.

7. Improving professional training by undertaking well-planned subject orientation or content courses.

8. Removing the isolation of teacher training institutions by bringing them into the mainstream of the academic life of the universities, on the one hand, and school life and education on the other.

Revitalization and Modernization

The Commission suggested the following measures to improve teacher education:

1. Increased Working Hours.
2. Competent Teacher Educators.
3. Adequate Physical Facilities.
4. Use of Technology in the Training of Teachers.
5. Comprehensive Content-cum-Methodology.
6. Systematic Internship of Practice of Teaching.
7. Due Emphasis on Practical Skills.
8. Study of Education as a Discipline.
9. Restructuring the Curriculum.
10. Four-year Integrated Course.

National Commission on School Teachers: Findings

and Suggestions

Drawbacks in the existing system of Teacher Education - The National Commission of School Teachers lamented that what obtains now in the majority of our Teachers Colleges and Training Institutions are woefully inadequate in the context of the changing needs of India today. It found the following major drawbacks and problems of the present system of teacher education :

1. Dearth of new technology of teaching.

2. Shorter working hours.

3. Lack of physical facilities.

4. Less qualified teacher educators.

5. Faulty methods of assessment of trainee's work.

6. Ineffective supervision of the teaching practice by an supervisors.

7. Meager training in the art of organising co-curricular activities.

8. Insufficient training in the art of communicating with the community.

9. Isolation between the Colleges of Education and the schools.

10. Insufficient time and attention paid to the actual practice teaching.

11. Inadequate training in practical skills.

12. Neglect of duty of eduction as a discipline.

13. Obsolete and irrelevant methodology of teaching.

14. Lop-sided curriculum.

Recommendations

1. Networking arrangement will be created between institutions of teachers education and university departments of education.

2. The National Council of Teacher Education will be provided necessary resources and capabilities to accredit institutions of teachers education and to provide guidance regarding curriculum and methods.

3. Secondary school teacher training colleagues will be upgraded to complement the work of State Council of Educational Research and Training.

4. District Institutes of Education and Training will be established with capacity to organise pre-service and in-service courses for elementary school teachers, and for personnel working in non-formal and adult education.

5. New teacher-education programs will lay emphasis on continuing education and the needs of teachers to meet the thrusts envisages in the NPE-86.

6. Teachers education is a continuous process and its pre-service and in-service components are inseparable. System of teacher education will be overhauled, revamped and revitalised.

NPE- 86 and Teacher Education

Observations

1. Teacher's association must play a significant role in upholding professional integrity, enhancing the dignity of the teacher and in curbing professional misconduct. National level associations of teachers could prepare a Code of Professionals Ethics for Teachers and ensure its observance.

2. The methods of recruiting teachers will be re-

organised to ensure merit, objectivity and conformity with conformity with spatial and functional requirements. The pay and service conditions of teachers have to be commensurate with their social and professional responsibilities, with the need to attract talent to the profession. Efforts will be made to reach the desirable objective of uniform emoluments, service conditions and grievance removal mechanisms for teachers through out the country. Guidelines will be formulated to ensure objectivity in the posting and transfers to teachers. A system of teacher evaluation-open, participative and data based, will be created and reasonable opportunities of promotion to higher grades provided. Norms of accountability will be laid down with incentives for good performance and disincentives for non-performance. Teacher will continue to play a crucial rolc in the formulation and implementation of educational programs.

3. The status of the teacher reflects the socio-cultural ethoes of a society: it is said that no people can rise above the level of its teachers. The government and the community should endeavour to create conditions which will help motivate and inspire teachers on constructive and creative lines. Teachers should have the freedom to innovate, to device appropriate methods of communication and activities relevant to the needs and capabilities of and the concerns of the community.

Qualitative Improvement of Teacher Education

Qualitative improvement of teacher education refers to the increase in teacher's ability, skill and broadening of his mental and attitudinal horizons to make him feel responsible and accountable for his role in nation building. Quality teacher education, therefore, must aim at giving adequate and right knowledge, useful communication skills and socially desirable attitudes toward profession and society. If envisages reorganization at all levels along following dimensions:

1. Improving Methods of Teaching and Evaluation - In training institutions the methods for evaluating the performance of student- teachers are the traditional ones. Students adopt the following methods for getting the highest possible grades in the practical examinations:

a. Offering gifts and services unconnected with their calling. One may refer to Batti's satire on this which reckoned the entire nation by exposing the exploits and woeful conditions, though restrict only to Ph.D. level. Nothing could be more disgraceful.

b. Pleading with the principals/faculty/examiners in a manner derogatory to the noble profession of teaching.

2. Vitalising Professional Studies - Many of the topics forming a part of professionals or vocational studies at present lacking utility should be eliminated. Professional studies should consist exclusively to topics which are useful for student-teachers. It has been suggested that the real need is for the synthesizing and harmonising various curricula according to Indian conditions. The Commissions's view is that these curricula suffer from the following defects:

a. Teacher education is unfortunately replete with platitudes. The reason for this lies in the absence of a tendency to read the best books on the science of education. At the primary level, there is a distinct tendency to read cheap guides or notes.

b. In Indian conditions because of the total absence or a minimum of research, the teacher educators generally talk only of theory, and their elaboration is replete with examples taken from foreign countries, and are, therefore, hackneyed.

3. Reorientation of Subject Knowledge - The purpose of such a scheme is that, during training at the primary and secondary level, the trainees should be imparted knowledge of the subject apart from information upon the modalities of teaching. The Kothari Commission's caution is that such a programme should be carefully planned. In it, the use of the given information, in the light of basic facts and school subjects, should be made sharply explicit. In addition, text level as a measure of aid and help. At least 20% of the entire training time should be given to a study of the subject itself.

In the context of any training there is the Internal question regarding the period of training essential for a specific level. In this context, the Kothari Commission has given two kinds of suggestions:

a. At the primary level, the training period should be of two years. Where the period is at present of one year, it can conveniently be extended to two years.

b. At the secondary level, where the existing curriculum extends over one year, it should be extended to two years, as justice is never done to the curriculum in the short period prescribed at present.

However, the biggest obstacle in this context is that it is neither desirable from economic viewpoint nor is practical. Consequently, the Education Commission and most wisely suggested that the working days in a year should be increased, from the present 180 or 190 days to at least 230 days. Since such an experiment has proved eminently successful in some training institutions, the Commissions suggested that the change should immediately be implemented else where also.

At the secondary level, the cooperation of teachers of the other departments of universities should also be sought for improving content knowledge. The Commission suggests that any such reorientation programme should be composed of the teaching method relevant to the subject as well as special techniques. The traditional ways of preparing lessons should be abandoned.

Types of Teacher Education Institutes

1. Summer school- cum- Correspondence Courses - An improvement step taken in this direction and been the organising of summer schools-cum-correspondence courses leading to B.Ed. degree at all the four Regional Colleges of Education. This course includes full time training at the summer and instruction through correspondence during the ten months period between the two summer vacations.

2. Comprehensive Colleges - A comprehensive college of education prepares teachers for several stages of education and/or of a number of special fields. Some institutions of this type already exist and have shown good results. The Education Commission recommends that planned attempt should be made to develop more institutions of this type and add sections for training primary and/or pre-primary teachers to training colleges that now prepare teachers for secondary schools only.

3. Regional Colleges of Education - Another important project for teacher education in the diversified system of secondary education relates to the setting up of the Regional Colleges of Education and their attached demonstration multi-purpose schools at Ajmer, Bubaneshwar, Mysore and Bhopal. The first three were

started in 1963 while the latter in 1964. These colleges are designed to represent a new enterprise in teacher eduction, to train competent teachers and teacher educators in certain critical areas like science, technology, industrial crafts, commerce and agriculture, so that they can function in their selected subject fields, in any system of education like technical, commerce and agricultural schools, and not only in multipurpose schools. These programs are: Four-year bachelor's degree programs in science, technology, commerce, agriculture and English. One-year training programs in science, commerce and agriculture; industrial craft programs of one, two and three year duration; and tow-year Master's degree programme. The colleges have undertaken a crash programme of training teachers to clear the backlog through correspondence-cum-summer schools, which may be regarded as sandwich course.

4. State Institutes of Education - In 1964, a chain of State Institute of Education was set up in all the major States with the assistancc of the Union Government. The main purpose and functions of the institutes, are among others, to provide various training courses for the supervisors of schools or teacher educators; organise conferences and seminars for senior State education officers, or non-official office-bearers of local bodies connected with education; to provide, conduct and supervise extension services training institutions for elementary teachers; organise research to provide correspondence courses for teachers; to improve the programme of teacher education in the State and, to assist the State Education departments in the preparation and implementation of educational plans.

5. Training Colleges for Special Subjects - these are separate classes for colleges for preparing teachers in

certain subjects like physical education, home science, crafts, languages, etc.

6. Training Colleges or Colleges of Education or University Education departments for higher degrees - These institutes provide opportunities to take up Master of Education and Ph.D. Courses.

7. Training Colleges or Colleges of Education - The minimum qualification for entrance is graduation. The duration of the course is one year. Degree awarded is B.Ed. or B.Ed. These colleges provide teachers for secondary and senior secondary schools.

8. Training for Middle and Secondary Teachers - These schools provide teachers for the middle and junior secondary schools and are gradually disappearing.

9. Pre-primary Teacher Training Institutions - Catering to the needs of teachers for Kindergarten, Montesoori, Bal Vihars etc. minimum qualification for admission to this course is higher secondary and the duration of the course is one year. May institutes impart training for two years.

Suggestions

In view of this, the Commission suggested that student-training should be split in to two stages:

1. The Student-teacher should, at the second stage, be made to teach for a continuous period of at least eight weeks. Such teachers must be made to work as integral part of the teaching staff and not as mere appendages.

2. The student-teachers should be made fully aware of the conditions in the school as well as the actual conditions prevailing in the classroom during teaching.

3. Revision and Improvement of Curriculum - The

Commission expressed to hope that the curriculum be revaluated in the light of the suggestions of the Teacher Education Commission. This revaluation should be oriented primarily toward utility. Its suggestions in this regard are:

a. For the purpose of practice teaching, conditions which are in consonance with the needs of modern society should be created. Fundamental facts should be kept in view while seeking solutions to problem.

b. At the primary level, general education should be coextensive with training. They need a curriculum which can evolve a suitable social and cultural attitude to life.

c. The curriculum of teacher education is divided into two parts. In the theoretical part art the principles of education, child development and child psychology, modalities of teaching, organisation of schools, and health education. In the practical aspect are such activities as practice teaching, craft, community life, etc. These subjects should be so reoriented as to create insight in the teacher regarding the school system.

4. Development of Special Programme and Courses - As already pointed out it is essential for the development of education that new curricula and courses be developed. The Education Commission has spoken in terms of introducing education as a subject at the graduate and post graduate levels. There should be special courses for principals, and short term courses for those about to assume the charge of principal. Short courses should also be devised for educational trainers at the primary and secondary levels. There should be other bridge programs after the completion of which they could teach higher classes. At the primary and

secondary levels, there should be composite courses. The Commission stresses that the devising of such programs should be the combined responsibility of NCERT, the Department of Education, and the National Council of Teacher Education.

National Council for Teacher Education

The NCTE been established as a national level statutory body by the Government of India vide its notification dated 17 August 1995. The main objectives on the Council are to achieve planned and coordinated development of the teacher education system, regulation and proper maintenance of norms and standards of teacher education. The NCTE has laid down norms and standards for pre-primary, elementary and secondary teacher education institutions and for B.Ed correspondence/distance education mode.

National Bodies, National Council of Education Research and Training

In 1961, and event of great significance in the field of teacher education was the establishment of the National Council of Educational Research and Training. The Council has set up a National Institute of Education as a national organisation to offer high level teacher-education and to investigate into the problems of education and suggest solutions for them. Its objectives, among others, are to examine, evaluate and coordinate the programs of teacher-education conducted by the State Departments of Education and the universities and to take all such measures as will lead to an improvement in teacher- education at elementary and secondary level.

Suggestions

For this purpose, the Commission offered the following suggestions -

1. Improvement of Student- Teaching - The lessons imparted to student teachers for training are not suitably planned, examined or evaluated. Most of the lessons are not examined at all, and, in addition, the period of practical teaching work is almost never more than 2 or 6 weeks.

2. In the developed countries, methods of teaching are constantly changing and developing. Such tools as radio, television, film-strips, programmed instruction, language laboratories, etc. have come into common use there. In India, too, ratio and television have begun to broadcast lesson for schools and even higher learning.

Besides, an equally necessary improvement is the change in the system of examination. As in schools, so too in training institutions, arrangements are made for external examinations. As long as examinations are not modified and improved, teaches will not adopt the modern methods of evaluation, and hence, there will be no improvement in evaluation through examinations at the school level. Hence, internal assessment must necessarily be recognised as an essential part of evaluation. Training schools should maintain cumulative the proper analysis of such records.

3. The attitude of the students should be developed and made nature on the basis relations, and stress should be laid upon the importance of social values in the development of education.

4. Student- teachers should be brought to the required level maturity through contact, experience, study and debates, for which independent study and the cooperation of students is essential. Unfortunately,

they do not come with the preformed habits of self-study and independent thinking. Training institutions must try to overcome this handicap and accustom students to thinking, self-study and discussion. Individual work in the work, seminars, debates, conferences, etc., should be an integral part of the curriculum of training institutions.

A teacher is a nation builder. It is in his hands that the future of a country shapes up, slowly unobserved yet definitely. As such, no study on teacher education could be worthwhile. If is does not observe, study and discuss him in all totality to gauge his present lot and to prepare a road map for his active and willing participation in social reconstruction, reformation and progress. Teacher, therefore, is central to all educational theories and practices: it is in him that society finds its fulfillment, culmination and reckoning. He needs to be understood and looked after so as to enable him give his unstained and unreserved best toward the stupendous task of nation building.

A society that does not respect and honour its teachers would not go very far. No wonder, free India decided to celebrate 5 September as the Teachers Day in recognition of their services and devotion to national being and prosperity. Special awards are made to special teachers of all levels, their services recalled, contribution recounted, dreams shared, with applause and aplomb. But it is resources and status, One cannot last on laurels alone: there are more basic needs of a teacher as a simple, unassuming and even uncaring, human being. Society owes it to him, and he must get what he deserves, if not more.

It is in this context that a reference is made by the

Secondary Education Commission to the study of a teacher's present lot and to suggest a rainbow that may bring colours and smiles to this long neglected standard-bearer of human and cultural values in our fast developing, dynamic society.

Major Problems of Teacher Education

1. Careless in teaching and absence of a sense of purpose.

2. No provision of Model Lessons.

3. Non availability of Demonstration school and lack of professional commitments of school Principals and Management.

4. Traditional Influence and Conservation - Even today, the curriculum is ancient, traditional, the ideal lessons are patently unpsychological, teaching aids are not used effectively and intelligently, indifferences and neglect are often displayed. In addition, the opportunities for fruitful discussion are few and far between hostel facilities are often lacking, and opportunities for mutual contact and co-operation and negligeable. S.N. Mukerjee pointed out that in order to raise the standard of teacher training attention should be paid to a proper management and organisation of the teachers' education programme, administration, finance educational institutions' selection for admission, preserves education, practical training, in-service education, research, and its publication, preparation of college teachers and lack of course.

5. In-service Training - In-service training includes in its ambit such activities as refresher courses, short term intensive curricula, practical knowledge of workshops, seminars, professional conferences, etc.

However, even those suffer from numerous inconsistencies.

6. Problem of Selection for Training - Training colleges were facing the problem of granting admissions, and undoubtedly, the choice of able and suitable individuals for training as teachers was the major problem.

7. Absence of Free, Untrammeled Atmosphere - In training schools, the atmosphere of freedom was conspicuously lacking, and because of the oppressive atmosphere, students were often seen indulging in flattery so that they may obtain good grades.

8. Neglect of Human Values - During training, the entire focus was upon objectives, goals, etc. , while human values were completely neglected. In the opinion of K.G. Saydian, the candidates were unable to visualise the fact that education was a specific social and cultural process. Because of lack of foresight and undue emphasis upon minor details or technical necessities, the close relationship of the school with society, the living problems of schools, and other important issues were lost sight of.

9. Lack of Suitable Curriculum - The curriculum of training was defective wherein student was compelled to study subject which bear no relationship whatsoever to actual teaching.

10. Imbalance between Theory and Practice - Training schools normally lay too much stress upon the principles or theory of teaching, whereas equal importance should be given to practice teaching as well.

11. Lack of Coordination between School and Training Institutions - According to K.G. Saiyidain, the

candidate's knowledge of theory and their actual conduct in the classroom, remain two distinct elements, instead of blending with the strengthening or reinforcing each other. Hence, it is necessary that there should be a balance between theory and practice, so that the gap between the schools and the training establishments is effectively bridged.

Observation of Secondary Education Commission

We are, however, convinced that the most important factor in the contemplated reconstruction is the teacher, his personal qualities, his educational qualifications, his professional training and the place the he occupies in the school as well as in the community. The reputation of a school and its influence on the life of the community invariably depend on the kind of teachers working in it. Priority of consideration must, therefore be given to the various problems connected with the improvements of their status.

Suggestions to Improve

Prof. K.G. Sayidain suggested the following suggestions for overcoming the shortcomings and problems of teachers education:

1. Predagogy of Teaching - As it the case in some universities, the science of education should be made on of all alternative or optional subjects.

2. Understanding the Progression - Individuals interested in adopting the teaching profession should keep in mind the needs of their future profession so that they do not acquire piecemeal knowledge and then seek admission to a training establishment. Such individual should shun all knowledge which bears no relationship to teaching, which is to be their future profession.

3. Selection of Trainees - The rough shod and stereotyped methods in use for the selection of new candidates should be replaced by more effective, adequate and scientific techniques of selection. These techniques should be capable of accurate evaluation of the aspiring candidate's moral and mental qualities.

4. Prospective Teachers - Having made arrangements for the training of Veteran and experienced teachers in the manner outlined above, the question now remains of those individuals who, having completed their college or university admission, wish to secure admission to a teacher's training institution. From among these candidates, only those individuals, who really posses the potential for becoming able and successful teachers, should be chosen.

5. Short term Courses - Short-term curricula should be prepared for the veteran and experienced teachers, who, for one reason of the other, could not take admission on training colleges. On receiving systematic training, these teachers will add to their efficiency, win promotions to higher ranks and feel more secure and satisfied in their jobs.

6. Manpower and Planning - State should, with the assistance of its training colleges and department of education, carry out a survey at least once in every five years to ascertain the need for male and female teachers in all the schools of the state. Admissions to teacher training establishments should be based exclusively upon this estimate.

Meaning of Isolation

In common parlance, isolation means the tendency of teachers of different levels living in aloofness. They work in their areas narrowly and do not like to meet or exchange their views with one another. They have no common platform where they can sit jointly and discuss serious educational issues and challenges faced by the country. By and large, the university teachers look down upon the college teachers and similar is the situation at other levels of education. Teachers of different levels of education are not on talking terms and suffers from a sense of inferiority complex. This is a dangerous trend and is causing great harm to the teaching profession as a whole and ultimately to the social fabric.

Similarly, the teachers of teacher education departments have no liaison with the school teachers. They are sitting in ivory towers and suffer from superiority complex. They forget the their main job is to prepare secondary school teachers. There is no coordination those praised in schools. Similarly, there is isolation between the teachers of B.Ed and B.T.C. training institutions. The teachers of post-graduate colleges also look down upon the teachers of B.Ed departments with great suspicion and contempt.

For all-around development of teacher education there is an urgent need to minimise and thus eliminate the prevailing isolation. All should act in unison for the welfare of students, teachers and the community.

The Teaching community, today is divided into a number of classes of sub-classes, among which their is little or no interaction. The primary teacher regards himself as inferior to the secondary, college or university teacher, just as the university teacher regards himself as far superior to all these classes of teachers an, remains proudly alienate from them. This alienation can be seen at three levels:

1. Alienation from Each Other - In various ways, the

various teacher training institutions are also alienated from each other, with the result that they have failed to create a cohesive community even among themselves.

2. Distant from School Life - Teacher's education at the primary and secondary levels is distinct and distant from the modern development of colleges and college educations.

3. Isolation from University Life - The professional education of the primary teacher if not seen from the viewpoint which applies to university education. The professional education of the secondary level is related to universities but even there relationship with the other subjects taught in the university is very little.

Isolation of Teacher Education

It is firmly believed that all teachers, irrespective of their level, proficiency and status, share and common bond that runs through their professional callings, needs and obligations. It is however, seen that teachers associated with higher education and level of learning do not appreciate the drills and procedures, techniques and methods, strategies and tactics, very kindly. On the contrary they are rather curt and even ridicule these procedures of school teaching, and consider themselves beyond such overtures.

It is nothing but crisis of status in which a poor school teacher suffers indignity in silence even amongst his won kind. Teachers must perform, and it is here that all teachers share the same touchstone: that all teacher must lead to learning by generating appropriate learning situations so as to make learning interesting, satisfying and memorable.

This criterion may vary at various levels of teaching,

but nevertheless is the basis of all successful classroom encounters. The phenomenon of disparity amongst teachers of various levels is generally referred to as isolation of teacher education wherein aloofness or, touch-ne-not attitude creeps in the system with disdain toward and neglect of a very great number of teachers associated with school and pre-school teaching. It cuts at the very roots of teacher fraternity which is one and indivisible. When teacher constituencies for electing teachers to the state legislative Councils do not discriminate the rights of a teacher on the basis of status and level, why should teacher community have such indifferent attitude toward the performance, objectives and commitments of their junior brethren who, infact, are the pre-condition of their existence and survival. The alienation and segmentation must be guarded against.

Strengthening Teacher Educational Programme: 9th Five Year Plan (1997-2002)

1. Reaching out to Primary Schools Teachers in Remote areas - To supplements the efforts to improve school effectiveness, an institutional mechanism will be put in place to provide on-the -spot counselling and guidance to teachers located in remote areas. This will be in the form of Mobile Teams of Resource Persons. Logistic arrangements will be location-specific, based upon felt needs and environment.

2. Upgradation of Infrastructure - The process of strengthening Teacher Education Programme will be given a further impetus by upgrading the physical and academic infrastructure of:

a. Institutes of Advanced Studies in Education. District Institutes of Education and Training, Block

Resources Centres/Cluster Resources Centres.

b. Departments of Education in University.

c. National Council of Teacher Education.

d. Colleges of Teacher Education.

e. State Councils of Educational Research and Training.

3. Initiative for North-Eastern States - The North-Eastern States, which have a larger percentage of untrained teachers in elementary schools, will launch programme to cover this gap by adopting the following measure:

a. NCTE will establish a Regional Committee for North-Eastern States to provide the necessary fillip to the teacher training institutions.

b. A Diploma Programme for Primary Education developed by Indira Gandhi National Open University will be launched in collaboration with the State Governments.

4. Curriculum Development - The draft curriculum framework developed by the National Council for Teacher Education will be finalised and made the basis for curriculum change in institutions for teacher education. This will help to improve the quality of Teacher Education Programme.

Conclusion

1. In the context of teacher education, Dr. Radhakrishnan observed that teacher occupies a very important place in society because he brings about the transfer of the intellectual tradition from one generation to the next. At the same time, he maintains the level of technological skill and keeps the light of civilisation

burning bright. He not only guides the individual, he shows the whole nation the right direction. The Kothari Commission, too was constrained to observe that the most important thing is to create satisfactory conditions of work for the teachers of our country.

2. Dr. Sampurnanda stated that the nation should be conscious of the sentiments and needs of its teachers. On the other hand, it is expected of the teachers that they will provide able and devoted leaders in every sphere of life, despite the fact that the teachers themselves are compelled to live in circumstances which are not conducive to efficiency, skill or even self-respect.

Other Effective Measures

1. Part-time Teacher Education - Proper arrangements should be made for part-time education.

2. Period of Training - The period of training for those who have received secondary education should be two years, while graduates should receive training for one year.

3. State Board of Teacher Education - State boards of teacher education should be established.

4. Status of Training Institutions - Training colleges should be raised to the same status and level as that of other colleges of universities.

5. Barriers should be Removed - The distance and barriers between particular subjects such as arts, physical education, etc., should be done away with.

6. Extension Services - In order to bridge the gap between training institutions and schools, there should be extension service departments at the pre-primary, primary and secondary levels in each establishment.

There should also be an organisation of old students which should offer suggestions regarding the curriculum of training. Candidates receiving training should be sent to recognised schools. The supervisory staff should be transferred from one school to another at regular intervals.

7. Colleges of Education - Universities should set up colleges of education which may provide assistance in training teachers and research.

8. Elective Subject - Education should be introduced as an elective subject for the first as well as the second degree.

Eradicating Isolation from University

Kothari Commission had felt that the nature of education is different from that of other academic subjects, but despite this, it should be available to the common masses. In its vies, education should be included in the main flow of the academic life of the university. In India, education is mainly associated with pedagogy, i.e., it is taught almost exclusively in training institutions, and only to those who have decided to enter the teaching profession at school level whereas, in the advanced countries, education if regarded as a separate, specific subject, comparable to any other social science.

After assuming that education is a process of social, political and economic change, it is regarded as far removed from implementability or practicability like other philosophies or subjects. It is also worth mentioning that philosophers as well as social scientists, or recent years, have begun to pay special attention to education in their respective fields of specialised reflection,. Having considered these factors, the Education Commission had put forth the following suggestions for putting an end to this distance from the universities.

In order to make education significant and to increase its scope, it is essential that education be recognised as a social science, as an independent subject of academic study. In addition, education as a subject for study at the graduate and post-graduate levels, i.e., as an optional subject, should be offered on the basis of the following:

1. In each of these curricula, there must be a certain minima of teaching practice as compulsory just as laboratory work is a compulsory part of science. The student may be required to go through a period in internship or compulsory in-service summer course teaching so that he may become a fully qualified teacher.

2. At the postgraduate level, there should be provision for an M.Ed. degree. After the conclusion of the first degree, the time period of this latter degree should be two years. Besides, at this level, it should also be possible to combine the various subjects of the sciences and the humanities with education. Initially, it should be kept as an additional option and in order to encourage its study, scholarships may be offered to those who study it in on their way to becoming graduate and past-graduate teachers.

3. At the graduate level, the curriculum laid down should be oriented into three spheres-sociological, philosophical, and psychological bases of education. The contributions of the greater educationists, comparative education and, some modern education problems should form part of the curriculum.

Kothari Commission recommended that, to bring about the desired result, the foregoing programme should be implemented by the University Grants Commission. In addition, it has also recommended the setting up of schools of educating in certain selected universities. In these, in addition to the normal teaching of various subjects, there should be provision and facilities for training and research in education.

Functions

1. It has also been the considered view of the Commission that reputed scholars in various subjects should be attached to these institutions for short periods of time. These scholars should create acquaintance with the progress that has taken place in various disciplines. Such programmes will have two advantages:

a. Many talented students, after studying these subject, will be attracted toward teaching.

b. The study of education will take place without teacher training or combined subjects.

2. Encouraging and developing research in education and considering the potential for interdisciplinary approach and research into it.

3. Conducting research in the curricula as well as methods of teaching with the help of student of all kinds.

4. Organising summer courses and in-service courses in professional and other courses of study.

5. Arranging for the setting up of Extension Services in some training institutions at every level.

6. Making arrangements for the vocational training and education of teachers of various grades at the pre-primary, primary and secondary levels.

7. Laying down the curriculum for the graduate and postgraduate levels.

Eliminating Distance From Each Other

At various levels there is complete absence of harmony of exchange between the teachers themselves. Teachers working at the pre-primary and primary level have secondary level qualifications. Besides, there is a difference in their pay scale also. The distance between them shows up as under:

1. The Pay-scales differ from each other.

2. Training institutions at the primary and pre-primary levels differ from those meant for the secondary level.

Having reflected on both these factors, the Kothari Commission declared that an important reform in this direction is to develop the training establishments for the pri-primary and primary levels to the level of training colleges. Thus, the distance in teachers training will diminish, and teacher education will be in the mainstream of educational activities at all levels.

Eradicating Isolation from Schools

1. Apart from the internship programme, other schemes can be devised for eradicating this harmful tendency. These are, for instance:

a. Teacher from the training colleges should go to the assisting schools for teaching work at regular intervals.

b. Teachers working in schools may be invited, from time to time, to participate in programmes organised in the training colleges.

c. Progressive teachers working in schools may be appointed on deputation to training colleges.

2. In addition, the Education Commission also

suggested that this alienation may be ended by introducing internship programmes in training institutions. Under these, the teacher-students should spend their entire time in designated schools and participate in every activity of the school. But for the success of any such internship programme, close cooperation between schools as well as training institutions is essential. Obviously, teaching experience through actual practice can only be the consequence of a partnership between the produces, and the consumers. The education department should give special recognition to schools selected for practice teaching, and as assisting schools, they should be given a special maintenance grant.

3. The distance from schools emanates from various causes, the main ones begin the notion of status and the idea of being superior or inferior. Training colleges can offer their cooperation for putting amendment to this alienation by offering their advice, at least to neighbouring schools, on such matters as planning of work, modes of teaching, etc. This extension work will benefit the training institutions as well as the schools. The Education Commission recommended that at every level of training- pre-primary as well as secondary- there should be extension service centres, and their creation should be an integral part of the programme of training establishments. Members of the staff should participate in it regularly.

Advantages

1. Schools will also come gradually to offer their cooperation in professional studies and educational research, and thus become active partners in a process intended, ultimately, for their own benefit.

2. Teachers will implement new methods of teaching and the principles of training and thus benefit the student-teachers directly.

3. Teachers of the training colleges well teach at least one unit of subject to the students of a school for at least one month; the effect of this can then be accurately evaluated.

7

HIGHER EDUCATION—MAJOR PROBLEMS

Introduction

Higher education is defined in the International Standard Classification of Education Handbook as more specialised study normally undertaken after successful completion of a good basic education lasting for at least eleven years.

Within higher education three sub-divisions are recognised, numbered 5, 6, and 7 sometimes referred to as levels or stages. Level 5 courses are below degree standard and are often geared more to specific occupations. In the U.K. these include the Dip. He; HBTEC, Higher National, Nursing and other professional qualifications. Level 6 covers first degree courses or other equivalent while level 7 consists of programmes which are usually post-graduate in content.

Higher education can take place in a variety of institutions only some of which are called universities, the designation of institutions being according to each country's traditions and conventions. Universities always provide for a wide range of subjects, with opportunities for post-graduate work, while the range and level of work at other institutions varies, with some concentrating directly on vocational courses, sometimes in one specific area such as teacher training.

Objectives of Higher Education

1. Kothari Commission 1964-66

a. Generating and nurturing in students and teachers, and through them in the whole of society, the values and attitudes which are required for the true life both by society and the individual.

b. Encouraging equality and social justice through the spread of education and side lining culture differences.

c. Giving to society educated individuals who have received training in agriculture, are, medicine, science, and technology and various other techniques, and who are also infused with social responsibility; in other words, giving society truly cultured individuals.

d. Providing the right king of leadership in every sphere of life recognising the talents of young men and women, developing their potential abilities, training them in physical and mental health and inculcating in them the desired attitudes and health interests, and the right moral and intellectual values.

e. Obtaining new knowledge and nurturing it, searching for true with courage and complete dedication, elaborating traditional knowledge and beliefs in the light of new needs and discoveries.

2. Radhakrishnan Commission 1948

a. A university should instill among its students thoughts leading to universal brotherhood.

b. It should teach students the lesson of morality, good behaviour and ideal citizenship.

c. In a democracy, the chief aim of higher education

should be to provide useful knowledge necessary for leading a democratic way of life.

d. Intellectual development of students should be possible through university education.

e. The main objective of higher education should be to give birth of new values of life.

f. It aims at producing intellectuals who will be able to direct guide, preserve, and revive our national culture, civilisation customs and traditions.

g. The aim of higher education is to give birth to great personalities, who can provide proper leadership in field of politics, administrations, commerce, trade, agriculture, industry and other avocations of life.

For the fulfillment of these universal objectives, the Commission formulated an outline of various programmes, based on the following foundations -

(i) Reforms in the organisation of universities.

(ii) Development of higher education for the purpose of fulfilling the aspirations and ambitions of the people, to some extent, so as to meet thereby the manpower needs of national development.

(iii) Total reform in hither standards.

3. NPE - 1986

a. Redesigning Courses - Courses and programmes will be redesigned to meet the demands of specialisation. Special emphasis will be laid on linguistic competence.

b. Autonomous Colleges - In view of mixed experiences with the system of affiliation, autonomous colleges will be helpful to develop in large numbers until the affiliation system is replaced by a free and more creative association of universities with colleges.

Similarly, the creation of autonomous departments within universities on a selective basis will be encouraged. Autonomy and freedom will be accompanied by accountably.

c. Protection - Urgent steps will be taken to protect the system from degradation.

d. Consolidation - There are around 230 universities and about 8,000 colleges in India today. In view of the need to effect an all round improvement in these institutions it is proposed that in the near future, the main emphasis will be on the consolidation and expansion of facilities in the existing institutions.

e. Dynamic - In the context of the unprecedented explosion of knowledge, Higher education has to become dynamic as never before, constantly, entering unchartered areas.

f. Social Issues - Higher education provides with an opportunity to reflect on the critical social, economic, cultural, moral and spiritual issues facing humanity. It contributes to national development through dissemination of specialised knowledge and skills. It is therefore, a crucial factor for survival, Being at the apex of the educational pyramid, it has a key role in producing teachers for the educational system.

Higher Education in India: A Brief Retrospect

Pursuant to the Wood's Despatch, two universities were established at Calcutta and Bombay under the Act II of 1857. Indian University Education Commission 1902 designated uniformity in the nomenclature of the examinations and degrees in the different universities on all-India basis, Under this, universities were also granted the right of teaching alongwith the right of conducting examination, Calcutta university Commission- 1919 fixed the minimum standard of entry into a university as Intermediate passed, or any other examination after completion of 12 years of study at a school or an Intermediate college. Secondary Education Commission 1952 changed this structure go to with its Higher Secondary Scheme making the first degree course of three years.

Kothari Commission 1964 visualised a three years or more course for the first degree followed by courses for the second or research degrees of varying durations. National Policy of Education 1968 considered a broadly uniform educational structure in all parts of the country, Its ultimate target was adoption of 10+2+3 structure as later advocated by to be shifted to school as part of school education throughout the country.

Structural Pattern of Institutions of Higher Education

The pre-factory note of the Radhakrisnan Commission declares universities to be an essential part of culture. Universities must carry on the task of nation-building and this is conceivable only when a country's civilisation and culture are enriched. The building of a modern India depends upon the structure and pattern of its universities. The team pattern includes two elements- Organisation and Method of working of the universities. These are organs of universities. Academic, Administrative, both are intimately related to each other. Educational administration, as compared, for example, to civil administration, is more academic than civil.

Three kinds of universities exist in India-

1. State Administered Universities - All universities other than the ones mentioned above are administered

by the state- governments.

2. Centrally Administered Universities - Among these are the Kashi Hindu University, the Aligarh Muslim University, Delhi University, Vishwa Bharti University, the Jawahar Lal Nehru University, North East frontier University, and are administrated by the Central governments.

Both centrally administered as well as state administered universities are classified again as follows:

a. Federal Universities - Universities of the king have following features:

(i) Teaching is carried on under the guidance of the university.

(ii) The colleges are themselves autonomous.

(iii) Each college functions at the university level.

(iv) The colleges linked to them are near the university.

b. Unitary Universities - Such universities exercise complete control over the colleges located at their own centres. Teaching is done either by teachers appointed by the university itself or by teachers working under the supervision of the staff of the university,

c. Affiliating Universities - The function of such universities it to hold examinations in the colleges affiliated to them. The task of teaching is performed by the affiliated colleges. The university exercise administrative and academic control.

In addition, some institutions have been recognised as universities of a third kind. They are deemed to be universities. The pattern of universities, depends, to a large extent, upon their activities and achievements. The situation with regard to this is determined in the following manner:

(i) Universities are not created to fulfil the wishes of the people or in response to their extra academic demands and aspirations, or for any other non-academic considerations.

(ii) In universities, the standard takes the form of symbol. But unfortunately in democratic countries, it has become a matter of leisure, and a situation exists in which the future of universities is being formulated rather lightly.

(iii) The existence of universities is determined by an act of Parliament of Legislature, which also sets out the basic principles and the educational programme of the universities.

(iv) Higher education comes into existence with the creation of universities. Their nature is clearly distinct from the education-government officials, and affiliated colleges. The university places its stamp of approval, or otherwise, upon the working and standard of the colleges.

Functions of University: Kothari Commission

1. Inculcate healthy and positive attitudes and values among teachers, students, and community.

2. Develop the concept of equality and social justice among students.

3. Prepare healthy and broad minded citizens for a healthy society.

4. Search for new knowledge and envisage its application to new emerging situations.

Autonomy

The institutes of higher learning including universities, are the gifts of the state and are established under an Act of Parliament/state Legislature for a specific purpose and having clear territorial jurisdiction and area of operation. The governments is therefore, obliged to ensure that the activities of these institutions are in keeping with the aims and objectives enshrined in respective Acts. However, certain uncalled for deviations and acts of commission and omission may force the official machinery to put it foot down and demand adherence to the existing framework or to any proposed change in the system/structure. At times, pressure may build up from both sides, for whatever reasons, as is evident from the recent litigation between the Government and institutes of higher learning, such as Indian Institute of Management and Indian Institute of Technology, who claim to be above government interference and direction as may seen from the following brief reference:

1. Government Interference/ Directions - What the Supreme Court had also addressed in its judgement was the fear of governmental tinkering with IIM functioning., After all, Joshi has had the occasional brain-wave of introducing astrology in the university curricula.

To ally such fears, the apex court had extracted a promise from the government that fee reduction would not amount to any interference. As for an increase in the number of seats, the IIMs should seriously consider such a move- something that needed to be addressed even if there was no fee-cut debate, On his part, Joshi should think with equal seriousness about setting up more quality. Schools to make equality management education much more accessible than simply through the existing IIMs.

Even as the Ministry of Human Resource Development is engaged in a war of attrition with Indian Institutes of Management, the government want to open another front against another centre of excellence - IIT Powai.

The ministry is uncomfortable about the hi-tech and luxurious hostels complete with sky bridges, spacious television- viewing rooms and other state of the IT infrastructure at Powai, designed by architect Hafeez Contractor.

Human Resource Development Minister has however, said that irregularities in some the Indian Institute of Management may emerge in the coming days. There is a fear psychosis being generated by those who skeletons will be out when financial irregularities come out.

2. Fixing Fee Structure - The wrangle between the government and those opposed to its February 4 decision of slash admission fees in the six IIMs could have been sorted out in a quieter manner. Instead, a flash-point was reached with both sides refusing to budge an inch. In the end, the government position of slashing fees has been upheld by the Supreme Court, with a three-member bench headed by Chief justice V.N. Khare, dismissing the petition field by three members of the IIM.

According to the HRD ministry, by cutting fees- from Rs. 1.5 lakh to Rs. 30,000- less economically well-off, meritorious students would find themselves in one of India's premier educational institutions. Critics, including IIM Ahmedabad chairman and Infosys chief N.R. Narayana Murty, pointed out that slashing fees would not make IIMs more accessible to the poor instead an increase in the number of seats and the setting up of new quality institutions would widen the net. HRD Minister Murli Manohar Joshi rightly maintained throughout the debate that a fee reduction would not affect the quality of education imparted. Even with the change of Government at the Centre, the premier Management institutions refused to budge and stuck to their earlier stand, making the Government look at dismal sector.

3. Fixing the Admission Norms - In a major ruling the Supreme Court held that state Governments could fix norms higher than those fixed by the All India Council for Technical Education for admission into professional colleges.

This ruling was given by a Bench headed by Justice S. Rajendra Babu while allowing an appeal filed by Tamilnadu Government challenging a Madras High Court order.

While AICTE considers a candidate eligible for taking the Common Entrance Test if he has passed the +2 level, the Tamilnadu Government had provided that a candidate would be eligible for the CAT only if he had secured 60 percent marks at the +2 level.

The High Court had earlier ruled on a petition challenging the additional norm fixed by the State Government that it could not fix the norms higher than those fixed by AICTE, the apex regulatory body for technical and professional courses.

However, the Supreme Court, setting aside the High Court order, said that to maintain excellence of professional courses, it is permissible for the States to prescribe higher qualification than those fixed by AICTE..

However, the Court directed the State Government

and the Anna University to regularise the admission of 13,000 students made during the academic year 2003-04 on the basis of the norms fixed by AICTE.

Meaning of Autonomy

Autonomy means a chain of responsibilities, acceptance of functions and creation of economic and performative efficiency. Institutions of higher learning should create modes of working suited to their organisation.

Comments

In fact, what is at stake is the matter of autonomy and freedom of work-culture, and perhaps, mutual distrust which do good to none, and should be amicably stored out without damaging the structured and organisation of higher learning.

Areas of Application

Autonomy of a university applies in three areas:

1. Selection of curriculum, methods of teaching, problems of research.

2. Progress and promotion of teachers.

3. Selection of students.

Why Autonomy

A university or any other institution of higher learning needs a whole lot of freedom to achieve performative efficiency and fulfillment of its formative modes. But, does autonomy really exist? In fact, autonomy is generally skewed by various built-in mechanisms wherein the government appoint the Voice chancellor, or the Chairman in case of Institutes, who do not run their charge as a corporate body thus affecting its performative efficiency and specific mode.

Other factors like teachers salaries and perks, students fee, work schedule and even the curriculum, atleast in social sciences are tinkered with. Hence, in the face of countless Government orders, Directives, norms of procedures and practices etc. dilute autonomy perhaps rightly because in the present day scenarios, absolute or total autonomy may bot be workable whereas some sort of enlightened control and direction may bring in transparency and accountability. That power corrupts, and absolute power corrupts absolutely, is no less true of educational management as of statecraft.

In order to maintain autonomy, it is essential to remove the following aberrations:

1. Undesirable pressure also comes into play in matters of admission and appointments.

2. Universities are also found to be suffering from structural defects.

3. Even the Academic Councils are subjected to pressure in the determination of the curriculum.

4. Members of the Senate of the university do not fulfill their responsibility and the Syndicate often takes advantage of this situation.

5. In Indian universities, there is a lack of mobility. Students, too generally lack any inner inspiration or drive. The stink of official pervades the whole atmosphere. Students resort to repressing their juniors and make not attempt to develop their own talents. These are major drawbacks.

Dr. Laksmiswami Mudaliar did not what the kind of autonomy often spoken of by people as the existing autonomy is no autonomy at all.

Stressing partial autonomy, Dr. C.D. Deshmukh, a

former Union Education Minister, and Delhi University Vice Chancellor said that autonomy often becomes responsible for disorder and a defective administration. This happens only in the absence of control. Some universities have become converted into centres of internal jealousy and politics. But the university should not acquire the nature of Eduction Ministry, and should be responsive to public opinion, demand and aspiration.

University Grants Commission

The University Grants Commission was created by an Act of Parliament in 1956 on the basis of the recommendations of the Radhakrishnan Commission, which defined its functions in the following terms-

1. Guiding the university with regard to development and spread of higher education.

2. Advising a university on such matters as the recognisation of a degree.

3. Finding out the curiosities being harboured by the universities as well as the government.

6. If and when necessary, giving advice regarding the setting up of new universities.

7. Making arrangements for the distribution of grants to universities.

8. Examining the financial position of universities and making necessary arrangements with the help of the current government.

9. Creating the interest of central government in the problems of higher education.

Higher Education Today

India occupies the second position in higher education worldwide as an unprecedented growth has taken place in this sector during the last five decades. This revelation came from former vice chancellor of Deen Dayal Upadhyay Gorakhpur University, Prof. R.K. Mishra.

He was delivering a special lecture on Challenges of Higher Education on the occasion of the fourth anniversary of the Academique, a discussion group, recently.

However, Prof. Mishra added that despite the quantitative increase in the number of institutions of higher learning, there was a lack of quality education. He said due to the pressure mounted by political parties, new colleges and universities were opened without paying attention to quality.

He said earlier higher education was the monopoly of the elite but situation had changed. 80 lakh students were being imparted higher education in the country,

Prof. Mishra alleged that the teachers and vice-chancellors being appointed now were not able to provide academic leadership in the true sense.

Prof. Mishra observed it was unfortunate that state funding on higher education had decreased considerably even though the universities were expected to impart quality education.

He said foreign universities were on the verge of entering the country and they would lay greater stress on financial gains. He described the commercialisation of higher education as a negation of the varsity system.

Speaking about the pattern of universities, of Kothari Commission had spoken of the setting up of leading universities in which each department would work on the lines suggested by the advisory tolerance, rational thought courage and the search for truth. It exists to bring about progress of the human race, in fact, for even higher purposes. If a university really fulfils its obligations, it will bring about the welfare both of the nation and of the people. Thus, it is obvious that the clearer the pattern of universities, the higher will be the standard of education.

Kothari Commission

1. Mechanisms of this kind contribute to the development of higher education. They also bring about the growth of a proper material outlook and lay the right stress on freedom of thought and action.

2. Kothari Commission suggested the setting up of similar commissions at the state level also. Other institutions of a similar nature should be set up to create harmony between agriculture, medicine, engineering etc. as well as to create harmony between them and general education. The Kothari Commission visualises the functions of the U.G.C. in the following terms-

a. University Grants Commission should be set up in the states also.

b. The U.G.C. should be given adequate financial resources.

c. The U.G.C. should set up permanent committees to perform its various functions.

d. The membership of the U.G.C. should be between 12 and 15 one third of whom should be high officials of the government.

e. Institutions similar to the U.G.C. should be created for education in agriculture, medicine, engineering, etc.

f. Higher education in its entirety should be regarded as a unit and the U.G.C. should direct it.

3. The Kothari Commission strongly felt that every activity concerned with higher education should fall within the purview of the U.G.C. Agriculture, Medicine, etc. are directed by their respective Councils though they are as much integral parts of hither education. It is for this reason that the commission accepted the recommendations of a committee on higher education composed of Members of Parliament. According to it, the whole stream of education should be regarded as a single composite unit, vocational education cannot be separated from general education. Hence, it is necessary that the jurisdiction of the U.G.C. should extend over agriculture, medicine, engineering etc. also.

National Accredition and Assessment Council

National Accredition and Assessment Council is a very important and powerful organ of UGC. It monitors not only the educational standards but also the level of teaching excellence, facilities, vision for the future and all relevant facts for running a monolithic empire that effects the life of lakhs of its students and teachers. A good grade from the NAAC would open the doors of the UGC coffers in favour on a university's development and growth, and make its brand more attractive in the job market. The NAAC should, however, be not only revitalised but its functioning should be transparent and fair, without favour and prejudice, to make its gradings creditable.

Improvement of Educational Standards

Standard of Education and UGC. The coordination and maintenance of standards in institutions of higher education and research is a central responsibility. To discharge this responsibility adequately the UGC has to assume several roles and functions.

1. The leadership and catalytic role of the UGC has to be supported by the creation of appropriate organisations at the university and State levels. These would include a mechanism for surveys of undergraduate colleges in relation to well-defined norms and guidelines so as to ensure that further proliferation of sub-viable colleges is arrested, and for similar surveys of post-graduate colleges so as to ensure that they satisfy the UGC norms, and maintain certain minimum standards. It would also be necessary for the UGC to persuade the universities to establish academic planning, evaluation and implementation boards to look after the post-graduate and research programmes in a long-germ perspective, and College Development Councils to advise and guide the colleges to improve their academic standards with the help of various UGC schemes.

2. The UGC should actively promote through the creation of an appropriate pattern of recognition and appreciation, the maintenance of values in the academic community so that its commitment to the pursuit of truth and excellence is enhanced and it is enabled better to discharge its responsibilities of society.

3. The UGC Should strive to remove regional imbalances in the development of higher education in different parts of the country and to relate such development to the programmes of socio-economic advance, and cultural growth of the people in various regions.

4, The UGC has to play an increasing role in promotion of high quality research in universities because of the symbolic relationship between teaching and research. At the same time it must promote applied research which has an immediate impact on the social and economic conditions of the people.

5. It is the responsibility of UGC to strive to provide leadership to the entire educational system and assist it to bring about the needed transformation. This can be done by encouraging the universities to play an increasingly active role in improving the quality of education in colleges and schools, by intensifying the R and D effort in education and by promoting the philosophy of extension whereby teaching, research, service of the community and the building of character become an integrated activity.

6. It has a major role of providing leadership and impetus for reform and development. Toward this purpose, the Commission must continuously review the emerging problems of education, the status of teaching and research in different disciplines and the standards of teaching and research in the universities. It should, through its committees and panels and other means, evolve a consensus within the academic community regarding desirable changes in higher education.

Comments

Economics Department of Allahabad University has earned another feather in its cap. It has become the first ever Economics Department of a Uttar Pradesh based state or Central University to be awarded a special grant by the University Grants Commission under its Departments Special Assistance Scheme. The Rs 22 lakh grant has been awarded to the Department in appreciation of its academic as well as research performances.

It is a great achievement for our department as we made it through after a through and a rigorous screening process. The grant will help us upgrade the existing facilities of the Department. The sum sanctioned will help the Department purchase 10 computers and two printers worth Rs 10 lakh, spend Rs 2 lakh on its computer lab, Rs 1.5 lakh for two LCD cameras and Rs 1.5 lakh for a Reprographic facility.

Beside this, Rs. 1.80 lakh has been sectioned for purchase of books and journals, Rs 1.20 lakh for emergency and Rs. 1.20 lakh for holding needs, seminars besides Rs. 90,000 for visiting fellow, Rs. 90,000 for the Advisory committee spending and Rs. 90,000 for works related to the technical Industrial Secretariat Assistance programme,

The UGC has also sectioned a post of project Fellow at the Department whose salary as well as allowances will be paid by the Commission. The money sanctioned under the scheme has to be utilised by us before March 32, 2007, Prof Malhotra informed.

Other Allahabad University Departments which too have received grants of varying amounts under the UGC's Department Special Assistance Scheme include the Departments of Ancient History, Physics, Chemistry, Mathematics, Psychology and Philosophy.

Privatisation of Education: Kothari Commission to NPE- 1986

1. National Education policy- 1986 - Following are the salient features of privatisation of education:

a. To provide optional courses for general education.

b. Job opportunities for partially unemployed.

c. To provide opportunities of contact programmes for students of vocational courses.

d. Government and private sectors to share the responsibility to establish vocational and professional institutes.

e. To develop knowledge, skills and attitude toward self employment through vocational education.

f. To development industrial training centres to make vocational education go with integrated approach.

g. To maintain balance between the demand and supply of skilled manpower, as there was no money in the government offers for his purpose.

Privatisation of Higher Education

Once a dirty word in the field of higher education, privatisation came into prominence during 1990s as a means of reduction of public expenditure on and self-sustenance of higher education. It was believed that higher education should be able to garner its own resources without being a parasite on government agencies and funds leading to a spurt of such colleges and universities all over the country. Higher education was considered to be a big drain on the exchequer. With privatisation, the public expenditure shrunk year after year without any possibility of any improvement in the near future. The Government of India's 1997 Discussion Paper of Government subsides in India provided of revealing insight into government thinking. The paper classified higher education as Non-Merit goods for which the government subsidy would need to be reduced drastically. Later, there was a revision of the situation wherein higher education was categorised Merit 2 goods which need not be subsidised by the state at the same level as merit goods. Even secondary education was classified as a merit good with reduced subsidy.

Withdrawal/ reduction of subsidy on education necessarily turns it into privatisation for its subsistence and sustenance by arranging its own resources and being on its own without compromising standards, aims and objectives and national needs and aspirations. In the present context, privatisation of education would stay and play its role in prescribed manner.

Comments

It may be observed that privatisation is necessary corollary of vocationalisation, liberalisation and globalisation in the face of the growing pressure of world trade and internationalism in education wherein the Government have no resources for additional institutes of higher education, to match with the foreign thrust in this regard.

The historic judgement of the Supreme Court in 1992 banned capitation fee as patently unreasonable, unfair and unjust, yet its another judgment of 1993 paved the way for the growth and expansion of self-financing colleges/institutes which were allowed by the government on the condition that no financial assistance would be expected. At the same time, colleges/institutes would confirm to the norms laid down by various Councils. Consequently, there was a mushroom growth of colleges as compared to the corresponding number of colleges funded by the government over a given period of time, in such diverse areas as engineering medicine, agriculture and management, adversely affecting the equity and quality of higher education in the country. Nevertheless, privatisation of education is a way of life today.

Advantages of Privatisation

1. Able persons find opportunities to display their

talents.

2. New spheres of jobs have been creates for example, canteens, Mess, Publishers, Multimedia, Internet, Stationers, Printers, are getting opportunities for their advancement.

3. Unemployment problem tackled to some extent.

4. Private sector resources are being channelised in positive and constructive work.

5. Those who do not get success in competitive examinations can get admission in private colleges.

6. Vocational and academic education is expanding and is available to all those who can spend money for their words.

Disadvantages of Privatisation

1. Not manpower planning while opening new institution.

2. English language dominates life.

3. Social discrimination has been developing day by day.

4. There is no place for disabled and weaker section of the society.

5. Profit is the only motive of the management.

6. There is tension due to anarchy and organisational management.

7. There is decline in educational and intellectual development.

8. There are few competent teachers in the institutions.

9. Faculty teachers are exploited. They are not given proper grade and service benefits. No security of jobs for them.

10. Big industrialists started educational institutions as corporate industry.

11. Education becomes costly.

12. Poor persons cannot get the benefit of education.

13. Education becomes business oriented and a consumer-producer relationship is developed.

Why Privatisation

1. Educational Policy 1986 :

a. In sum, education is a unique investment in the present for the future.

b. Education develops manpower for different levels of the economy. It is also the substrate on which research and development flourish being the ultimate guarantee of national self-reliance.

c. Education has an acculturating role. It refines sensitivities and perceptions that contribute to national cohension, a scientific temper and independence of mind a spirit, thus furthering the goals of socialism, secularism and democracy enshrined in our constitution.

2. Profiteering and commercialisation of education.

3. Attitudinal changes and demand for autonomy and academic freedom at the cost of denial of subsidy.

4. Easing out problems of globalisation which entail diversion of limited government resources to areas other than education.

5. Vocationalisation necessarily leads to privatisation.

6. Knowledge explosion and variety of course.

7. Population explosion and resource crunch.

8

CONSTITUTIONAL PROVISIONS AND SAFEGUARDS

Constitution of India

The very fact that India is a Sovereign Socialist Secular Democratic Republic is representative of the values cherished and desired by the people of this country. This representation has no meaning, bearing and significance for some other country which may be inspired by some other concept of values. Nevertheless, certain values have universal application and relevance and may, therefore, be common in the Constitutions of some like-minded countries.

Fundamental Rights

The Indian Constitution bestows upon its citizens some necessary pre-requisites, for a just and equitable life. These are called the Fundamental Rights. These rights are the guarantees which are the fundamental, firstly, because the Constitution delivers them, and secondly, because they are considered necessary for the over all development of a person keeping in line with social and moral status, meaning and significance ascribed to him. Once again, these Rights are also value based as they are the manifestation of the values cherished, aspired and practised by the people of this country. Rights to equality believes that all are equal and that there are no social, religious and sectarian discriminate, angularities and dispositions. The Indian constitution guarantees safeguard against discrimination- social, economic and cultural.

Right to Freedom guarantees, freedom of movement, faith and profession irrespective of caste, creed, religion, region, and gender. The right, if at all it is to be curtailed, will have to be in accordance with the constitutional provision. This restriction forces the government to enact special acts like TADA and POTA to meet special and exceptional circumstances. Prevention of Detention Act is a safeguard in this regard.

Besides, there are other rights like Culture and Educational rights which ensure freedom of faith, culture, language, etc., and protect minority institutions to conserve develop and transmit their culture, and language. Recently, the Hon'ble Supreme Court ruled total control on admission and courses in such institutions to the respective governing bodies. However, no one can be discriminated against in such educational institutions run or aided by the government, admission to which is no merit. Even this has to be done in a transparent manner.

Preamble

The Preamble of the Constitution spells out the national objectives and goals that the people of India give upto themselves. It is more of a policy statement which promises certain basis guarantees and privileges to the citizens. That India is a secular, democratic republic entails that we do not have any state religion and that there is no distinction between citizens on the basis of caste, creed, region and gender, and that all have freedom to follow their own religious tenets in an environment of mutual trust and tolerance.

The fundamental objectives enshrined in the

Constitution are Liberty, Equality, Fraternity, and Justice. These are nothing but the democratic values cherished and practised by like-minded people all over the world. Of these Justice, perhaps, is the most vital value because short of it there would not be a just society, and even the tenets of liberty, equality and fraternity may be infringed.

Directive Principles

The Directive Principles of state policy, in fact, are the directions given by the Constitution to respective governments to adopt policies that commensurate and further the cause of social justice and create such situations and circumstances in which every citizen has ample opportunities for self-fulfillment, development and progress, socially, economically, politically and vocationally. These principles are the safeguard against exploitation and violation. Work and livelihood, education, equal wages for equal work, ban on child labour and safeguard against child abuse and exploitation, social and economic justice, free medical and legal aid to poor and destitutes, Panchayati Raj, protection of milk-giving animals, prohibition, protection of natural resources like forests, etc., wild life, protection of ancient monuments, and equitable distribution of wealth, are some of the Directive Principles that entail upon the government to frame and [promote policies and agencies that may help achieve these in the normal course of governance.

A little introspection and one would realise that these Principles of State Policy, in fact, are nothing but the manifestation of the value-aspirations of a people recognised and held sacred and mandatory by the Constitution. Thus, Constitution is a major sources of values; it preserves, promotes and transmits mandatory by the Constitution. Thus, Constitution is a major source of values: it preserves, promotes and transmits these values to all the citizens who owe allegiance to it, generation after generation, for all times to come.

Education of Minorities

Article 30 (i) reads 7 All minorities whether based on religion or language, shall have the right to establish and administer educational institution of their choice.

Article 30 (ii) lays down - The State shall not, in granting aid to educational institutions discriminate against any educational institution on the ground that it is under the management of a minority, whether based on religion or language.

Equality of Opportunity in Educational Institutions

Article 29 (i) states- No citizen shall be denied admission into any educational institution maintained by the State or receiving aid out of State funds on grounds only or religion, race, caste, language or any of them.

Main Educational Themes covered in the Constitution

Free and Compulsory Education

Article 45 of the constitution state-

The State shall endeavour to provide within a period of ten years from the commencement of this Constitution, for free and compulsory education for all children until they complete the age of fourteen years.

The expression State which occurs in this Article is defined in Article 12 to include. The Government and

Parliament of India and the government and the Legislature of each of the States and all local or other authorities within the territory of India or under the control of the Government of India.

Thus we notice that the responsibility for universal elementary education lies with the Central Government, the State- Governments- the Local Bodies and Voluntary organisation.

Religious Education

Article 28 states-

1. No person attending any educational institution recognised by the state or receiving aid out of State funds shall be required to take part in any religious instruction that may be imparted in such institution or to attend any religious worship that they may be conducted in such institution or in any premises attached there to unless such person or, if such person is minor, his guardian has given his consent thereto.

2. Nothing in clause (I) shall apply to any educational institution which is administered by the State but has been established under any endowment or trust which required that religious instruction shall be imparted in such institutions.

3. No religious instruction shall be provided in any educational institution wholly maintained out of State fund.

Education in the Mother-tongue

Article 350 A reads it shall be the endeavour of the State to provide adequate facilities for instruction in the mother-tongue at the primary stage of education to children belonging to linguistic minority group and the President may issue such directions to any State as he considers necessary or proper for securing the provision of such facilities.

Language Safeguards

Article 29 states that any section of the citizens, residing in the territory of India or any part there of having a distinct language, script or culture of its own shall have the right to conserve the same.

Education of the Weaker Sections

Article 46 states, The State shall promote with special care the educational and economic interests of the weaker section of the people, and in particular, of the Scheduled Castes and the Scheduled Tribes, and shall protect them from social injustice and all forms of exploitation.

Promotion of Hindi

Article 351 states, It shall be the duty of Union Government to promote the spread of the Hindi language, to develop it so that it may serve as a medium of expression for all the elements of the composite culture of India and to secure its enrichment by assimilating without interfering with its genius, the forms, style and expressions used in Hindustani and in the other languages of India specified in the Eighth Schedule, and by drawing, wherever necessary or desirable, for its vocabulary, primarily in Sanskrit and secondary in other languages.

Education of Scheduled Castes and Tribes

Article 15 reads, Nothing in this article or in clause (2) of article 29 shall prevent the State form making any special provision for the advancement of any socially and educationally backward classes of citizens or for the scheduled castes and the scheduled tribes. Article

15 (3) says, Nothing in this article shall prevent the State from making any special provision for women and children.

Higher Education and Research

Entry 63 of the Union List- Institutions of National Importance. The Institutions known at the commencement of this Constitution as the Banaras Hindu University, The Aligarh Muslim University and the Delhi University and any other institution declared by Parliament by law to be an institute of national importance.

Entry 64 - Institutions of Scientific and Technical Education, financed by the Government of Indian wholly or in part and declared by the Parliament by law to be institutions of national importance.

Entry 65 of the Union List, Union agencies and institutions for -

a. Scientific or Technical assistance in the investigation of detection of crime.

b. The promotion of special studies or research.

3. Professional, vocational or technical training, including the training of police officers.

Entry 66- Co-ordination of any Determination of Standards in institutions for higher education or research and scientific and technical institutions.

Education in the Concurrent List

The Constitution provides educational functions at three levels- Central, State and concurrent. Till 1976 education was a State subject with certain provisions at the Central level. The Forty-Second Amendment, 1976 brought about drastic changes in the Indian

Constitution. It affected the status of education also by putting it on the concurrent list. Hitherto, education was a State subject with certain provisions for the safeguard of the interests of the minorities etc.

The implications of making education a concurrent subject is that both the Centre and the Sates can legislate on any aspect of education from the primary to the university level. In case of any dispute, legislation framed by the Central government will have overriding authority. By having education in the concurrent list, the Centre can implement directly any policy decision in the States.

Conflicting views have been put forward by experts relating to this aspects. Education on the Concurrent List was put on the recommendations of the Swaran Singh Committee in 1976 which observed Agriculture and education are subjects of primary importance to country's rapid progress towards achieving desired socio-economic changes. The need to evolve an all India policy in relation to these subjects cannot be ruled out.

The Kothari Education Commission examined this problem and concluded that position given to education in the Constitution is the best and therefore the status quo should continue for, say, ten years. The Commission says, We are not in favour of fragmenting education and putting one part in the Concurrent the other in the State List- education should, under any circumstances, be treated as a whole.

In 1976, during emergency Swaran Singh Committee suggested 42nd Amendment in the Constitution which states that education is to be included in the Concurrent list. The amendment was passed by both the houses of Parliament and it was endorsed by several state assemblies. Since then education is included in the Concurrent List.

On the 26th September, 1991 Inter-State Board accepted the recommendations of Sarkaria Commission on the relation of State and the Centre and opined that the Central government must consult the state before beginning of any Legislation on the subjects included in the Concurrent List. This makes it clear that the central laws on concurrent subjects will supercede all State Laws but before such laws are enacted state government would be consulted beforehand. Education would also be such a subject.

Education in the Union Territories

Article 239 of the Constitution reads, Save as otherwise provided by Parliament by law, every Union Territory shall be administered by the President acting, to such extent as the thinks fit, through an administrator to be appointed by him with such designation as he may specify.

Educational and Culture Relations with Foreign Countries

Entry 13 of the Union List- Participation in international conferences, associations and other bodies and implementing of decision made thereat.

9

EDUCATIONAL AGENCIES

Introduction

The whole of the environment is the instrument of man's education in the widest sense. But in that environment certain factors are distinguishable as being more particularly concerned. Society has, therefore, developed number of specialised institutions to carry out these functions. These institutions are called the agencies of education and are instrumental, in their own characteristic manner, in transmitting information and in controlling the behaviour of the child on his way to growth and development.

Meaning

The means or sources that interplay in the act of transmitting information and knowledge to the child are called agencies of education. These agencies have great impact upon the growing child as they influence the development of the child in their own characteristic manner. It may be seen that these agencies impart formal and informal education in their own characteristics fashion, and prepare the child for specific and general types of education.

Active agencies of education act and react upon the growing child and make him to react in response. Here the child is actively involved and may even become interactive, whereas passive agencies of education do not influence the child to act, react or interact. These are one-way street.

Formal Agencies

1. Created agencies which restrict the freedom of the child.

2. Also called direct agencies as they work for modification of the child's behaviour in a direct manner.

3. Fixed programmes under its specific rules and regulations.

4. Directly planned, aim at the modification of the child's behaviour.

Informal Agencies

1. Natural agencies doe not curtail the child's freedom.

2. Also called indirect agencies as they influence the child's behaviour in an indirect manner.

3. Neither fixed programme nor specific rules.

4. Spontaneous. Not pre-determined.

5. Influence the child's behaviour in an indirect and natural manner.

Merits of Informal Agencies

The child if informally educated by living with others and the very process of living together educates. It enlarges and enlightens experience, stimulates and enriches imagination, creates responsibility and vividness of statement and though.

Limitations

1. Children might go astray due to lock of control and supervision.

2. Does not help acquire skills whereas education has to be specific and direct.

3. Generally wastes time in random experiences.

4. Not much of planning.

5. Does not educate for citizenship.

6. Imparts vague knowledge, nothing specific.

Comparative Study of Formal and Informal Agencies of Education Merits of Formal Education

Without formal education, it is not possible to transmit all the resources and achievements of a complex society. It also opens a way to a kind of experience which would not be accessible to the young, if they are left to pick up their training in informal association with other. Formal education makes education a serious, purposeful, well-directed, meaningful, interactive experience.

Limitations - Formal education easily becomes remote and dead. Dull and drab classroom proceedings hamper the transmission of knowledge where students lose interest and suffer from referent confusion where the child interprets constructed experiences with reference to that his own, each drawing his own conclusions.

Definition

Derived from Greek word schola or skhole meaning leisure. In ancient Greece. Leisure places were used for self-development. Gradually, these places came to be known as schools where teachers, under a pre-planned system gave specific information during a fixed time.

1. School may be regarded as a social invention to serve society for the specialised teaching of young.

2. The school must be thought of primarily not as a place of learning where certain knowledge is learnt, but as the place where the young are discipline in certain forms of activities, namely those that are the greatest and most permanent significance in the wider world.

3. School is a special environment, where a certain

quality of life and certain types of activities and occupations are provided with the object of securing the child's development along desirable lines.

4. Schools are institutions devised by civilized man for the purpose of aiding in the preparation of the young for well-adjusted and efficient membership of society.

Comments

The formal and informal agencies of education influences the behaviour of the child directly respectively. One transmits knowledge under specifically controlled conditions whereas the other does the same in an informally free atmosphere. Both are complementary to each other and jointly provide a wholesome educational experience.

The school is an active, direct and formal agency of education. It has evolved as a residual institution to catch up an preserve social patterns otherwise in danger of loss or neglect. A school is a vibrant community centre, radiating life and energy all-around, and a well conducted school in a happy home. In fact, the transition from home to school should be so smooth that the latter becomes the extension of the former.

Importance of School

1. Co-operation of Different Agencies - School is the only agency through which cooperation of different agencies namely the family, the community and the state may be successfully achieved. It is why all these agencies try to extend their full co-operation in all the activities of school. Without the active co-operation of these agencies school cannot achieve its objectives.

2. School a Better Place of Education than Home - Under the influence of group life in school a child learns many social qualities and courtesies. Since the physical surroundings of school are healthy, there is a simple

provision for games, sports and various kinds of cultural activities. A family cannot provide all these facilities. Hence, school is a batter place than home for the socialisation and culturalisation of the child.

3. Creation of Education Citizens - In democracy, school has a special importance. Children learn their rights and duties and develop love, affection, sympathy, co-operation, tolerance and responsibility in school. With the development of these socially desirable values they prove useful citizens when they become adults.

4. Encouragement to Corporate Life - Individual life needs socialisation. The child should be encouraged to be more and more social in his outlook and behaviour. School provides these experience for the child to understand social behaviour and develop in him a sense of social responsibility and corporate life.

5. Perpetuation and Development of Society - Society reviews and develops itself through the active cooperation of school. All social problems and needs of society are flashed in one way or other in school which provides the desired solutions for all the problems of society. In this way, social progress goes on with the help of school.

6. Propagation to Ideals and Ideologies of State - School is an important agency for the propagation of ideals and ideologies of each state in the shortest possible time. It is why all the democratic, fascist and communist state have assigned due importance to school today.

7. Development of Culture Pluralism - In school children belonging to different religions, castes, creeds and social hierarchy come together and mix up freely with each other in friendly atmosphere with the result that they develop sympathy, co-operation, tolerance and

respect for the views and cultures of others in a natural way. It is how school is an important agency to develop cultural pluralism amongst children.

8. Harmonious Development of Personality - The family, the community and the church with other informal agencies do not have set aims and objectives of education. Their plans and schemes of education are also indefinite. Sometimes, the vagueness of activities affects the personality of the child adversely and develops in him undesirable habits and attitudes. On the contrary, the aims and activities of school are pre-planned. This ensures the harmonious development of the child.

9. Provision of a Special Environment - Informal agencies do not impart education according to pre-planned scheme. Hence, the effect of such indefinite environments affects adversely upon the growth and development of the child. On the other hand, school provides a simple, pure, interesting and well-organised environment before the child according to pre-planned scheme which ensures the physical, mental, emotional and social development of the child in natural way. Hence, school is an important agency of education.

10. Connecting Link Between Home and the World - The family develops in the child various qualities and values namely love, sympathy, sacrifice, cooperation, tolerance and service. But all these qualities remain connected with the members of the family and its four walls. This makes the child narrow-minded. School is a connecting link between he family ad the external world. In school he child comes in contact with children belonging to different families. This contact widens his outlook with the result that the child becomes capable enough to face the challenges and multifarious problems

of life and their wider society outside. Raymont has rightly remarked. The school is a half way house between entirely domestic life of early childhood and the larger life that await the youth when he quits his parental roof.

11. Extensive Culture Heritage - In modern knowledge has become so vast and varied, cultural heritage so extensive that in formal agencies like the family and the community are quite incapable to shoulder the responsibility of transmitting this huge treasure of knowledge to the rising generation. School is the only formal agency to complete this task.

Special Features of Modern/Progressive School

1. Centre of Community Life - Progressive schools are such centres of community life where children are developed according to the demands of community. This indicates the inseparable link between school and community-community projects its requirements and school is actively responsive to such social pressure/ projections.

2. Emphasis on the Development of Personality - The true end of education is the complete realisation of the ideal personality its balanced personality.

3. Emphasis on Social Values - Children are made actively conscious of their obligations to the community, society and nation.

4. Emphasis on Practical Knowledge - Education is no longer restricted to bookish knowledge. Modern/ progressive schools impart useful, constructive and practical knowledge to the children based on real life experiences.

5. Importance of the Principles of Activity - The environment of a progressive school is simplified, purified and balanced. Under such as atmosphere the child is afforded ample opportunities to experiment for

himself and acquire many social ideas. Modern Schools are no longer dull and drab centers, but motivate and stimulate children for self-learning.

6. Importance of Child's Personality - The modern/ progressive school seeks to replace information by experience for it subject-matter and theory makes school life active and meaningful.

Modern Concept of School

While discussing the modern concept of school. Pestalizzi remarked our unpsychological schools are essentially only artificial machines that destroy all the resist of power and experience that nature herself brings to life. The traditional schools tyrannically stop the delightful course of the unrestricted freedom of the children, pen them like sheep, piteously chain them for long durations to attend to dull and drab classroom experiences and drills. Modern educationists like Pestalizzi. Herbart, Froebel, Montessori, Nunn, Parkhurst and a host of other western and Indian thinkers like Tagore, Gandhi and Vivekanand, lay exclusive emphasis on child-centered education.

Informal Functions of Schools

Informal functions of a school relate to the physical, social and emotional development of children. We discuss them in some detail as under -

1. Emotional Development - The third most important informal function of school is to develop the child emotionally. For this, the entire environment of school must be artistic. In other words, there should be garden flower plants and other beautiful natural objects. The school building and the campus should be neat and clean. The walls of the rooms should be white-washed annually and the rooms be decorated tastefully. Tips, tours, exhibitions and debates also stimulate the

emotional and aesthetic sense of children who can further be infused with a sense of administration toward Truth, Beauty and Goodness, the high ideals of human life.

2. Development of Social Feeling - The second informal function of school is the development of social feeling in all the children of school. As a matter of fact, school is a miniature society. Hence, the school should provide such a social environment before children by organising students unions, social service camps, social functions and parent-teacher associations etc. so that all the socially desirable values namely sympathy, cooperation, tolerance, social awakening and above all discipline develop in them in a natural way.

3. Physical Development - The first informal function of school is to develop the child physically. For this, the entire environment of school should be such that leads to the physical well-being of the children.

Formal Functions of School

Formal functions are mainly concerned with the mental development of the child. In this connection the following are the functions of school-

1. Development of Character - The most important formal function of school is so develop children morally and socially so that they are able to acquire firm and noble character. In early times the family and the church developed the character of children jointly, but bow it has become the function of school to develop the character of children by allowing them to participate in such moral, ethical and social activities which may inculcate in them the socially desirable values and lead to the formation of a strong good character.

2. Development of Citizenship - The sixth formal function of school is to develop in children the essential

qualities of citizenship so that they may become active and responsible citizens imbued with qualities of leadership leading the nation on the path of progress in all spheres of national life.

3. Re-organisation and Re-construction of Human Experience - The fifth formal function of school is to re-organise and re-construct human experiences. As a matter of fact, the function of school is not to preserve the continuity of society alone: it has to meet social problems, to reform the society and ultimately to purge it off its dead wood. For this, a continuous process of research in all the higher branches of knowledge is a must and the school should be equipped to do it.

4. Vocational and Industrial Education - The Fourth formal function of school is to impart vocational and industrial education to children according to the demands of society. In a poor and developing country like India, the school must be alert to impart vocational and industrial education to children according to their interests and capabilities so that they are able to support themselves and serve the country with sincerity.

5. Preservation, Improvement and Transmission of Culture - The third formal function of school is to preserve and improve the national culture and to transmit it to the coming generation.

6. Cultivation of a Dynamic and Adaptable Mind - The second formal function of school is to impart such knowledge to the child which is not an end in itself but a means to achieve some end. The end is cultivation of a dynamic and adaptable mind which is resourceful and able to create new value for future life.

7. Development of Mental Powers - The first formal function of school is to develop the mental powers of the child so that he is able to think freely, clearly and

logically. To complete this function the school structures such experiences for the child that he is able to develop his inherent mental faculties according to his needs, interests and capabilities for his own good and good of the society.

Suggestions to Make Indian Schools An Effective Agency of Education

1. Centre of community life to develop morality, character, self-reliance, emotional and national unity. It should make children willingly responsive to social demands and needs.

2. Provision for teacher's training programmes, seminars, work-shops and refresher courses to help teachers to learn and acquaint themselves with the latest teaching technology and practices. To attract suitable personnel the job should be given necessary face-lift.

3. Emphasis on constructive and creative activities such as exhibitions, competitions, social and cultural programmes.

4. Emphasis on practical knowledge.

5. Provision of vocational education and earn while you learn programme to make students feel economically independent.

6. Character formation and moral development helps one acquire resilience and capacity to bear all types of stresses with grace and dignity.

7. Emphasis on individual differences.

8. Dynamic method of teaching to make learning mor meaningfully, enduring and useful. Use of appropriate strategies, technics and techniques will make classroom situations interesting and memorable.

9. Flexible curriculum to meet the needs and requirements of children and other social conditions.

10. Psychological and conducive environment.

11. All round development of the child.

12. Cooperation of other agencies, such as, family community and state.

13. Democratic nature of school.

School and Society - Functions

Individual and society are not on cross purpose. In fact, society may be said to exist in and by communication between individuals in a social matrix. It is sharing of purposes that constitutes society and are mutually inclusive. Much the same way, the social process and educational process are intrinsically one and the same, as the two are inversely related and find consummation in each other. Any clash between the two must be resolved as the school has to perform some definite functions with regard to social change and progress, and the two must share a common outlook.

1. Natural Functions - The values carried forward by school should be transmitted to posterity. Transmission, therefore, is another function of school. It should be active and dynamic in its approach and functioning, but while doing so, it should remain neutral, not take sides, and transmit things as they are. The school should not acquire an attitude of aloofness from the controversial social issues- remain apolitical. Even if it exercises opinion, it should be in all fairness without subscribing to any political thought and practice: without fear or favour.

2. Normative Functions - Liberals and progressive, however, maintain that school is not simply a residual institution to catch up an maintain things as they are but vehicle by which to forge ahead as well. It is in this light that the normative function of the school is considered to be creative rather than conservation.

School, as such, must take the responsibility of initiating social progress based on the harmony of the values cherished and conserved by it, over a period of time. It should move with time, all the while refining and sharpening what it is carrying forward.

3. Conservation Functions - By far the oldest theory of mutual relations of the school and the social order, and the one most widely honoured in practice, is that the school should conserve the existing social culture won only at a greater cost of time and suffering. The school must preserve the best of the culture and mores. Even if the times are not conductive, the school must perform the conservative function as it is the guardian of social and cultural heritage.

4. Schools performs threefold social functions-preservation of cultural values, norms and mores, their refinement and updating-and finally, their transmission to society at some given point of time, in a continuous process of social change and evolution.

10

NON-FORMAL EDUCATIONAL AGENCIES

Introduction

Non-formal education is a flexible teaching-learning process. This education includes the characteristics of both formal education as well as informal education. An illiterate or semi-illiterate adult wants to take degrees of formal education but due to various circumstances, he cannot fulfil the rules of formal education. In non-formal education, courses are nearly the same as in the formal education but there is no compulsion for an adult to attend the classes or to pass an examination with in a certain period or to study under college teachers. He is free to adopt courses of his choice, takes counsel whenever necessary from the local centres and give examinations at that centre which is best suited to him.

According to Ward and Delton, Non-formal education is a planned instructional design which uses both overt and covert procedures in a more flexible environment to reach towards a goal determined by a regulated policy,

The main characteristics of non-formal education are-

1. Management of Non-formal Education Programmes is decentralized.

2. Besides being flexible, non-formal education is planned and systematic.

3. Teaching-learning material used in non-formal education of different type.

4. The responsibilities of the director of non-formal education are different from that of average teachers.

5. The curriculum and learning activities of non-formal education are more liberal according to specific needs of the students.

6. The time-duration and other things are determined, keeping in view the convenience of the students.

National Policy of Education has mentioned the following points about non-formal education-

1. Much of the work of running NFE centres will be done through voluntary agencies and Panchayati Raj institutions. The provision of funds to these agencies will be adequate and timely. The government will take overall responsibilities for this vital sector.

2. Effective steps will be taken to provide a framework for the curriculum on the lines of the national co-curriculum, but based on the needs of the learners and related to the local environment. Learning material of high quality will be developed and provided free of charge to all pupils. NFE programmes will provide participatory learning environment and activities such as games and sports, cultural programmes, excursions etc.

3. Modern technological aids will be used to improve the learning environment of NFE centres. Talented and dedicated young men and women from the local community will be chosen to serve as instructors and particular attention will be paid for their training. Steps

will be taken to facilitate their entry into the formal system for deserving cases. All necessary measures will be taken to ensure that the quality of non-formal education may be comparable with formal education.

4. A large and systematic programme of non-formal education will be launched for school drop-outs, for children from habitations without schools, working children who cannot attend whole-day schools.

Continuing Teacher Education

The National Council of Teacher Education has made the following recommendations about Continuing Teacher Education.

The country is facing the task of orienting a large number primary and secondary teachers to meet the following needs of new curriculum-

1. Methods and Modes of Continuing Education - there are many ways, somc of thc modes have be mentioned as - Workshops and summer-instruction, Orientation programmes, Correspondence-cum-contact courses.

2. School complexes are essential to improve competence and fostering professional growth of in-service teachers.

3. Teacher and Teacher-Educators Centres should be established after examining the viability of a place at district level or regional level.

4. Centers of continuing education are to be established at the university departments and State boards of Teacher-education.

5. Need for upgrading teacher-educators to meet the demands for introducing new curriculum in our schools

- Pre-school Teacher, Primary Teacher-Education and Secondary Teacher-Education.

6. Continuity between pre-service and in-service teacher-educator programmes.

There may be the full correspondence course and professional educator courses. The mode of distance education can also be used by employing print and non-print media of instruction.

Here, we will discuss about the mode of correspondence course. The following recommendations have been given by Kothari Commission regarding correspondence course-

1. Opportunity to take examination conducted by Secondary Education Board and Universities in the country should be made available to those who wish to work on their own without any assistance.

2. The Ministry of Education is collaboration with other ministries should establish a National Council of Home-studies, for the purpose of aggregation and evaluation of agencies which provide correspondence courses, identification of the areas in which different types of correspondence courses through proper agencies and for conducting evaluation and research.

3. Correspondence courses would be developed for the teachers in school to keep them abreast with new knowledge as well as with new methods and techniques of teaching.

4. Correspondence courses should be made available to those who desire to enrich their lives by studying subjects of cultural and aesthetic value.

5. Correspondence courses should not be confined to prepare students for the university degree but should

also provide agricultural, industrial and other such special courses of institutions as would help them to improve production.

6. Correspondence courses should be supported by well coordinated Radio and Television programmes.

7. Student taking correspondence courses should be provided opportunities to meet the teachers occasionally, they should be given the statues of recognised students and where possible, be attached to some colleges in order to enable them to make use of the library and other facilities.

8. In order to give education to those who are unable even to attend part time courses, widespread correspondence courses should be organised.

Continuing Education

Kothari Commission has recommended continuing education and said about it the following things-

1. Special institutions such as those run by the Central Welfare Board for Adult Women and Vidya Peeths in Mysore state should be enable them to be of service to the rural community.

2. Further education should be provided for workers for improving their knowledge and skills, widening their horizon in life, inculcating in them a sense of responsibility towards their profession and improving their careers. Special part-time sandwich courses should be offered to them which would lead them step to hither courses.

3. Educational institutions should give the lead in organising adhoc courses which will help people to understand and solve their problems and to acquire wider knowledge and experiences.

4. A parallel part system of education be created to provide adults with opportunities for taking the same diplomas and degrees as students in schools and colleges get.

With a view of deriving optimum results from eradication of illiteracy, a nation wide network of continuing education will be established through new institutional structures, better utilisation of the existing infrastructures, open and distance learning etc.

Norms Prescribed for Functional literacy

The mission has prescribed levels in the three R's be achieved by the target groups.,

1. Reading Norms - A person, to be declared a literate, must be able to read aloud a simple passage at a speed of 30 words per minute. While reading silently small paragraphs in simple language, a speed of 35 words per minute should be achieved.

The neo-literates must also be able to read and understand road signs, posters, simple instructions and newspapers specially produced for them. Ability to follow simple written massage relating to one's working and living and living environment is another requisite attribute.

2. Writing Norms - In respect of writing, the mission has laid down that a neo-literate should be able to copy with understanding at a speed of seven words per minute. He should be able to take dictation at five words per minute. He should be able to write with proper spacing and alignment.. He should be able to write independently short letters, application and forms of day-to-day use.

3. Arithmetic Norms - Proficiency in numerals has

also been laid down. The new learner must be able read and write 1 to 100. He should also be able to do simple calculations without fraction involving addition, subtraction upto three digits and multiplication and divisions to two digits.

The mission also expects the neo-literates to have a working knowledge of metric units of weights, measures, currency, distance and area, and units of time. They should also have a broad of proportion and interest and their use in working and living conditions.

Main Features of the Strategy

1. To universalise the outreach by providing facilities for literacy, learning, continuing education and vocational training.

2. To institutionalise continuing education for post-literacy, particularly through establishment of Jana Shikshan Nilyams and better use of existing institutional facilities.

3. To undertake technology demonstration in 40 districts for development, transfer and application of technology pedagogic inputs and thereafter covering more districts after evaluating the results.

4. To allocate finances.

5. To make available standard learning material on a wide scale, in print and non-print media.

6. To launch mass movement by involving educational institutions, teachers, students, youth, military and para-military personnel, housewives, ex-servicemen, employers trade-unions etc.

7. To involve suitable mechanism for staff selection and development, collection, flow and utilisation of

information, systematic monitoring and evaluation.

8. To establish effective management system at different levels.

9. To improve substantially on-going programmes.

10. To secure people's participation through media and communication, creation of local participatory structure, taking out of jathas, training of cadres of youth etc. These efforts are expected to create an environment conducive to learning.

11. To increase motivation of the leaner by taking up learner need-based programmes.

12. To increase significantly the involvement of voluntary agencies.

National Literary Mission

The National Literacy Mission was launched in the month of May, 1998 to impart functional literacy to 80 million illiterate persons in 15-35 age group, 30 million by 1990 and additional 50 million by 1995. The NLM will concentrate on the 15-35 age group which is important for the country's development. On its understanding of the significance of national and social integration, of productivity and a new work ethics, and of family planning depends the course of our country's future.

11

ROLE AND FUNCTIONS OF THE TEACHER

Introduction

The role of headmaster is very important and comprehensive because educational expansion is still in its infancy and various traditions and evil practices, like casteism and provincialism, are prevalent in our country and society. The position of the headmaster in a school is like that of the caption in the ship. On his policy depends the social prestige of the school as well as the future of the country.

The principal or the headmaster has to eradicate all these evils with the help of his associates so that high ideals may be projected before the students. The headmaster is the leader of the school and the guide of the teachers and the students.

Qualities of Good Headmaster

The headmaster should possess various qualities which make him effective in the discharge of his duties. We shall study them under the following heads:

1. Personal Qualities - The headmaster should possess the following personal traits or qualities :

a. Touches life at many points.

b. Tolerance for other's seriously without taking himself seriously.

c. Self-confidence and courage.

d. Solves problems.

e. Identification with work.

f. Devoted and dedicated.

g. Frank and forceful,

h. Common-sense and tact.

i. Creative and constructive.

Physical Qualities

The headmaster should possess the following physical qualities or traits :

a. Immaculate behaviour.

b. Sober life-style.

c. Shuns affectation and posing.

d. Robust, healthy, agile.

e. Regular habits.

d. Natural and good manners.

e. Clear and resonant voice.

f. Simple and sober dress sense.

g. Good physique.

h. Active, smart and strong.

i. Attractive and clean appearance.

Moral Qualities

The moral qualities of the headmaster can be enumerated as follows without going into undue detail : a. Sense of absolute values.

b. Self-respect.

c. Self-realization through social service.

d. Self-control.

e. Ready to admit mistakes.

f. Highest ideals.

g. Good character.

i. Belief in democratic values.

j. Ethical.

k. Ability to discriminates between right and wrong.

Social Qualities

Since the role of headmaster has important social connotation, he should possess the following social qualities too:

a. Knowledge of others problems.

b. Insight into social forces acting on education.

c. Humility in achieving.

d. Honest in dealings.

e. Goodwill for all.

f. Helpful in difficulties.

g. Good human relations.

h. Good relationship with colleagues.

i. Cooperation.

j. Should avoid unnecessary criticism.

k. Active and socialised citizen.

Emotional Qualities

The emotional qualities of the headmaster can be described under the following headings :

a. Optimist and hopeful.

b. Strongly motivated.

c. Should not be susceptible to be upset by difficulties and disappointments.

d. Not easily excitable, should be able to keep his cool under adverse circumstances.

e. Free from nervousness, tension, and worry. Full of confidence and a strong desire and ability to lead from the front.

f. Free from anxiety and conflicts, and have a balanced state of mind and attitude.

g. Happy and contented.

h. Cheerful and pleasant to talk to or work with.

i. Emotional stability.

Intellectual Qualities

The headmaster should necessarily possess the intellectual qualities which can be briefly mentioned as under:

a. Should have scholarly bent of mind, and a vast store of correlated knowledge and information.

b. Should be able to understand and utilise individual differences to draw the best out of everyone.

c. Sense of systematic and planned work.

d. Excellent communication skills, both spoken and written.

e. Knowledge of social problems and possible solutions.

f. Should be an authority on his subject and be abreast with the latest trends in the theory and practice of teaching and education.

g. Knowledge of pedagogy, child growth and development.

h. Awareness of his position and ore.

i. Attitude of enquiry, should encourage putting forward views by the subordinates and should not shut them off.

Moral Qualities

The moral qualities of the headmaster can be enumerated as follows without going into undue detail:

a. Sense of absolute values.

b. Self-respect.

c. Self-realisation through social service.

d. Good character.

e. Belief in democratic values.

f. Ability of discriminates between right and wrong.

We can detail a few of this qualities for the benefit of our students:

1. Optimism - The headmaster should be optimistic, otherwise, he will dampen the spirits of the students and teachers at every step. He should have an interest in life and faith in human power. His way of thinking should be ideal so that the others may follow it and realise their objectives in life. He should also have implicit faith in his profession, that is, in teaching. If he is not optimistic, he will infect has colleagues also.

2. Ideals - The headmaster should be a man of high ideals, for then only will he able to make the teachers and the students love and pursue high ideals.

3. Efficiency in Work - It is natural for a school to be faced with different situations and circumstances and the headmaster should have the ability to take the right step. It was thought that the headmaster was a horrible creature who inflicted heavy punishments on simple matters. But, now under the democratic system, he is regarded as a king-hearted, just and sympathetic individual. He now treats the students, the staff of the school and the guardians with love and regress. He takes interesting all the activities of the students and fully considers their representations. His aim is to prepare students not only for examination but for life.

4. No Haste in Introducing Reforms - The headmaster should not show undue haste in introducing any reform. Before launching any scheme of reform he should understand its ins and outs and, as far as possible, should consult the teachers, students, and guardians.

5. Health - Good health is the key of success in life. To be a torchbearer to others it is necessary that the headmaster exudes cheer and its radiant with high spirits. This comes only with good health.

6. Interest in Mankind - The headmaster has to come into contact with teachers, students and guardians of different status and temperament. Hence, he should have an interest in solving the problems of all these, else his influence will not be very widespread.

7. Administrative Capacity - The headmaster should be a good administrator. The progress of the school depends, to a great extent. On his management of the affairs. The headmaster should know how to secure the best services of the students, the teachers, the clerical and other staff of the school.

8. Learning - It is necessary for him to be a master of his subject while being ahead of his colleagues in general knowledge. To succeed as a headmaster it is necessary that he should command respect from his colleagues for his learning. Hence, he should possess a personal library with a good collection of books on education. He should also read magazines dealing with researches in the field of education so that he may be acquainted with the latest advancements.

9. Politeness or Culture - The conduct, behaviour and general conduct of the headmaster should be extremely polite and polished and he should be capable of inspiring confidence and commanding respect from others.

10. Professional Knowledge - The headmaster should have a good knowledge of literature pertaining to education as also of the education code and the various rules and regulations of the Education

Department.

Knowledge and Professional Training

Only a highly trained headmaster can show the way of the members of the staff on teaching techniques. He must have mastery of educational, child and social psychology. To refresh himself and keep his professional knowledge up-to-date, he must study educational journals and latest books on education. He must have a progressive outlook and be ready to experiment with new ideas. As W.H. Ryburn observes, "As leader of this cooperative group, it is the headmaster's duty to keep himself up to the mark. If he is not to be blind leader of the blind, he must keep himself in touch with modern movements in education, with experiments which are being tried out in different status of the India and in other countries with new ideas." He should take part in educational seminars and workshops.

Role of the Headmaster

Hodgkinson points out the following four maxims for the leadership in school administration;

The headmaster is the monarch of the school, students constitute his army, the staff forms of the body of officers, the school building corresponds to state and the school management is state administration. The end of state administration is justice or doing good, so is the end of school management. The maxims resemble with Tennenbaum's four forces Hodgkinson's first maxim is all the more important because of its scope on which depends the whole functioning of the school, that is, to know the task both short term and long term.

His second maxim can be taken to include the rotational situation, and, of course, the third maxim on followership would also imply a knowledge of following invariables that include a knowledge of the environment as listed for management tasks. There is, in fact, relative discussion in the literature of the skills required and strategies entailed in the leader transforming the forces in the environment into a mission for the organisation; among them knowing himself and his own qualities and capabilities by the headmaster is no less important and significant. Hodgkinson gets much closer to this in his concept of administration as philosophy.

We can explore some of the implications of the construction and presentation of the mission for the head. The headmaster is expected to be alert to the forces in the environment of the school which have potential relevance for its internal activities. These forces can be divided into two clusters. One cluster will contain relevant knowledge of what is happening in the broader educational world. According to General Grant, "these are no poor regiments but only colones." And so is the case with the school. The success or failure of the school depends upon its Headmaster. He is responsible for the smooth running of the school. He is responsible for carrying out policies and programs for the Departments of Education. He is the coordinator of educational work.

He sets the tone of the school. He is the chief force in moulding the traditions which develop as time goes on. This would largely entail the knowledge of existing and emerging educational policies at national and local levels. This knowledge would be acquired through a reading of policy statements, reports, the educational press, and thorough interacting with other heads, advisers, lectures, etc., through policies will be a body of educational and curricular theory and associated research on which the well- prepared head could call, to put them in a wider philosophical and empirical context. The second cluster relates to the clientele of the school and would include knowledge of social background, parental aspirations, community resources, job opportunities, etc. The head who would create a mission for the school would have the continuous task of selection from these factors within the head and within the teachers currently teaching in the school and such other organisational forces as structures and resources, would fashion set of goals for the school which could be construed as a mission.

P.C., Wren explains the role of Headmaster in the following words, "What the mainspring is to the watch, the fly-well to the machine or the engine to the steamship, so is the headmaster to the school. The character of the headmaster. He is the seal and the school is the wax. He is the organiser, leader, governor, business director, coordinators, superintendent, teacher's guide, philosopher and friend Different leadership styles entail differences in the degree to which heads construct missions alone or in collaboration with members of staff who would have been encouraged to contribute to the negotiation of a mission on the basis of their knowledge of environment forces and forces within themselves. To the head would fall the task of retaliating and presenting the mission

Dr. Jaswant Singh says, "What the school is and what is does, is determined largely by the intelligence, scholarship, imagination, initiative, personality and social skill of the headmaster, it includes everything in the school- the plant, the staff, the curriculum, methods and techniques of teaching curricular activities. Human relationships bear and impress on the personality of the head of institution and reflect his leadership. The school is as great as the headmaster. This would be achieved though verbalisation, through the deliberate deployment of symbols, or through a series of less obstructive symbolic acts. At this point the task merges into the middle elements of Hodgkinson's model - politics and mobilising. This involves securing of staff commitment to the mission. The task then moves to the operationalisation stage and merges with the managerial components of the Hodgkinson model.

This involves the fulfillment of the two dimensions of leadership task achievement and social needs satisfaction. The basic distinction is between those heads who lead from the front and, if successful, inspire teachers to follow, and those who are lacking and degree of mooted charisma, though succeed in building a mission through democratic means involving much negotiation. The former kind is more likely to be carriers, to articulate the mission via language and symbol, and to be committed to greater and more radical change.

The school is aptly called the lengthened shadow of the head-master because the character of the school reflects or proclaims the character of the school reflects or proclaims the character of the headmaster. No scheme of educational reconstruction will produce the desired result unless it is administered with vision and efficiency. The person who plans with vision and executes with responsibility is an exact headmaster.

A scholar writes It must not only be known by his staff and scholars that he is their headmaster by appointment but it must be felt that he is their headmaster by superior ability, energy and character. Secondary Education Commission, 1953 said, "On the headmaster the proper working of the school ultimately depends. The reputation of the school and the position that it holds in the society depends in a large measure on the influence that he exercise over his colleagues, the pupils and the general public. Similarly the discipline of the school and its esprit de corps are the special responsibilities of the headmaster. He holds an important place in the life of the community, where he can exercise a very healthy influence. By this contact with the parents and the general public he can to forge that link between the school and the large community which we have repeatedly stressed. He is also responsible for carrying out the policies and the programme of the Department of Education and he acts as a liaison between it and the management of the general local community."

The Headmaster must have knowledge in social science, psychology, philosophy, sociology and economics. He must also remain in touch with the latest scientific development. He should remain in touch with the latest scientific developments. He should not only know his own subject of specialisation, but should also know the latest thinking in other school subjects. The headmaster should possess adequate and effective professional training because educational administration is a specialised job.

A good headmaster thus agree all educationists, needs to have a sound philosophy of education based on careful study of latest knowledge and research. The philosophy must be constantly examined and received, for any defensible philosophy must be constantly open to scrutiny, re-examination, and revision as new problems arise and new insights are gained. This philosophy must not be opposed to the modes of the community, though it should not be subservient to it. It must be sold to the community through a well-organised programme of public relations. All school plans, policies and methods must evolve from this philosophy, and the achievement of the school must be measured and evaluated in terms of the objective derived from this philosophy. Without this the curricula and techniques will lack right direction, and therefore, would fail to assure the goals of education.

Functions of the Headmaster

A nation is built in its schools. In this way there comes very important responsibility on the headmaster. The foremost duty of the headmaster is attainment of objectives of education. The chief duty of the school is to achieve maximum number of objectives which have been fixed by keeping requirements, ideals and desires of individuals, society and the nation in mind. Thus being leader of the school, the headmaster has to bear the following functions and responsibilites :

1. Evaluation - One of the important duties of the headmaster is to evaluate his total arrangements form time to time. He has to implement his planning, besides he has also to evaluate not only his policies, processes and activities of students, but also it is essential for him to examine his associates and actions of other functionaries of school. At the time of evaluating the activities of these officials, the headmaster should keep in mind the following points:

a. He should conduct evaluation for bringing about improvement in their working.

b. To make human relations appropriate, he should have sympathetic and helpful attitude towards his subordinates. He should not conduct the evaluation with the viewpoint of destruction.

c. He should know merits and demerits of his colleagues.

d. He should develop feelings of self-evaluation and self-development in his workers.

It is important to know how far the level of the teachers has improved and what principles and processes have been used for them, and how far the extent of realising co-curricular activities of the organisation and the objectives of education been successful or helpful? Discipline of school and its general tone, how far have they been helpful in developing social and moral qualities in children? To know all these things, the requires to conduct evaluation. For the knowledge of these things, the headmaster should use various method, slide observation, probes, interview, questionnaire and record methods, etc. He should pay attention on the following points for knowing about progress, promotion, capacities and difficulties, etc., of his students.

He should watch that question papers of examinations are not too easy or too hard, and weekly and monthly tests should be arranged and unkeep of record of these should be maintained.

Cumulative Record of children should be prepared. In these records, a detailed description of test of various aptitudes and qualities should be given, for instance, general knowledge, practical capability, social and citizen activities, expression, service motive, cooperation, health progress, traits of personality, character, firmness, leadership, industriousness, self-confidence, self-control, sociability and presence of mind. These qualities of students should be recorded and maintained in the office records. It is very essential for him to know the opinions and ideas of teachers and guardians as well.

2. Supervision - The headmaster requires vigilant supervision. Through supervision only, he can have the knowledge of all the activities of the school and be successful. His awareness of the fields of weakness would enable him to take action so that some steps may be taken to improve them. No part of the school is out of the vision of the headmaster because every section of the school plays some role in making or unmaking of students.

It is not sufficient to pay attention do outside, the school games and sports are the life of hostel, it is also necessary to see how students lead hostel life. The supervision of all these things should be done not only for the mental development of the students but also for physical, social and ethical development. Supervisory responsibility of a headmaster could be studied under the following heads;

a. General Administration - The headmaster should also look after the co-curricular activities in the school. He should pay full attention to the sports and games for the students as also educational activities like monitorial, dramatic and literary associations, etc. He should himself occasionally take part in these and encourage the teachers of the school to do so.

b. The Tone of the School - It is difficult for the school to fix its tone or tis definite policy overnight as is takes several years to shape. The tone of the school should influence the students and teachers in such a manner that they may become imbued with a sense of duty and their all-round development may be brought about. The headmaster has a duty in this regard also. In such a school the conduct of students is more or less flawless; and they do not cause any harm to anybody and the foundation of their ideal character is laid during their school life.

c. Guardians - The headmaster should maintain good relations with guardians. They should be invited to the school from time to time so that they may see how the work goes on in this school on the occasions of social functions and otherwise. A get-together of guardians and teachers should also be organised at regular intervals, at which the headmaster should explain the general policies of the school and invite suggestions for improvement in the school. Whenever the guardians visit the school they should be treated well by the headmaster. By establishing good contacts with the guardians, various difficulties pertaining to students can easily be resolved.

d. Textbooks - The headmaster should see that such textbook are selected out to the approved ones which will be most suitable for the students. He should consult the teachers in this regard. He should not select a textbook under the pressure of an author of a publisher. In the selection of textbooks he should be guided by the following considerations:

(i) Is the price of the book reasonable?

(ii) Are the given questions are exercises appropriate?

(iii) Are the facts given in the book correct?

(iv) Does it include all the suitable maps and illustrative figures?

(v) Is the style such as would develop in the students the power of self-thinking?

(vi) Is it good from the point of view of printing and language?

(vii) Does the subject of the book co-relate itself with others?

(viii) Has the book been written in accordance with the prescribed course?

(ix) Is its paper and lay out good?

(x) Has the matter been presented coherently?

4. Supervision - The headmaster requires vigilant supervision. Through supervision only, he can have the knowledge of all the activities of the school and be successful. His awareness of the fields of weakness would enable him to take action so that some steps may be taken to improve them. No part of the school is out of the vision of the headmaster because every section of the school-plays some role in making or unmaking of students. It is not sufficient to pay attention on the teaching programs alone, notwithstanding, what students do outside, the school games and sorts are the life of hostel, it is also necessary to see how students lead hostel life. The supervision of all these things should be done not only for the mental development of the students but also for physical, social and ethical development. Supervisory responsibilities of a headmaster could be studied under the following heads:

a. General Supervision - Supervision means actual inspection. The teacher enjoys a certain amount of prestige with the class and if he is rebuked in the presence of the class, his headmaster encroaches upon the dignity of the teacher. If the headmaster feels that the teacher needs correction, he should send for him after the period is over. In this post-visit conference details may be discussed. The headmaster should deal with the teacher very tactually. Advice should have friendly attitude toward his teachers. He should regard himself and his staff as a team, as a small family. He is the head of the family to guide all other members.

b. Office Record and Office - It is necessary for the headmaster to inspect the working of the office and unkeep of office record. For running the schoolwork efficiently, full attention should be paid towards daily correspondence and replies sent as soon as possible. Besides, he should inspect various records of the office.

c. Hostel Supervision - It becomes a duty of the headmaster to supervise the hostel too. He should keep a watch on the food of students, management of food preparation, arrangement of drinking water, dinning room, cleanliness of utensils, etc. So, it is necessary for him to inspect all these things and sometimes he should eat food with the students so that he should know what king of food is served to the students. He should look after the hostel activities. He should inspect the sleeping rooms of the boys for cleanliness and proper lighting and ventilation. Besides, he should manage to know that the children do not study while lying in the bed or other unhealthy postures and, that they keep their rooms in order. He should inspect the arrangement of bathroom and latrine etc. In addition to that he should also inspect the hostel bye-laws, logbook, stock register, attendance register and other records.

d. Supervision on Teaching - The principal should see that the teaching work in the school goes on well. The students and teachers should go to their respective classes as soon as the bell rings. The headmaster should also occasionally go to classes while teaching is going on, not as a critic but as a friend and collaborator.

He should not criticise any teacher in any class before the students. If he has to make any suggestions to a teacher, he should do so in his own.

The headmaster should also periodically inspect the written work done by the students. This will acquaint him with the work and the teaching of the teacher. He should give instructions to the teacher so that all the written work with the requisite details may reach him in time. He should inspect all or most of the copies and see whether the mistakes have been marked in tend and necessary instructions have been given to the students. There should be a separate notebook for each teacher in which he should express his opinion in regard to the written work, e.g., good work much attention has not been given to the mistakes of a particular student etc.

In order to improve the method of teaching, ideal lessons should be occasionally planned and the headmaster should also take part in these. He should also keep a check over the teachers in regard to private tuitions, else many will devote most of their time to this. It would be best not to permit the teacher to undertake private tuitions, but this is not possible for various reasons, such as, low salaries.

The headmaster should supervise the register and accounts of the school; cleanliness of the school, students and the surroundings; the school farms and the craft work; games, discipline, etc. Dr. Hart has described seven abilities which every administrator and supervisor should possess, and we have mentioned them on the preceding pages. These qualities and abilities should guide a headmaster toward running the school administration.

e. Supervision on Teaching - The principle should see that the teaching work in the school goes on well. The students and teachers should go to their respective classes as soon as the bell rings. The headmaster should also occasionally go to classes while teaching is going on, not as a critic but as a friend and collaborator.

He should not criticise any teacher in any class before the students. If he has to make any suggestions to a teacher, he should do so in his own office.

The headmaster should also periodically inspect the written work done by the students. This will acquaint him with the work and the teaching of the teacher. He should give instructions to the teacher so that all the written work with the requisite details may reach him in time. He should inspect all or most of the copies and see whether the mistakes have been marked in red and necessary instructions have been given to the students. There should be a separate notebook for each teacher in which he should express his opinion in regard to the written work, e.g., good work much attention has not been given to the mistakes of a particular students etc.

In order to improve the method of teaching, ideal lessons should be occasionally planned and the headmaster should also take part in these. He should also keep a check over the teachers in regard to private tuitions, else many will devote most of their time to this. It would be best not to permit the teacher to undertake private tuitions, but this is not possible.

5. Organisation and Administration - The next important task of the headmaster is organisation. His organising duties consist of the following tasks:

a. To maintain friendship, respect and confidence towards the workers.

b. To assign duties and responsibilites.

c. To secure sustained and persistent cooperation of all workers.

d. To define the positioning of workers on the basis of law and conventions.

e. To ensure individual and group satisfaction through group interaction and consideration.

f. To lay down the structure of the organisation, the pattern of positions and relationships.

g. To ensure security and durability of the group through pleasant relations, encouragement, self-expression and self-direction.

h. To promote effectiveness and efficiency for accomplishment of purpose.

i. To make the organisation democratic through personal relationship, active participation and sharing of power and responsibility.

j. To ensure group behaviour towards achievement of purposes through action, procedure, communication and evaluation.

6. Planning - The chief duty of the head of every educational institution is to plane before conducting his various programs and functions and activities. He has to plan out all his duties and responsibilities for the whole year; he should plan them mainly on the following three levels:

a. At the End of the Session - The headmaster has to organise the following works and activities:

(i) To formulate the rules of class promotion.

(ii) To organise annual sports and games and

celebrate functions such as Guardians Day, Culture Programs, Annual Prize Distribution Day, etc.

(iii) To prepare annual reports of students.

(iv) To discuss essential steps for preparation of the next session.

(v) To get the attendance, accounts of fees etc., checked so that it may be known that no student is left without depositing the dues of the school before announcing the results.

b. During the Session - The headmaster should plan for the following functions during the session -

(i) To appropriately arrange for correspondence with Education Department, Managing Committee and others.

(ii) To arrange for broadcasting school programme.

(iii) To organise the guidance-services.

(iv) To arrange for verification of written work of students, records of students and school records.

(v) To arrange for room invigilation at examination period.

(vi) To organise lectures of experts.

(vii) To arrange for examination and evaluation.

(viii) To organise various projects or teaching aid activities.

(ix) To organise teaching work.

c. On the Opening Day of the School - Planning should be done for arrangement of the following functions within one week of re-opening of the school-

(i) Arrange for physical facilities as per requirement

in the school.

(ii) To arrange for school assembly. Set rules for the organisation of the school rules and traditions etc.

(iii) To undertake selection of textbooks, and direct students for buying them.

(iv) To plan for arranging various teaching aid activities and distribute the responsibility of arranging them on the basis of ability and interest of teachers.

(v) To prepare plan of their activities and lesson plan from each teacher.

(vi) To get prepared the inventory of teachers, inventory of students, and inventory of classrooms.

d. Before Re-opening of the Schools - At this stage he has to necessarily plan the following functions:

(i) He should get the calender of activities for whole session prepared.

(ii) Required registers and files are to be arranged.

(iii) Whitewashing of the school buildings and polishing of furniture should be arranged.

(iv) Formulation of rules regarding admissions. At the same time, to form those committees to which this responsibility is to be handed over.

(v) To announce the date of the re-opening of the school after the summer vocations. Last date of receipt of application forms for admission, if the admissions are to be done by some sort of examination, fixation of its data and to arrange the examination on that date.

(vi) He is to see in the school that furniture, other equipments, availability of books etc., in the library meet satisfactory stocking; if not, he should arrange for them.

If the furniture is to be repaired, he should arrange for it.

Delegation of Authority

The delegation of authority is a necessary feature of an able headmaster. The headmaster should delegate to the other members of the staff supervision of the examinations, school cleanliness, morning assembly, funds, hostel, scouting, literacy and social activities, etc. The delegation of power will develop in them a sense of responsibility for the school. He should consult his colleagues regarding improvement in school discipline and instruction. The headmaster should have good relations with controlling authorities like the state department of education. Only then he can bring about the desired improvement in the school. In the case of private schools, the managing bodies are the controlling authorities. These bodies are concerned with the selection of school staff, construction and raising of funds for the school. The headmaster should try to carry the members of the managing bodies with him. He should convince them of his point of view through sound arguments. The advantages will be that a spirit will be instilled in them that they belong to the school and area as responsible to it as the headmaster himself is.

The teachers have a great role to play in the educational, social and even political reconstruction of India. The teacher is essentially a nation-builder. He is the torchbearer of the race. On him depends the future of the school , the village, the country and infact, the future of mankind. The headmaster should work in active contact and cooperation with the public. He is the main agent who forms the link between the school and the public. He should create an interest in the school among the general public. He should create call staff meetings from time-to-time. Full freedom should be given to the teachers to put forward their problems in these meetings.

Supervision of Each Teacher's Work

The Headmaster should have friendly attitude towards his teachers. He should regard himself and his staff as a team, as a small family. He is the head of the family to guide all other members. Supervision means actual inspection. The teacher enjoys a certain among of prestige with the class and if he is rebuked in the presence of the class, his headmaster encroaches upon the rights of the teacher. If the headmaster feels that teacher needs correction, he should send for him after the period is over. In this post-visit conference details may be discussed. The headmaster should deal with the teacher very tactfully. Advice should be given in a pleasant and friendly manner. The teacher should come out of the headmaster's room after a post-visit conference as a better person, wiser and in a more pleasant mood than when he went to him. The headmaster should supervise the registers and accounts of the school, and also the cleanliness of the school students and the surroundings, the school frame and the craft work, games, discipline, etc.

Dr. Hart enumerates seven abilities which every administrator and supervisor should possess in ample degree to discharge his duties.

1. The first is to set goals that are within the reach of an individual.

2. The second is to organise the school system such that essential worthwhile things are discovered and spread through the whole system.

3. The third is that of helping everyone in the system to grow professionally and in service to society.

4. The fourth is to overcome the inefficiencies of others without losing their goodwill.

5. The fifth is to make those who work for the administrator or supervisor personally happy.

6. The sixth is the ability to recognise the essentially worthwhile changes that are taking place in the school system.

7. The seventh is that of making everyone in the school system feel the worthwhileness of his job.

Winning of Faith

The headmaster should be a man of faith. As Ryburn says, "It is essential, therefore, that he be not only a man of high character but also that he be a man of faith; faith in vocation, faith in his pupils, faith in human nature and faith in his staff."

Headmaster's Relationships with Others

The chief responsibility of organisation and administration rests upon the headmaster. The tone and efficiency of a school depend largely on his personality and professional competence. A headmaster has to maintain the following relations:

1. Relationship with the Managing Committee - Private institutions are run by managing committees. In all matters of internal administration, the headmaster should deal directly with the committee. In all matters pertaining to external management of the school, the committee may correspond directly with the department.

2. Relationship with the University of School Education Board - In certain states the University

conducts the school leaving certificate examination, while in other states the School Education Board does so. Certain rules and regulations concerning the examination are fixed, curriculum is drawn and textbooks are prescribed. The headmaster should know all these details.

3. Relation with the State Department of Education - The headmaster should maintain the following type of relationship with the States Departments of Education.

a. Recognition - The headmaster should know every detail about recognition of schools and about the advantages of recognition. He should know what he has to do and what he must not do.

b. Rules and Regulations - The headmaster should know fully well the rules and regulations as fixed by the State Department of Education from time to time. For the administration of secondary education there are rules regarding admissions, withdrawals, attendance, school timing, promotion, time table, size of classes, medical examination, physical education, leave, courses of study and textbooks prescribed for different classes as well as regulations regarding schools and hostel buildings, equipment and furniture, rules regarding recognition of schools and finance, grants-in-aid, accounts, tuition fees, scholarships; procedure for this maintenance of records, etc.

4. Relations with Public - The headmaster can maintain relation with the public in the following way:

a. Handling Inter Personal Relation - The headmaster has to play a delicate role of balancing the demands of the parents, the opinion of the public, perception of teachers and the needs and aspirations of the students. He should be adept at handing the delicate inter-personal relationships. He should remember the advice Polonius gave to his son Laertes, to lend his ear to everyone but none his tongue. Patient listening will tell him what the speaker is trying to communicate.

b. Content - To serve the school, the headmaster must enlist the cooperation of the parents. No headmaster can be successful if he does not look beyond the four walls of his school and is contented only with organising and directing its internal activities. He should utilise every opportunity of getting in touch with the parents of pupils. This will add to the effectiveness of the work of the school and make its scope more comprehensive. It will enable the parents and teachers to pull in the same direction. His relations with the public must be cordial but he must not take sides.

5. Relation with Pupils - The headmaster can maintain relationship with the pupils in the following way:

a. Access - The headmaster should be respected but not feared; he should be easy to access but certainly not one to be trifled with. He should be able to maintain the prestige and dignity of his office without giving the impression that he is harsh, indifferent or callous to his students.

b. Student Associations - Students should be associated with the school administration through students council students panchayat, students parliament, etc. They should be entrusted with organising and running of co-curricular activities and entrusted with positions of responsibility.

c. Direct Contact - This may be done taking some period in the lowest class. This will also solve the problem of discipline because the pupils will come to know their headmaster. Contact with the pupils of the school is an important secret of success of a headmaster. He should not see the pupils only through the eyes of his assistants. He must try to know as large a number of children in his school as possible.

6. Relations with Teachers - The headmaster should maintain the following king of relationship with the teachers:

a. Democratic Relations - The teacher should be given a much bigger share in the actual day-to-day administration of the school. The headmaster should strive to establish true rapport within the staff through informal and formal individual and group causations and conferences. The headmaster must establish democratic relationships. The attitude of mot to reason why, but to carry out orders, good, bad, or indifferent, will create deep frustration and issues among teachers. There should be frequent meetings of the whole staff or section of the staff. Where full and frank discussion and two-way traffic of ideas should flow on all matters pertaining to the welfare of the school. To get the best of the cooperation of the staff should be the major concern of the headmaster. He must assist staff members in improving their competencies, in making their individual contribution as well as gaining competence in working together with others on specific assignments. The headmaster and teachers can educate each other about new developments of educational theory and practice- this will promote healthy and creative teamwork.

b. First Among Equals - The headmaster should remember the wise statement of Ronald Gould, "No quality education is possible without good personal relationships." The headmaster is the head teacher. Many teachers are as well qualified, and experienced as the headmaster. They must be given a positive say in matters of school policy. When teachers are treated as allies and colleagues, are consulated and given responsibility they respond resulting in better teaching.

12

DISCIPLINE

Introduction

The concept of good conduct varies with the political institutions and social traditions of the community. Education has two aims, namely institutional training and good conduct. Indiscipline is a serous problem everywhere, but it hits the hardest in big cities where classes are large, where huge percentage of the student population leads its social behaviour not in stable middle classes home but in poverty-ridden slums; where children have more economic deprivation and mor emotional and physical problems than they bring to school with them; where inadequacy in language is often a barrier to good communication.

There are no easy answers to the discipline question, and most of those that have been proffered- such as educating children who chronically misbehave in separate- school as educating children who chronically misbehave in separate facilities until they are ready to return to the mainstream- requires additional funding. But unless we deal with discipline, we are sacrificing not only the education of the other children, those who are short-changed when a teacher's time is taken up with one or two disruptive or even violent students, but also the capacity to attract the best teachers to the urban schools that need them most. Until we make all schools in our big cities safe and calm places where teachers can teach and students can learn, we will be confronted with a serious disincentive for the best and brightest to join or remain in teaching ranks. The teachers want to teach the subjects they love, and not to be policemen or jail wardens. Moreover, the teachers tend to have come from working-class homes where teaching was seen as a way up and out. Many teachers simply do not want to return to the climate of urban disruption and violence they had hoped to leave behind.

When there was a hierarchal organisation proceeding from the self by gradual stages up to God, chief virtue was obedience in the middle ages. Children were taught to obey their parents and to revere their social superiors, to feel awe in the presence of respectable elders and submission in the presence of the Lord. Only the Emperor and the Guru were free, and since the morality of the time afforded no guidance to free men, they spent their time in fighting with one another.

Meanwhile propaganda has become persuasive rather than forceful, and has learnt to proceed by instilling suitable sentiments in early youth. The modern man differs from the man of the earlier centuries both in aim and method. Democracy has substituted cooperation for submission and herd-instinct is to be most operative has become the nation, which was formerly rendered unimportant by ideas of univesality. Music, school songs, and the national flag determine, by their influence on the boy, the subsequent action of the main in moments of strong emotion. Against these influences the assaults of reason have but little power. The influence of political conceptions on early education is not always obvious, and is often unconscious on the part of the educator.

When it is sought to produce a certain kind of behaviour in a child or animal, there are two different techniques which may be followed. By a suitable distribution of rewards and punishments, it is possible to control a very large part of overt behaviour. Usually the only form of reward or punishment required will be praise or blame. We may cause by means of rewards and punishments, the child or animal to perform or abstain from certain precise acts; or we may, on the other hand, seek to produce in the child such emotions as will lead, on the whole, to acts of the king desired. By this method the boys who are naturally timid can acquire physical courage, and the children who are sensitive to pain can be taught a stoical endurance. Good manners, if not taught at an early age, can be learnt in adolescence by means of no worse punishment than the contemptuous lifting of an eyebrow. As a social force, the behaviourist method of conditioning is therefore very powerful and successful. It can does make man to act in a way quite different from those in which he would otherwise have acted, and it is capable of producing an impressing uniformity of overt behaviour. Nevertheless, it has its limitations. What is called good form it is acquired by almost all who are exposed to it, merely from fear of the bad opinion incurred by infringing it.

Those who have been taught from an early age to fear the displeasure of their group as the worst understand nothing, rather than suffer the contempt of fools. The English public schools have carried this system to perfection, and have largely sterilised intelligence by making it cringe before the herd. This is what is called making a boy manly.

For our purposes, the essential discovery of psychoanalysis that an impulse which is prevented, by behaviourist methods from finding overt expression in action, does not necessarily die, but is driven underground, and finds some new outlet which has not been inhibited by training. Freud propounded these limitations first in a scientific manner, though men of psychological insight had long ago perceived them in an intuitive way. Often the new outlet will be more harmful than the one that has been prevented, and in any case the deflection involves emotional disturbance and unprofitable expenditure of energy.

It is, therefore, necessary to pay more attention to emotion, as opposed to overt behaviour, then is done by those who advocate conditioning alone as sufficient in the training of character. What is less recognised is that we all suffer, to a greater or lesser degree, from nervous disorders having the emotional origin. A man is called sane when he is as sane as the average of his contemporaries; but in the average man many of the mechanisms which determine his opinions and actions are quite fantastic, so much so that in a world of real sanity they would be called insane.

It is dangerous to produce good social behaviour by those means which leave the anti-social emotions untouched. So long as these emotions, while persisting, are denied an outlet, they will grow stronger and stronger, leading to impulses of cruelty which will at last become irresistible. In the man of weak will, these impulse may break out in crime, or in some form of behaviours to which social penalties are attached. In the man of strong will, they take even more undesirable forms. He may be a tyrant in home, bellicose in school, persecuting in his social morality, for all these qualities other men with similar defects in character will admire him.

Correct behaviour combined with bad emotions is not enough. Therefore, to make a man contribute to the happiness of mankind, which is our criterion of desirable conduct, something more must be sought in the education of character. Such consideration, as well as the sympathetic observation of children, suggests that the behaviourist methods of training a character is inadequate, and needs to be supplemented by a quite different method. The institutional idealistic philosophies of the nineteenth century did not make the nation state the agency of securing ideals as these narrowed the concept of the social aim to those who were members of the same political unit, and tended to reintroduce the idea of the subordination of the individual to the institution.

Significance of Disciplines in Schools

Discipline is also very much important with social viewpoint. Discipline in schools generally means order and system in doing things, regularity and obedience to commands. Discipline is not synonymous with class-order. It should bot be identified with orderly behaviour in the classroom and other forms of school activities. Outward show of order can be maintained by force or fear. That is not real discipline. Real discipline implies persuasion while order implies compulsion, It is, therefore, imperative that school discipline should be the result of a gradual building up of habits of self-control and cooperation and carried out by pupils, not because it is imposed from above, but because of the recognition of its necessity and value. Ultimately school discipline should imply the cultivation of certain desirable attitudes, habits and values in individual pupils.

Discipline has great significance in life. For want of it man cannot utilise powers properly given by nature. Through discipline only, man can attain good power, and by this power he becomes capable in developing his natural tendencies with personal viewpoint. The great philosopher Aristotle said, "A nation is not built by mountains and trees, notwithstanding it is built by character of its citizens." This statement is completely true. The statement of P.C. Wren is very relevant, "As in the Army, the Navy of the state, so in the school, the pre-requisite, the very condition of existence is discipline." When the citizens of some country would be disciplined, they could be capable to take their country on the path of progress. A disciplined person is of good character, and pious by mind, words, and actions.

In this way, it is clear that for nation or entire society disciplinc is vcry important. Great educationists T.P. Nunn is of the opinion, "Discipline consists in the submission of one's impulses and powers to regulation which impose from upon chaos and bring efficiency and economy where it would otherwise be ineffective and waste." This fact can be made clear with the help of history also. History is witness, when a country becomes prey of indiscipline, it has to accept slavery of external powers. Through discipline, a man and entire society or nations are taught alertness among them. For wand of it, this power parishes which results in terrible condition. In this way, the personality of a man, a nation and a society can be made great by discipline.

In the absence of it, entire working of school cannot be run properly, in want of it, there would be a reign of anarchy in it. Thus, discipline is that power through which person, society, nation and school are taken on the path of progress and their personality is made splendid.

Any activity with an aim implies a distinction between an earlier incomplete phase and later completing phase, with intermediate steps. An aim denotes the result of any natural process brought to consciousness and made a factor is determining present observation and choice of ways of acting. It signifies that an activity has become intelligent. Specifically it means foresight of the alternative consequences attendant upon acting in a given situation in different ways, and the use of what is anticipated to direct observation and experiment. A true aim is thus opposed at every point to an aim which is imposed upon a process of action from without. The latter is fixed and rigid; it is not a stimulus to intelligence in the given situation, but is an externally directed order to do such and such things. Instead of connecting directly with present activities, it is remote, divorced from the means by which it is to be reached. Instead of suggesting a freer and better - balanced activity, it is a limited set of activity.

In education, the currency of these externally imposed aims is responsible for the emphasis put upon the notion of preparation for a remote future and for rendering the work of both teacher and pupil mechanical and slavish.

Interest and discipline are correlative aspects of activity having an aim. Interest means that one is identified with the objects which define the activity and which furnish the aims and obstacles to its realisation. The time difference between the given incomplete state of affairs and the desired fulfillment exacts effort in transformation; it demands continuity of attention and endurance. This attitude is what is practically meant by will. Discipline or development of power of continuous attention is its fruit. The significance of this doctrine for the theory of education is twofold. On the one hand, it protects us from the notion that the mind and mental states are something complete in themselves, which then happen to be applied to some ready-made objects and topics so that knowledge results.

The developing course of action, whose end conditions are perceived, is the unity which holds together what are often divided into an independent mind on one side and an independent world of objects and facts on the other. It shows that mind and intelligent or purposeful engagement in a course of action into which things enter are identical. Hence to develop and train mind is to provide an environment which induces such activity. On the other side, it protects us from the notion that subject matter on its side is something isolated and independent.

It shows that in learning, to start with, subject matter is identical with all the objects, ideas, and principles which enter as resources or obstacles into the continuous international pursuit of a course of action.

Meaning of Discipline

The word discipline is supposed to have been derived from the Latin word Discipline which means management, rule, education, practice, teaching and trained condition. The derivation of English word Disciple is supposed from the Latin word Discipulum which means pupil. This is expected from the pupils that they should obey the teachers respectfully and they should develop necessary and required qualities in themselves for successful life.

The main focus of educational administration is to realise the educational objectives. For this purpose several types of activities and programs are organised in a school. These activities and programs are required for the conducive climate of a school. The smooth functioning of a school depends on the maintenance of discipline and coordination among the headmaster, teachers, students and other staff of the school. The maintenance of discipline and coordination generates the academic climate of a school which leads to the growth and development of the school, teachers as well as students. The climate is the process while health is its end product which is also the result of growth and development of an institution. In this way, the meaning of discipline is to create regularity in conduct. Lot of words are used in Hindi for discipline, control, regulation, self-restraint, courtesy and discipline etc. The use of the word control would be appropriate at the place where someone is to be kept forcibly in position.

Where according to some fixed rules, the man is asked to do work, "regulation" would be used. The term "discipline" refers to a state of orderly conduct of an individual which is gained through training in self-control and in habits of obedience to socially approved standards of thought and action. It implies a good and an adherence to such standards as are just and necessary. It includes the socialisation of behaviour, the manner of working and living in cooperation and the subordination of individual interests to group interests. True discipline, therefore, provides for both individual interests to group interests and group welfare in a democratic society. In words of Sir Percy Nunn, "Discipline consists in the submission of one's impulses and powers of the economy where there would otherwise be ineffectiveness and waste. Though we, as part of our nature may resist this control, its acceptance must, on the whole, be willing acceptance" Where the child obeys his elders with courtesy and respect, there the word "courtesy" all those be proper to use. But, "discipline" is the word which covers all those mentioned above. The use of this word "Discipline" is more prevalent.

Modern concept of school discipline in which self-discipline and social discipline are stressed especially or particularity. According to modern educational thinking, the meaning of discipline is taken in widespread form. Today, where the objective of education has been understood to develop qualities of successful citizenship and sociability in child, at the same place, school discipline is meant internal and external discipline which should develop physical, mental, social, and ethical values. The great educationist John Dewey has influenced separation in school between intellectual and moral training, between the acquiring of the information and growth of character, is simply one expression of the failure to conceive and construct the school as a social institution having social life and value within itself.

Each experience in life a child, may be psychological, and mental or moral value, leaves its impression on his personal development. Thus, the school should be imagined in the form of such a place where other kinds of developments are also achieved equally along with mental development through co-curricular activity. We can say that according to maximum modern thinkers, the meaning of discipline is to prepare boys and girls for life in a democratic society meaning thereby, to provide help to man in achieving knowledge, strength, habits, interests and ideals which are envisaged for the amelioration of self, his companions and whole of the society.

Dewy says, "Out of doing things that are to produce result, and out of doing these in social and cooperation way, there is born discipline of its own kind and type." This is the self-discipline which is based on the recognition of the society. The kind of discipline would need moral or character training. Thus, according to John Dewey's opinion, discipline lies in social conditions of the school.

The Role of Parents in Maintaining Discipline

Discipline at home may complement or conflict with the discipline at school. In the normal case parental discipline should enhance the discipline of the school and be enhanced by it. Parents have a greater responsibility today than they had in the past as far as freedom of the child is concerned. The adolescent can no longer be expected to grow automatically from childhood to maturity without problems, mal-adjustments and those unanswerable curiosities that parents and teachers have to cope with. Adolescence must be recognised as a difficult period in which an essentially good and kind child, who will eventually achieve maturity and wisdom, passes through a period of adjustment, unhappiness, weariness, fatigue, discontent, frustration and irritation with the world at large.

These irritations are particularly focussed on parents and teachers, and parents and teachers have to necessarily go through this period of questioning, scrutiny, and criticism in fulfilling their respective roles. Few chores of child rearing are more frustrating and fraught with emotional conflict than discipline. Now some researchers believe they do not know why discipline is being applied to children be it should first be applied to their parents.

But new findings suggest that it may be surprisingly easy for parents to get out ineffective disciplinary rut. Researchers caution that beyond the importance of combining love with limits, there is no one approached that every parent should adopt. Not only do disciplinary occasions differ, but all children are different and parents cannot be convincing disciplinaries when they are using a tactic that makes them uncomfortable. Most parents lack a good grasp of what to do when they rely on their emotions they often end up feeling guilty. "One size doesn's fit all," said Carolyn Webster Stratton, a nurse-practitioner and child psychologist at the University of Washington in Seattle, "Basic disciplinary principles must be tailored to each child and family."

There are recent findings which suggest that most parents can, with a little help, improve the behaviour even of a difficult child Simple self-help techniques, with or without professional support, can help parents sharply reduce discipline problems. Parents who are sensitive to their children's needs have more obedient children. Too much permissiveness hurts a child's efforts to develop self-control.

Behaviour problems should be reversed early-waiting until the pre-teenage years diminish chances for success and puts children at higher risk for drug use and other problems. Praise and love alone are not enough to instill good behaviour. Permissiveness alone does not work well because the parents, while warm and living, do not provide enough structure or monitoring of their child's behaviour. In his eight-year study of 200 families, a researcher in Houston found that when parents failed to set limits, the child does not know when to stop and act out more.

Dr. Susan O' Leary, a Stone Brook psychologist, found that lax parenting is as bad as harsh parenting. Both for teachers in the classroom and for parents of two-years old, the timing, tone of voice and length of the reprimand determine its effectiveness. If maladaptive behaviour is not revised early in a child's life, studies have shown that highly aggressive and non-complaint children are at high risk for delinquent or socially deviant behaviour like drug abuse when they reach their teenage years.

It has long been known that frequent spanking, yelling or threatening non-compliant children with harsh punishments can foster misbehaviour. It is the duty of parents to take care of every aspect of the child development. Dealing with the role played by the home do parents unconsciously make their wards dull or backward? What can be done to prevent this? Our evaluation system evaluates only superficial parts of the child personality and how many parents realise this? According to Dorothy Fernandez, the home, like the school, plays a positive role in moulding the personality of the child. In this the attitude of the parents is crucial.

Education is a triangle- and equilateral triangle comprising the parent, the student and the teacher; all three playing equal roles to achieve the same goal. Hust as teachers who are important constituents of society in moulding children spend a good lot of their time in school on working days and the rest of it at home. Some tend to lag behind in class due to maladjustment, frustration, irritation, unhappiness, weariness, fatigue, discontentment, etc. This does not mean that they are academically backward but have been made so by certain factors, such as the home, the school and the society.

Children should be allowed to learn at their own pace and not determined by the parents' wishes. These days with both parents working children start school from the age of two to two- and half years. Starting so early can often be harmful. Attending school regularly, paying attention in class, a daily revision, a revision every weekend, month end, term end, etc., pays without overburdening the student thus avoiding opportunity of making them victim of an inferiority complex hindering their self-esteem playing a vital role in education and on the child psychology. Children have a right to self-respect. Generous reinforcement serves better. The mental horizon of each child grows at different pace.

The Role of Teacher in Managing Discipline

Only desirable discipline is self-discipline. Self-discipline is not easy to achieve, and to ask students in elementary and secondary schools to achieve this is an impossible task. If anyone thinks that the schools can continue to treat teachers so unprofessionally indeed like children, and attract bright, young self-directed college graduates into teaching, he or she is sadly mistaken. Even after we have solved the problem of providing adequate compensation, dealing with discipline, reducing the workload, achieving a better match of teachers with students and with the teachers' professional interests, we are not going to think and question the authority that knows that anarchy and disorder are bad for the human spirit.

Today, the student in the elementary and secondary school needs for this development a larger measure of freedom than he had in the past. Conversely, it needs a different kind of discipline too.

The discipline which comes naturally to children in groups is a discipline exercised by that group. Rounding-off angularities, some rough edges, are all part of the business of being at school. This is the kind of incidental discipline that is good for all children and that no child ultimately regrets having gone through. There is, in addition, the inevitable discipline of a timetable and curriculum.

Kinds of Indiscipline in School

Indiscipline in schools finds manifestation in various forms, the following being the most obvious:

1. Bullying the Younger Students - The cases of bullying younger students, even to the extent of unlawful ragging are very common in schools. It will be good in this case to make the offender apologies and also realise his folly.

2. Making a Noise/Talking in the Class - The reason for this may either be an uninteresting method of teaching or a large number of students in the class. In order to make teaching interesting the teacher should try to get the cooperation of students along with other useful methods. Students who are found talking may be seated separately.

3. Rude Behaviour Toward the Teachers - First of all the cause for this should be found out. The headmaster may make the student apologies for his misconduct and warn him not to repeat it in the future.

If the offence is repeated, the offender may be given corporal punishment.

4. Coming Late to School - There can be many reasons for unpunctuality. It is possible that due to some domestic circumstances a student gets late or other students might be teasing him while he is on the way to school. Hence, before punishing the student on this score the principal or the teacher should find out the cause.

5. Use of Unfair Means - Some students have the habit of copying during examinations. For this the school should raise moral standard and instil in the students the spirit of morality. The students should be strictly warned when caught for the first time, but one who does this repeatedly, should be turned out from the examination hall. This may, however, involve administrative complications as the reason for expulsion along with evidence thereof, duly attested, may have to accompany the answer-book. It may be simpler to cross out the copied answer and obtain the signature of the examinee on that, and forfeit the copying material.

6. Damage to the School Property - The students should be punished for this and some fine should be realised from them as far as possible. If the students can repair the articles he should be required to do so.

7. Neglect of Homework - There may be several reasons for not doing the homework. It is possible that the amount of homework in various subjects becomes so much that the student cannot do it, or due to family circumstances he is unable to complete it, or his negligence may be responsible for it. In fact, the real cause should be found out before giving any punishment/remedy.

8. Bunking Classes - some students run away from the school. This may be due to disinterestedness in studies. Hence, the individual difficulties of the students should be attended to. It should also be found out how the student passes his time after running away from the school.

9. Thievery - Some students steal pencils, books, pens and other articles from their classmates. The reason for this habit may be an excessive fondness for the particular article, self-consent, exhibition- complex or the feeling of revenge. Hence, the real cause should first be found out. If excessive fondness is responsible for this, those articles should be provided to the student. If exhibition- complex is responsible, other means should be provided for the expression of this complex. The student should be treated with love in order to cure him of the feeling of revenge.

10. Telling a Lie - The students often tell lies for fear of punishment.

Principles of Maintaining Discipline

The principles of maintaining should discipline in an educational institution can be discussed under the following headings:

1. Self-Control - It is one of the demands or a democratic set-up that each individual should have control over himself. Only he, who can influence others, knows how to exercise control over himself. The students should be made responsible for the establishment of discipline amongst themselves, because in this way they will exercise control over themselves and will exert a good influence over others. Hence, the headmaster should give an opportunity to the students to control themselves.

2. Cooperation - The student remains in the school for about 6 to 7 hours a day and the remaining time is spent either at home or in society. Evidently, the responsibility of inculcating discipline in the students does not fall only on the school. The guardians and the society also have a responsibility in this respect. Hence, cooperation of the guardians should be elicited for establishment of discipline. Through discussions with guardians, the problems and difficulties of the students should be found out. If the cooperation of those persons who are closely related with the students is available, it will not be difficult to discipline the students.

3. School Climate - Discipline is necessary for the collective life of school. Its significance should be well explained to the students. This means that the breach of discipline should not be regarded as a revolt against the teacher but an attack on the collective life of the school. If a regard for the collective life in the school in created in the students, they will themselves understand the significance of maintaining discipline. Since it is related to the whole life, attention should necessarily be paid on the following:

a. To become liberal-minded.

b. To make constant efforts towards mental development.

c. To observe rules to maintain one's health and to avoid bad habits.

d. To avoid ill will against anybody and to be always imbued with the spirit of tolerance, love and justice towards others.

e. To inculcate in the student democratic virtues of dutifulness, and cooperation and the ability to discharge obligations and responsibilities.

4. Love, Trust, Goodwill - The basis of discipline should be mutual love between the teacher and the student. There should be no element of fear, because discipline based on fear does not serve its ends. The students should obey the teacher out of a feeling of reverence and not of fear. This spirit of mutual trust is the foundation of true and permanent self-discipline.

5. School Infrastructure - In the interest of discipline it is necessary to provide in the school the necessary facilities for study and teaching. In this connection the following things should be taken into account:

a. The Home - The environment of the home should be peaceful. The people at home should take an interest in the education of the student and should not place any hinderance in his studies.

b. The Principal and the Teachers - The principal and teachers should be efficient when discharging various responsibilities.

c. The School - The necessary means for the physical, mental and moral development of the students should be available in the school. The standard of teaching in the school should be of a high order.

d. Classroom - There should be sufficient and comfortable chairs and desks for the students.

Contributors of Discipline in School

The foundation of good discipline is deeply rooted in the total school programme and classroom situation. The headmaster, the teacher, the associates in studies, the school activities, the school building, furniture, equipment and playgrounds instill in the pupil positive regard or distaste for the school laws and thus, lead him to conform to or flout some of all of those laws. The following are the important contributors to good discipline in a school:

1. Self-Government in Schools - The pupils should be properly associated with the administration of discipline as well as with the health, sports, dramatic and other school activities. This sharing of authority and responsibility with sympathetic and friendly teachers, will provide first-hand practical training in democratic, citizenship, which is the real aim of modern education. Such an association will make obedience rules and regulations far more real, meaningful and willing than when the same are imposed from above.

2. Co-curricular Activities - co-curricular activities play an important role in shaping up the personality of a student. Sports, scouting, N.C.C., social service and community activities of the type, develop in pupils a sense of self-control and self-confidence, which is the cornerstone of good discipline. Such activities give our pupils practical lessons in subjugation of their will. Moral values, co-curricular activities also appeal to the tastes and temperaments of our pupils and help them in releasing their superfluous energies on the playground or in the clubs instead of the classrooms. Social cooperation, respect for authority and leadership training can pave the right way of instructing them in the fundamentals of true discipline.

3. Teaching Methods and Aids - The utilisation of modern progressive methods in which pupils' activity is brought into play and harnessed for educative purposes, eliminates the possibility of any type of indiscipline. If appropriate methods of teaching are employed, the

chances of pupils getting indisciplined or going astray, will be few and far between. Classroom methods should be directed towards producing well-adjusted and self-disciplined individuals and towards the building up of high morale.

4. Building up Traditions - The problem of discipline, like school work, in a continuous process and, therefore it is quite comfortable to work in a school with the tradition of good discipline. School discipline is closely connected with school traditions. The higher and nobler the traditions set by a school, the greater the efforts on the part of pupils and teachers to maintain those traditions. Traditions descent from one generation of pupils to the other and as such, if properly guided, pupils would never be a let down to lower the noble traditions established by those who have gone before them.

5. Suitable School Environment - The school environment should be made as conducive to learning and studies as possible. Besides a specious building and well maintained play-field, the schools should also be provided with adequate library and reading room faculties. In fact, school premises and a proper school atmosphere contribute greatly to shape the education which our children receive and to the maintenance of genuine discipline and adjustment, so essential in the democracy. Every school should prepare its calendar in the beginning of a new school session, giving a clear idea of the aims, the courses of study, administrative rules and regulations, as well as the plans of curricular and co-curricular activities of the institution.

6. Judicious Use of Rewards and Punishments - We shall discuss in the following pages how meritorious and

successful efforts on the part of pupils should be recognised and rewarded.

7. Effective Team-Workers - The headmaster should further try to coordinate the efforts of different individuals and groups, in the best interest of the school. A sense of unity, cooperation and fellow-feeling, prevailing among the school staff, is sure to reflect upon the pupils. The young pupils in the school watch very minutely the activities of their teachers and try to imitate them for good or bad, it must first be established and maintained among the members of the school staff.

8. The Teacher - Without good teachers even the best of systems is bound to fail. With good teachers, even the defects a system can be largely overcome.

9. The Principal or Headmaster - Success or failure of any school depends upon the personality of the headmaster. He must possess some philosophy of discipline. He must have some well-grounded fundamental principles to guide him in his dealings generally, against which to set each individual case of discipline as it comes before him. As a successful disciplinarian, he should be given an adequate share in the management of school affairs. He should organise the corporate life of the school in such a manner that it may provide ample opportunities for the expression of pupils impulses and a flow of their superfluous energy into worthy and fruitful channels. Such measures will surely help in the smooth-functioning of the school as a whole and in maintaining the desirable discipline and order in all school activities.

Negative Means of Discipline

P.C. Wren is of the opinion, "Punishment is a bad thing, and it should be neglected too. But the way knife of a surgeon is essential to cut a rotten part of body to save whole of the body, in the same way punishment is also necessary to get rid of human weaknesses. Thus, as the state is an essential evil, so is punishment a necessary evil which we have to adopt."

In order that the students may be completely disciplined and there may be no increase in indiscipline, many remedial measures may be adopts. We mention below some of the chief ones:

1. Attention should be directed towards the individual behaviour of each student and the cause of breach of conduct, if any, should be explored.

2. A study of the student's nature, proclivity and work should be made and he should be entrusted with responsible work suited to his ability.

3. Each moment of the student's life should be considered as useful and he should be kept busy all the time.

4. A close contact should be established with the students and they should be treated sympathetically and respectfully.

5. A complete meaningful contact should be maintained with the students' guardians and parents and they be maintained with informed about the conduct, work and behaviour of the students.

Positive means of Discipline

Positive means are classified into the following points:

1. Rewards - In maintaining discipline the rewards plays an important role because through them habit of good deeds and tendencies is developed in children.

Each person desires to be appreciated. Some persons seek recognition of the society by their good deeds. But the persons who do not seek recognition of the society through their good deeds, try to bring themselves into limelight by evil activities. Generally, in all schools, rewarding students for their good deeds and specific qualities is a prevalent tradition.

In school, through rewards for the satisfaction of the children, discipline is created. If the same child receives reward for his good performance and character qualities, the other children get inspiration from it. They become interested in receiving rewards and working hard for it. In this way they always try to demonstrate themselves better that others for receiving rewards. Thus, reward exerts very important role in maintaining discipline. The children develop spirit of competition with the hope of getting a reward for good deeds, with the result they become prepared for doing more good deeds one after another. The children get pleasure and inspiration from the attainment of the school performance and behaviour. The children learn to work regularly and become dutifulness for acquiring these behaviours.

Some scholars have criticised the rewards. Many students become ready to use unfair means for receiving rewards, which is injurious to society and for the students themselves. The scholars are of the opinion that rewards are useless from psychological and social point of view, because through these children develop feelings of jealously and rivalry. Secondly, rewards affect only a small number of students as they are given to selected few, and are restricted. Against these it is also said that there is a possibility to develop the feeling of inferiority complex among the children who do not receive this honour. For making rewards useful, it is essential that they should be awarded very carefully and impartially.

So, the following points should be kept in mind when giving rewards:

a. Rewards should not be given to children for demonstrating quality at one occasion alone; the basis of reward should be the work of the entire year.

b. Rewards should not be given in form of valuable things, because costly rewards may create greed and temptation in children. Alongwith it, it should also be kept in mind that the rewards should be given in the form of certificates and prase-letters instead of cash or valuable things. The letter or honour is more important than some material things.

c. Rewards should be given collectively, and not individually, so, that may banish personal jealousy and hostility.

d. Children are given rewards for the qualities and good deeds, which should be communicated to all students and highlighted for their importance in life, so that other students too may try to acquire those qualities.

2. Provision of Co-curricular Activities - Through these activities leadership, dutifulness, feeling of respect towards authorities, order and inclination towards regularity, is achieved. Thus, for maintaining discipline, appropriate programme of co-curriculum should be formulated, so that every student may participate in them according to his interest and ability, and may be capable of developing above mentioned qualities in himself.

3. Control on External Influences - As the famous educationist John Dewey says that the school is a special atmosphere that should be kept in tact from follies of life

outside. It is necessary to have control over external influences, that is, dirty politics of society, social tension, mutual struggles, etc. These should be prevented from entering the pure atmosphere of school. For this, only those elements should be selected which are valuable and educative. For maintaining discipline the school should not be affected by external influences and other aspects of indiscipline.

4. Provision for Moral Education - Moral education plays an important role. There should be provision for it in the school curriculum. Through this, faith towards high ideals and feelings should be developed in the children. But this should not be thought as a teaching subject, notwithstanding, it should be given place among teaching of all subjects. Besides, stress should be given on development of moral qualities in conducting various activities.

5. Rules and Traditions of Schools - Rules and traditions of a school occupy very important place in maintaining discipline of a school. Formulation of rules of school is done by the Department of Education; management committees; headmaster and teachers; students, union, etc. The students should also be intimated that it is necessary to sacrifice their personal interests for social interest. Mostly the rules made by the Education Department and management committee have to be followed without hesitation. The rules constructed by the headmaster and teachers relate to promotion, absence, maintaining arrangements, etc.

Along with it, it should be intimated to students that on doing work here according to rules, there would be no difficulty in future life in doing regular work. But here, one point is notable, less the rules, more appropriate it would be, because the youth generally do not take too many rules very kindly. Every school has some of its traditions. In fact, school discipline is should try for improving their prevailing traditions continuously. If there are good traditions of a school, there would be good level of discipline. If the conditions are otherwise, an atmosphere of indiscipline would prevail.

6. Parent- Teacher Cooperation - It is very essential to garner good relationship between teachers and guardians for the children to lead a disciplined life. In maintaining discipline, cooperation of these two components has very important place. The teachers with the cooperation of these two would able top know difficulties and activities of children. With this knowledge, they would be able to solve various problems of children. In the school, the knowledge activities of children by the guardians can help the teachers plan for their development. As we have seen above that the child spends most of his time at home. The school, in want of cooperation of guardians, cannot be successful in effecting their proper development.

7. Self-Government - The students can get help in maintaining discipline and affecting the vital parts of the atmosphere of school. The students themselves can frame rules regarding their conduct. In following these rules, they will not feel any hitch, because they themselves have framed them. Besides, they may be made responsible for cleanliness of the school, personal cleanliness, security of school property, problem of late comers, knowledge of rules regarding health, and extensions of those. To fix responsibility on children for general programme of daily routine of school is of great help in maintaining good discipline. With their

cooperation, the entire atmosphere may be made so lively that they may become capable of becoming disciplined themselves.

8. School Environment and Educational Facilities - There should be proper arrangement of library, laboratory and their equipment, playground etc., with the proper arrangement of these the children could make proper utilisation of their leisure and would learn to remain in discipline. The school environment plays important role. If the school environment is not appropriate, there would be great difficulty in maintaining discipline. For proper teaching it is necessary to have proper arrangements of cleanliness, air, light, furniture and necessary apparatus, etc. If adequate furniture or place is not there for sitting in the classroom, there would remain a possibility of indiscipline.

9. Mutual Cooperation - The functions of a school depend upon mutual cooperation. The headmaster is in need of cooperation perform any work successfully in tis absence. When all the people are ready to understand their obligations and are ready to perform them, discipline would come to be created of its own, because responsibility creates discipline. In this way, mutual cooperation is essential for maintaining discipline in the school.

Causes of Indiscipline in School

Indiscipline is a serious problem in our educational institutions. The following are some of the major causes of indiscipline in our schools:

1. Economic Drawbacks - Our economic condition has deteriorated while the population has increased and unemployment has become a national problem. The